A Historical Introduction To Library Education:

Problems and Progress to 1951

by

Carl M. White

The Scarecrow Press, Inc.

Metuchen, N.J.   1976

020.711
W

Library of Congress Cataloging in Publication Data

White, Carl Milton, 1903-
    A historical introduction to library education.

    Edition for 1961 published under title: The origins of
the American library school.
    Includes bibliographies and index.
    1.   Library schools--United States--History.   2.   Li-
brary education--United States--History.
    I.   Title.
Z668.W54   1975   020'.7'11   75-28086
ISBN 0-8108-0874-9

PREFACE

This is a revision and enlargement of Origins of the American Library School (Scarecrow Press, 1961).

Someone has observed that the roots of the present lie deep in the past and must be uncovered to understand fully how the present came to be what it is. This study is less a descriptive history of library schools and their work than a search for perspective within which major problems, as well as the course pursued in resolving them, can be more fully understood. The original study, begun in 1941-42, sought to throw light on how library education at that time came to be what it was. The present study continues beyond the early forming of the American library school to the re-forming of basic lines of policy and organization. A new title is used to reflect the broadened scope.

A double significance is attached to the year 1951, and this explains why it is used as a terminal point. It is significant as the year when the American Library Association adopted new standards for the accreditation of library schools; but in a longer perspective, it serves as a dateline to mark the first clean break with the unwritten standards that evolved from nineteenth-century technical education as well as the first concerted effort to accommodate library education to university standards. The story of developments since we entered this new watershed is of course an important one, but it is convenient--and a relief--to leave the writing of it to younger hands. Here is the prologue.

I have sought to catch the errors in the original volume, but certain imperfections, mainly of bibliographical form, I have allowed to stand. Ben Franklin provides a precedent of sorts for doing so. When he looked at his axe, you will recall, and then at his grindstone, he concluded that leaving a few rust spots has something to be said for it.

The treatment is limited to American experience.

1

ALAB refers to the <u>ALA Bulletin</u>; LJ to <u>Library Journal</u>. A few other abbreviations have been used, which I believe the context will make clear.

It is a pleasure to acknowledge the cooperation and encouragement I have received from many friends during the long, often-interrupted search that now ends. I particularly want to thank Jack Dalton and Alfred Lane for aid in obtaining material that was essential to finishing the job.

Special thanks go to Dorothy Gray for preparing the Index to this work.

Carl M. White

CONTENTS

Chapter 1

FORMATIVE NINETEENTH-CENTURY INFLUENCES

Essential facts about the beginning of library schools
are well known. How their programs came to take the form
they did is not. The first three chapters are devoted to this
neglected subject.

Vitality of the Library Movement

A good place to begin is with factors that explain the
growing potential for better library training. The growth of
libraries in number, size and complexity was one influence.
"So far as is known"--the monumental 1876 Report on Public
Libraries reads--"there were in 1776 twenty-nine public libraries [collections accessible without any, or with easily-
met, restrictions] in the thirteen American colonies and they
numbered altogether 45,623 volumes."[1] By 1800, the number had risen to forty-nine libraries with a combined total of
80,000 volumes. By 1850, there were 694 libraries with
2,202,632 volumes. Five libraries had collections totalling
50,000--more than all of the libraries put together in 1776.
By 1876, 3,682 libraries exclusive of district school libraries contained 12,276,964 volumes.

Total annual additions had, according to best estimates,
already shot past the 1,000,000 mark in 1876--half as much
as all of the holdings of all U.S. libraries open to the public
twenty-five years earlier. The school-district library was
losing ground by 1876; but to make up for it tax-supported
free libraries were gaining popular acceptance comparable to
that of tax-supported free schools, and were multiplying at
an unprecedented rate. College and university libraries were
multiplying less rapidly but were beginning to acquire a role
in instruction and research which, educators agreed, would
materially alter their character.

1

Second, there were too few qualified librarians to go around. In 1883, William F. Poole was fully occupied with his indexes and with creating in a booming Western city, Chicago, the greatest circulating library in the country; but totally inexperienced persons, newly in charge of libraries which were "springing up all over the Western states," would not let him alone. "Scarcely a day passes," he ruefully observed, "in which one or more of these tyros does not come to my library for information."[2] What was to be done? He and others similarly situated had gained their special competence through long years of paid experience during which they had "worked their way up," and he thought the larger libraries ought to provide the new crop of tyros similar opportunities. But how this haphazard method could be used to produce enough librarians for the new libraries when it was already being strained to supply enough to meet the growing staff needs of existing libraries was not explained.

The trouble went deeper, and here too the pace of library development helped build up pressure to do something about it. John William Wallace, in his address of welcome to the founders of the American Library Association in 1876, spoke of two interrelated occurrences: "the much-increased and still much-increasing issue of books from the printing-press" and "the establishment of common schools and colleges everywhere throughout this country by which both the capacity to write and the disposition to read are vastly increased."[3] The meaning of it all, he said before this celebrated gathering, was that if librarians were to meet the challenge of their times, they would have to develop a library science--an adequate and generally accepted body of principles for use in developing, organizing and administering libraries. This was a specialized job that would have to be handled by qualified people.

A third influence has to do with deeper background forces that further contributed to the accelerated demand for trained librarians. When Cornwallis surrendered, the colonies had achieved political independence, but they remained cultural dependencies of the Old World. The task of forging established ways to sustain the new life of freedom still lay ahead. The modern library movement was one of the slower outcomes of the century when the members of the colonies addressed themselves to the task of creating institutions that suited their needs. It was a movement which introduced a specialized division of labor which required specialists who were willing to devote their lives to it, and this was not

understood till long after the guns of Revolution had fallen
silent.   The first major experiment in taking library service
to the people occurred during the half century following 1835.
State after state, following the example of Massachusetts and
New York, poured money into school-district library collections on the assumption that access to a good book collection
is all it takes to produce good library service.   The experiment failed because the assumption was false.   It overlooked
a simple fact that is illustrated by the presence in our midst
of families of Smiths, Millers, Tanners, and Weavers--proper
names which identify people as the crucially important factor
in handling special divisions of labor which the human family
originates to sustain itself.   The assembling, organizing,
housing and promoting of the use of library materials began
to be recognized as a coming branch of public service as
early as the 1853 meeting of American librarians, and its
significance rapidly deepened after the Civil War.   The profession of librarianship may be said to have originated when
librarians accepted responsibility for developing this branch
of service as their common task.   Better methods of training were needed for the purpose.

Adaptation of Education to the Aspirations of the People

        Meanwhile, there was a great deal of ferment in edu-
cational thought and practice.   The English colonists had used
the educational models they knew best.   Our first colleges
turned out accordingly to be recognizable facsimiles of the
English college. [4]   The latter was primarily an ecclesiastical
and monastic institution where, as one writer in the Quarterly Review put it in 1840, studious men, removed from secu-
lar cares, were free to consecrate their time to deep reading.   The early Harvard course of study consisted of classical languages and literature, mathematics, logic, philosophy
and theology, with liberal allowance for writing, oratory and
forensics.   This pre-Revolutionary model underwent some
change during the first half of the nineteenth century, but
the classical tradition held pretty firm until after the Civil
War.   Its grip is well illustrated by the regimen prescribed
by the Yale charter two centuries after the founding of Harvard: all students the first year to be exercised in the
Greek and Hebrew tongues the first four days of the week,
beginning logic toward the end of the year; all of them to
continue logic and "the exercise of themselves in the tongues"
the second year; the third year to include physics, and the
fourth, metaphysics and mathematics, besides the former

studies; the last days of the week to be devoted by all classes
to rhetoric, oratory and divinity.

These early colleges were rooted so far back in the
past that any idea of consciously suiting the curriculum to
post-Revolution needs was an alien one, so as time passed,
a gap showed up between them and the people.   The backwoods farmer, for example, had no place to go for the specialized learning which Jefferson envisioned for him, and his
low esteem for book larnin' became part of the folklore of
the frontier.   The gap became more noticeable as the young
nation set to building a huge canal system, to building rail-
roads and exploiting vast mineral resources.   West Point perhaps contributed as much toward early technological development as all the colleges combined.   The war years, 1861-65,
accelerated the industrial revolution, brought passage of the
Morrill Act and underscored the need for fundamental changes
in education.   On the whole, the colleges had become so re-
mote from the grass roots which nourished them that reducing the gap became necessary for their survival.

The pioneering of Brown University illustrates how
readjustments were brought about.   In 1848, the trustees decided that something had to be done about professors' salaries: they had not been raised in twenty years.   Meanwhile,
rising costs of living had forced some of the men to fall
back on income from outside sources.   A campaign to raise
$50,000 failed; thereupon President Francis Wayland, one of
the stalwarts of his generation, resigned.   Pressed to recon-
sider, he produced a report which is a minor classic.   He
described Brown's plight as symptomatic of a sickness which
affected American higher education generally.   He showed
that the American college was losing ground in enrollment,
in effectiveness, in public esteem.   The trouble lay not in
the nation's capacity to support higher education, nor yet in
its willingness to provide support, but rather in the lack of
a program which the public could be convinced was worth supporting.   Such a program, he believed, would require a new
orientation.   Brown, along with other American colleges, was
too tightly organized around an older educational ideal which
made it unnatural to give adequate attention to the knowledge
arising in the 19th century from the newer sciences and practical arts.   The challenge facing the American college, he
argued persuasively, was the creative one of attuning higher
education to the realities of American life:

... with the present century, a new era dawned upon

the world. A host of new sciences arose, all holding important relations to the progress of civilization. Here was a whole people in an entirely novel
position. Almost the whole nation was able to
read. Mind had been quickened to intense energy
by the events of the Revolution. The spirit of self-
reliance had gained strength by the result of that
contest. A country rich in every form of capability, had just come into their possession. Its wealth
was inexhaustible, and its adaptation to the production of most of the great staples of commerce unsurpassed. All that was needed, in order to de-
velope [sic] its resources, was well directed labor.
But labor can only be skilfully directed by science;
and the sciences now coming into notice were precisely those, which the condition of such a country
rendered indispensable to success. That such a
people could be satisfied with the teaching of Greek,
Latin, and the elements of Mathematics, was plainly
impossible. [5]

Wayland's proposals were presented and adopted in
1849. The trustees returned to the public for $125,000: in
six months, the much-enlarged total was oversubscribed!
Salaries were raised. Four professors were added. A department of Civil Engineering was organized and a strong
Chemistry Laboratory established. Nearly twice as many
new students enrolled the next year. Brown had entered a
new era of usefulness. [6]

It should be added that the tone of this 1849 report
was a positive one. Wayland saw no black-and-white issue
between the classics and the newer sciences and arts. He
was sympathetic with, and worked to conserve, the liberaliz-
ing influence of studies which reached 19th century America
through the classics. The goal of the reorganization was essentially one of attaining a higher synthesis in which all studies having demonstrable relevance to a higher, indigenous
civilization would find a respected place. If the report placed
all productive labors of a self-reliant nation on a common
footing, it was to enhance the usefulness of learning, not to
lower academic standards nor yet to lower the dignity of
things of the mind. The report is perhaps best characterized
as an early apologia for professional education which shows
close kinship in spirit and aim to much later statements on
the subject.

Origins and Meaning of Nineteenth Century Technical Education

        The remainder of this chapter is devoted to the period
between the new start at Brown in 1849-50 and the launching
of a new program at Columbia for the training of librarians
in 1886-87. Dewey called the program, as we shall see, "a
purely technical course." The significance of this term
"technical" is not immediately transparent to twentieth-century readers. We speak of the flawless technical skill of the
poet or novelist, of technical points of law, of dull technical
routine, and in each case the term has a different shade of
meaning. It had not acquired its present ambiguity in Dewey's
time. Its meaning then was that given it by the "technical
education movement," to which we shall now introduce ourselves. Between 1850 and 1886-87, this movement achieved
spectacular popularity, and what has been said above explains
why. The collapse of the classical tradition in the years following the Civil War created an educational vacuum. Technical education had something new and specific to offer. To
many who were searching for an educational policy better
fitted to the aspirations of the people, it seemed to be exactly what was needed.

        The phrase, "Technical education," was too new to
find a place in the eighth edition of the Encyclopaedia Britannica of 1860; but anyone who examines educational literature
from then to 1886 will be struck by how quickly the term
caught on. It came to be used in too many connections to
continue to mean precisely the same thing on every tongue;
but, coined as it was by a generation that knew its Greek,
it retained a distinct idiomatic flavor for the rest of the century, as the following review brings out.

        One of the first works on technical education to appear
in this country was Charles B. Stetson's Technical Education:
What It Is and What American Public Schools Should Teach,
published in 1874. By technical education, Stetson meant education which would produce skilled laborers of all kinds--
farmers, artisans, merchants, manufacturers. He was concerned over the fact that apprenticeship was disappearing at
the very time when new conditions in production and trade
were placing a premium on skilled workmanship. He argued
that "something else must take [the place of apprenticeship]
in America, as its place has already been largely taken in
Europe by special schools, and give the American artisan
that technical instruction which he must have or perish."[7]

Stetson believed that this special training in occupational competence should be provided by the common schools, which he criticized for giving too much emphasis to education of the head and too little to education of the hands.

> It is not the business of the common school to make specialists--farmers, carpenters, accountants, engineers, cooks,--it is the business of such a school to teach at least the elements of technical knowledge .... Laborers cannot be satisfactorily educated for their work unless they have first received, in schools for children and youth, not only literary instruction, but also instruction in the elements of technical knowledge, scientific and artistic. [8]

A further explanation of this type of "elemental" instruction is given as follows:

> There are but few kinds of labor which require only the rude strength of the steady plodder.... Almost every laborer should possess skill; the more skill the better. Even in sawing wood, spading earth, tending a cotton-picker, there is a philosophy, a best way to proceed, which the intelligent but not the stupid laborer is sure to discover and to follow. [9]

Early technical education was broad enough to include all vocational pursuits of all people who work for a living. Thus Stetson threw engineers, cooks, and carpenters into one general category and similar inclusiveness reappears as late as 1902 in the following statement by the Dean of Armour Institute of Technology:

> Time was when the young practitioner began by driving the doctor's horse or sweeping out the lawyer's office; today he must attend a professional school. Trades could formerly be learned by the apprentice system, but that system is now become obsolete. The one influence felt by educators who are not wedded to medieval forms or classical models is the demand of the great masses of the people to be taught the scientific and technical features of their callings.... Besides schools of technology which train engineers, there are schools to teach barbering, manicuring, hairdressing, breadmaking, beermaking, the blending of whiskies, the

making of cocktails, and even the art of undertaking.... 10

Technical education did not originate in the United
States. 11 The earliest extended treatment of the subject in
English was a book published in 1869--Systematic Technical
Education for the English People, by John Scott Russell, a
prominent British shipbuilder. By "technical education," he
says,

> I mean that special training which renders the tal-
> ents of the educated man directly useful to that so-
> ciety in which its useful member is destined to pass
> his life. We English live in the midst of an ener-
> getic rivalry of competing nations. The aim of our
> national life should be to do the work of the world
> better, more ably, more honestly, more skillfully,
> and less wastefully than the skilled men of other
> countries. 12

In the 1840's, Russell had served as Secretary of the
Society of Arts, which was interested in improving "facilities
to enable a workman ... to become a better workman by
studying the science and art underlying his trade in the school,
side by side with practice in the workshop. "13 Thomas Twining, a vice president of this Society, published in 1874 a suggested plan (which attracted considerable attention but was
never implemented) for a national system of industrial instruction to head up in "a central technical university. " The proposal assumed that satisfactory training was already available
in mining, metallurgy, civil engineering, agriculture, pharmacy and the maritime industry, and that the university would
round out the system by providing practical training for workers in "the ordinary standard working trades" (of dyer, tan-
ner, brewer, baker, cook, etc.), the "mechanical trades"
(watchmaker, wheelright, carpenter, smith, tailor, shoemaker,
miller, etc.), the "artistic trades" (decorator, jeweller, sil-
versmith, engraver, etc.), and "commercial trades" (draper,
haberdasher, grocer, wine merchant, and ironmonger). 14

Experience with technical education revealed differences
between trades and professions; and it was found that workmen of one grade (common laborer) might need a different
type of training from one in a higher grade. These revelations affected the use of the term but the following definition
of 1884 in the Nineteenth Century Magazine shows little change
in fundamentals:

> Technical education is that specific training and
> teaching required to fit a person for any trade, pro-
> fession, or other calling in life over and above
> that general education which every person ought to
> possess according to age, sex, and other circum-
> stances.   Hence it is needed as much by lawyer and
> doctor, housemaid, ploughman, soldier, gardener,
> and cook, as by carpenter, bricklayer, bookbinder,
> or tailor.   At present, however, attention is being
> chiefly paid to the technical training of artisans and
> agricultural employees, on whom the prosperity of
> our manufactures, trade, and commerce so largely
> depend. . . . 15

The ninth edition of the Encyclopaedia Britannica (1888)
contains a similar definition:

> In its widest sense, technical education embraces
> all kinds of instruction that have direct reference to
> the career a person is following or preparing to fol-
> low; but it is usual and convenient to restrict the
> term to the special training which helps to qualify
> a person to engage in some branch of productive in-
> dustry.   This education may consist of the explana-
> tion of the processes concerned in production or of
> instruction in art or science in its relation to indus-
> try, but it may also include the acquisition of the
> manual skill which production necessitates.   The
> term technical, as applied to education, arose from
> the necessity of finding a word to indicate the spe-
> cial training which was needed in consequence of the
> altered conditions of production during the present
> century. 16

The New Movement Catches On

In support of the last sentence, Sir Lyon Playfair, one
of the founders of what quickly became known as the technical education movement, says the term was coined in 1855
when a group of interested persons decided that a "crusade"
should be launched to improve the training of workers. 17
This decision and the new movement grew out of a series of
international exhibitions which originated with the Universal
Exhibition of the Industries and Products of All Nations, held
in Crystal Palace, London, in 1851.   The effect was electri-
fying, and a second followed in Paris in 1855.

Each nation had in 1851 seen its inferiority plainly exhibited at one point or another. Britain, for example, had
been astonished by the superiority of some continental nations
in the beauty and grace of their glass and earthenware products. The French and German nations, on the other hand,
had taken account of their inferiority in the heavier industries
and had set out to catch up. They had reasoned that the only
way to compete with British superiority in raw material and
mechanical power was to invest their products with superior
workmanship. The exhibitions of 1855 and 1862 showed that
they were making rapid gains, but not until 1867 did the British come alive to what was happening. "By that exhibition
we were rudely awakened and thoroughly alarmed. We then
learnt, not that we were equalled, but that we were beaten--
not on some points, but by some nation or other on nearly
all those points on which we had prided ourselves.... A
whole generation of wakeful, skilled workmen had been trained
in other countries during the interval between 1851 and
1867. "[18]

British workers shared in this estimate of the situation. A delegation of eighty-eight artisans, representing all
major arts and crafts, had gone to the Paris Exhibition in
1867. They came away impressed by what technical education had done to improve workmanship in other countries, and
with how Britain, still complacent, was falling behind. A
chairmaker summed it up for the delegation as follows:
"Without the least doubt or hesitation, yet with the most ...
profound regret, I say that our defeat is as ignominious and
I fear as disastrous, as it is possible to conceive. We have
not only made no progress since 1862, but it seems to me we
have retrograded. "[19]

By 1881, Her Majesty's Government had decided to
come to terms with the new movement. A Royal Commission
on Technical Instruction, created by Queen Victoria, set out
to comb through the experience of all major nations to find
out what methods were being used to educate "the various
classes engaged in industrial pursuits. " A preliminary report, published in 1882, was devoted largely to France, where
certain methods to be discussed later had been well perfected.
The final report of 1884 is the most authoritative contemporary source on international practices in technical education.
Published in five ponderous tomes, it is a massive symbol
of popular and official interest which the movement had come
to command in not much more than a quarter of a century. [20]

Reasons for the Popularity of Technical Education

If one asks why this movement gained such sweep and power so quickly, the international exhibitions do not provide a full answer. They helped technical education catch on, but mainly because they helped dramatize the more basic influences enumerated below:

1. Changed Conditions of Trade. The national rivalry which has been noted was related, of course, to international trade. Free trade did not become a reality until after England abandoned her protective policy in 1846. International competition was in the meantime being affected by the railroad, steamship, telegraph, and by other mechanical inventions. If a man did his work well and as cheaply as those who went to the same church or sat on the same jury, he once had no further worry. He and his neighbors could fix the price of their products and sell them in a market in which competition was negligible, or perhaps non-existent. Changes in transportation and communication were now opening up competition with producers far beyond his locality.

Western European countries were experimenting with the uses of skilled workmanship in waging this competitive struggle. Bismarck declared, "the war of the future is the economic war, the struggle for existence on a large scale." But this idea had been spelled out to the Germans much earlier: "Among the weapons which are irresistible in this economic warfare the spread of knowledge holds the first place .... All nations which are striving for a share in the products of industry and commerce are at war with England.... When knowledge is better distributed and wider spread than in England, then we have nothing more to fear from her.... Simply to envy England, merely to gaze at her with admiration, profits us nothing; 'tis but to sit idly by with folded hands and to befool ourselves ... with the delusion that it were useless to fight against this full-grown giant."[21]

It was the advocates of technical education who warned England--well before she was ready to listen--that she would have to fight back with the same weapon. Stressing the need of equipping each individual in "commerce, manufactures, public works, agriculture, navigation, architecture" with practical training in addition to general education, Scott Russell made the point in these terms: "This, then, is what I mean by a technical education: that which shall render an English artilleryman a better artilleryman than a Frenchman; an Eng-

lish soldier a better soldier than a Prussian, an English loco-
motive builder better than a German; an English ship builder
better than an American ship builder; an English silk manufacturer superior to a Lyons silk manufacturer; an English
ribbon manufacturer superior to a Swiss ribbon manufacturer."22

    2. Decay of Apprenticeship. Benjamin Franklin be-
queathed £2000 for loans to young married workers who had
served an apprenticeship. He had no way of knowing that this
system, which had been one of the fixtures in social organization since the Middle Ages, would be on its way out by his
death in 1790. First came a procession of revolutionary
mechanical inventions--Hargreaves' Spinning Jenny; the water
frame of Richard Arkwright, the first manufacturer to employ
machinery on a large scale as a substitute for hand labor in
textile production; Crompton's Spinning Mule, which combined
the inventions of Hargreaves and Arkwright and greatly increased the demand for thread; Cartwright's loom, which began the modernization of weaving; and Whitney's invention of
the Cotton Gin, which made it easier to meet the increased
demand for raw material. These inventions all took place in
the thirty years between 1764 and 1794. Watt showed the
way to new sources of power by patenting his condensing steam
engine in 1769. By 1785, steam was being used in mining
and manufacturing, including the manufacture of textiles. Machine tools began to be produced soon afterwards, as the demand for machinery rapidly developed. Transportation began
to be affected early in the nineteenth century. Fulton applied
steam power to water transportation in 1807, George Stephen-
son to land transportation in 1814.

    Those trades where machinery was substituted for man-
ual tools and hand work were the first to be affected but the
chain of reactions went on to be caught up in the larger revolution. The new conditions which emerged from all these
changes gradually undermined apprenticeship in three ways.
First, machines brought about a reorganization of the fundamental process of manufacture. As the old hand-labor shop
was turned into a mechanically equipped factory, the apprentice, the same as other workmen, usually wound up working
with only one process or one piece of the article, which was
turned over to a single master craftsman to finish. Sometimes, the whole article would be produced by such piece-
work. This type of specialization gradually displaced master
craftsmen with wage-earners who did not need such a high
order of craftsmanship. The old stratification made up of

master craftsmen, journeymen, and apprentices thus gave way
to a different type of stratification made up of heads of factories at the top, a thin layer of supervisors and foremen
standing next to them, and finally, a thicker layer of factory
"hands" at the bottom.

Second, production was taken out of the home. As it
became unnecessary and even impractical for apprentices to
"live in," the distance between the apprentice and the head of
the shop widened. Employment became less personal, an
economic relation only. The responsibility for the boy and
his future came to rest more and more on the boy himself,
on his parents if he worked near home, and on a society
which had not yet developed a very sensitive conscience about
such responsibilities.

Apprenticeship was fundamentally a system of training.
If a boy had to sign away seven years between fourteen and
twenty-one, he could depend, if apprenticed to a good master,
on getting thorough vocational preparation for adulthood. The
factory system had nothing comparable to offer, and here we
come to the third factor in the dissolution of apprenticeship.
Many factory jobs could be done with little or no training,
while the higher knowledge involved in newer forms of production could in some cases not be learned on the premises at
all. The conditions were so different that many of the laws
which defined and upheld apprenticeship practice became first
unenforceable, then obsolete.

3. Discovery of the Uses of Schooling as a Substitute
for Apprenticeship. The decay of the system of apprenticeship could be looked upon narrowly as the misfortune of the
boy who wished to master a trade, but as just indicated, it
also interfered with established social procedure for passing
the worker's know-how down from one generation to another.
Why formal schooling did not come into use earlier to perform this function is in some ways surprising. Certainly apprenticeship was, as an educational method, far from perfect.
It was extravagant with the time of the pupil and of the teacher. It was unsystematic, uneven in its results, and readily
permitted exploitation of the apprentice.

We are to discuss the characteristics of apprenticeship
schooling in the next chapter. To linger here over the history of its substitution for apprenticeship would take us along
a path which, for all its interest, is too broad for the scope
of this book. In passing, however, it should be observed that

France took an early lead in the matter. The École Poly-
technique, the success of which influenced the establishment
of technical schools throughout Europe, was founded in 1794
as a result of the discovery made during the Revolution that
patriotism and courage could not make up for want of knowledge. This experience helped crystallize the French attitude
summed up by Jules Simon, "Le peuple qui a les meillieurs
écoles est le premier peuple; s'il ne l'est pas aujourd'hui, il
le sera demain." When France was able to turn from war
to peace, she found that a new form of industrial organization
had been growing up abroad, particularly in Britain, with
which she was unable to compete successfully. In the area
of hand trades, however, her success was so remarkable that
her competitors found it disturbing, and the secret of her success was trade schooling.

    4. Discovery of the Applicability of Science to Indus-
try. Interaction of the three factors named thus far explains
the "panic cry" for technical education which went up after
the first international exhibitions. Spurred by new conditions
of trade, every modern nation faced the same dilemma: find
a workable substitute for apprenticeship or lose out to nations
that do. As the century wore on, however, a fourth factor
began to assume ever-greater significance. In the more prim-
itive stages of business and industry, the nation which had an
abundant supply of raw material enjoyed a prize advantage
over all others; but industrial progress brought the insight
that, wherever superior intelligence could be applied in production, the advantage of mere possession of raw materials
was reduced. Thus Hindustan enjoyed an early advantage
over the rest of the world because of its cotton; but cotton
manufacture, though at first centered there, migrated west-
ward through Arabia to Spain, and eventually settled in England; the Arabians, the Spaniards, and the English had each
in turn learned to surpass their predecessors in the application of intelligence to production. Acting on the same principle, Switzerland had, by the time of the centennial exhibition in 1876, captured the ribbon trade from England and
was underselling American mills with goods made of cotton
grown in the United States. At about the same time, England was discovering that all, or nearly all, of the staple
manufactures which she continued to hold were "founded on
chemical principles, a knowledge of which is absolutely indispensable for their economical application."23

    Utilization of scientific knowledge was destined to be
the greatest breakthrough of the industrial revolution, but the

discovery was gradual. As of 1850-87, that commonplace of
modern industry, the research division, was unknown; even
the advancement of science was still fortuitous, not systematic. Much however was being said about "head" training: the
literature abounds in references like the one about how the
artist gets his color effects by mixing paints with his brains,
not just his hands. Certain trades moreover, like dyeing,
mining and agriculture, were by now supported by limited
bodies of "useful knowledge," and this lent an importance to
"head" training which did not exist in trades like carpentry
or masonry where good craftsmanship was manual. Old-style
apprenticeship was best suited to these hand trades, and was
poorly designed to compete with formal schooling in fields
where those who were to go to the top required specialized
"head" training.

        Early in the chapter, we noticed that "technical educa-
tion," although coined to express a definite idea, in time
gained different shades of meaning. The reason why is now
clearer. It is to be found in the multiplication of occupations,
criss-crossed by growing specialties. A definition of technical education originating within the chemical trades would lay
stress on "head" training, while definitions originating in the
older hand industries would quite as properly stress the training of "hand" and "eye. "

In Conclusion

        Three influences have been cited. First, a library
movement of unusual vitality spurred interest in some kind
of formal library training. Established libraries were quite
small by present standards, but were rapidly expanding in
size, complexity and usefulness. New libraries were springing up rapidly, too. But professional skill was accessible
almost entirely through personal contact with a handful of experienced librarians. Moreover, the body of library theory
and practice they shared showed no internal consistency,
lacked uniformity from library to library, and was recognized
as inadequate by librarians who were looking ahead. Like
birth pangs, these stresses attended the emergence of a new
division of labor having all the potentialities of a profession
except the necessary professional manpower.

        Second was a ferment of the times that stimulated ex-
perimentation. The young republic was still in process of
developing the institutional forms required for the success of

a democracy.   The Civil War had interrupted reconstruction
of higher education, but the postwar era made up for it.
There was a strong surge of interest in adapting education
to the aspirations of the people and their day-to-day vocational needs.   Classical education was on its way out for
failing to do this.

Third was the popularity of technical education as a
means of filling the vacuum left by classical education on
one hand and a crumbling system of apprenticeship on the
other.   Technical education's star rose to spectacular heights
in the quarter of a century following the origin of the movement in the 1850s.   A working assumption of this chapter is
that this vigorous movement supplied the educational model
for the first library school, so it is desirable to understand
the meaning of "technical education" at the time and why the
phenomenon gained such a grip on the popular imagination.
Contemporary definitions of the term differ in matters of detail but adhere closely to the basic idea of training in the
accepted practices of an art or craft.   The literature on the
subject in the years prior to the opening of the Columbia
School in 1887 is voluminous.   With its aid, it is possible to
sum up the essentials of the movement as follows: technical
education originated as a substitute for apprenticeship, and
this explains the form as well as the content of instruction.
Falling heir to the office of apprenticeship, technical education took its main purpose to be that of getting workers ready
for employment.   A related feature, to which reference is
made later, is that it was education designed for working
people as distinguished from those who govern them.

The movement gained rapid popularity because international trade had produced a new kind of warfare in which
the competence of working people was the decisive weapon.
Second, the industrial revolution which precipitated this rivalry led to disruption and eventual collapse of the old system
of apprenticeship.   Third, certain countries adopted early the
policy of substituting apprenticeship schooling for old-style
apprenticeship as a means of producing workshop competence,
and in the years between 1851 and 1887 this method clearly
demonstrated its superiority over the dying system of apprenticeship.

Technical education was at its best in the hand trades,
not in the scientific and technical fields where "head training"
was required.   Here we turn attention to the nature of the
educational process.   This subject, already touched upon in

introducing the movement, is discussed in the next chapter.

REFERENCES

1. U. S. Bureau of Education. Public Libraries in the
   United States of America: Their History, Condition
   and Management; Special Report. Washington:
   Govt. Printing Office, 1876. Pt. 1.

2. Library Journal 8:288-289. Sept.-Oct. 1883.

3. Library Journal 1:92. Nov. 30, 1876.

4. For a good secondary source on this early period, see
   Thwing, C. F., A History of Higher Education in
   America. Appleton, 1906.

5. Brown University. Report to the Corporation of Brown
   University on Changes in the System of Collegiate
   Education; Read March 28, 1850. Providence:
   Geo. H. Whitney, 1850. p. 11-12.

6. Brown University. Report of the Committee of the Cor-
   poration of Brown University Appointed to Raise a
   Fund of One Hundred Twenty-Five Thousand Dollars.
   Providence: Knowles, Anthony and Co., 1851.

7. Stetson, Charles B. Technical Education: What It Is
   and What American Public Schools Should Teach;
   an Essay Based on an Examination of the Methods
   and Results of Technical Education in Europe as
   Shown by Official Reports. Boston: James R. Osgood, 1874.

8. Ibid., p. 17.

9. Ibid., p. 13.

10. Alderson, Victor C. "The Need of Technical Education,
    a Paper Read before the Chicago Literary Club,
    October 20, 1902." n.p., n.d., p. 15.

11. Twentyman, A. E. "Note on the Earlier History of the
    Technical High Schools in Germany," in England.
    Ministry of Education. Special Reports on Educa-
    tional Subjects, Vol. 9, p. 465-74. See p. 465.

12   Russell, J. Scott.   Systematic Technical Education for
        the English People.   London: Bradbury, Evans and
        Co., 1869, 437p.   See p. 132.   The same year the
        British Government published a translation of the
        following comprehensive study made by the French
        ministry of agriculture, commerce and public works:
        Commission on Technical Instruction Appointed by
        Imperial Decree, 22nd. June 1863.   Report on Tech-
        nical Instruction in Germany and Switzerland, To-
        gether with Documents Laid Before the Commission
        (London, Her Majesty's Stationery Office, 1869,
        309 p.); and the same Commission's Report on
        Technical Instruction in Sweden, Together with the
        Translation of the Report of the Select Committee
        Appointed to Examine the Draft of the Bill on Tech-
        nical Education in France and Miscellanea Relating
        to Various Establishments for Technical Instruction
        in France and other Countries (London: Her Majes-
        ty's stationery office, 1869, 69 p.).

13.   National Association for the Promotion of Technical Edu-
        cation.   The Industrial Value of Technical Training;
        Some Opinions of Practical Men, reprinted from
        Contemporary Review, May 1889.   London: Coopera-
        tive Printing Society, Ltd., n. d., p. 34.

14.   Twining, Thomas.   Technical Training, Being a Sugges-
        tive Sketch of a National System of Industrial Instruc-
        tion, Founded on a General Diffusion of Practical
        Science among the People.   London: Macmillan,
        1874, 457 p.

15.   Nineteenth Century, 16, 1884, 304.

16.   See the article on "Technical education. "

17.   Playfair, Lyon.   "Technical Education, the Supplement
        of Free Trade and Protection," International Re-
        view, 7, 1879, 601-11.

18.   Russell, J. Scott, op. cit., p. 80-90.

19.   Ibid., p. 101.

20.   Great Britain.   Royal Commission on Technical Instruc-
        tion.   First Report of the Royal Commissioners on
        Technical Instruction.   Presented to both houses of

Parliament by command of Her Majesty.   London:
Printed by Eyre and Spottiswoode, 1882, 62 p.
(Parliamentary papers, 1882, Vol. 27).   Second
Report.   London: Printed by Eyre and Spottiswoode,
1884.   5 vols.   (Parliamentary papers, 1884, Vols.
29-31).

21. Twentyman, A. E. , op. cit. , p. 467.

22. Russell, J. Scott, op. cit. , p. 133.

23. The words are Sir Lyon Playfair's.   "Our Portrait Gal-
lery, Second Series, No. 38. " Dublin University
Magazine, 89, 1877, 306.

Chapter 2

THE PROCESS AND CHARACTER
OF TECHNICAL EDUCATION

One type of technical education simply used new methods to produce the same results as apprenticeship. It was
designed to initiate the beginner into workshop practices.
The second type had a more theoretical purpose. It included
the new schools and classes which were organized to disseminate the steadily growing fund of knowledge which had
industrial uses.

Initiation into Accepted Workshop Methods:
the Apprenticeship School

The programs under this heading were all alike in that
they provided more formal schooling than did apprenticeship.
The generic name applied to them was "apprenticeship
school."[1] This type of technical education provided two
kinds of training. One was the trade school. Its job was
to provide the beginner an opportunity to practice the calling
under competent supervision. The other sought to identify
the special procedures or skills which were the foundation
of standard practice and trained the beginner in these essentials.

Before describing these two varieties of technical education more fully, it should be pointed out that, while the
foundations of apprenticeship were crumbling, this system
still had its advocates. Their chief arguments were that it
still produced good results when given a fair chance; that it
held down the cost of education at public expense; and that it
accorded trade organizations more control over their work.
The Royal Commission on Technical Instruction, mentioned
in the last chapter, accepted these arguments and recommended, as the best means of protecting British superiority in

industry and trade, a revival of apprenticeship with such
changes as new conditions in industry required.

It was a solution that was generally regarded as too
conservative.

1. Trade Schools: Learning by Supervised Practice
of the Vocation. Certain French manufacturers had shown
such superior workmanship at the early international exhibitions that the superiority was at first ascribed to superior
native ability. But further inquiry, led by the Germans,
brought out the fact that the superiority was in reality due to
the way workers had been trained. Interest thereupon shifted
to the educational methods which the French had used. An
example of these methods is provided by the program of the
very successful Municipal School of Apprentices in Paris. [2]

While early trade schools usually limited themselves
to one trade this one, established in 1873, taught the trades
of the carpenter, wood-turner, pattern-maker, smith, fitter,
metal-turner and, after 1879, those of the locksmith and
maker of philosophical instruments as well. The period of
apprenticeship was three years, beginning at the age of thirteen or fourteen. Each boy was allowed a year in which to
choose a trade and during that first year, he would rotate
through all of the trades carried on in the establishment. Beginning with the second year, he would settle down to his
chosen trade and begin to produce finished articles. During
the first two years, the apprentice spent six hours a day in
the workshop and four additional hours in classes where he
had an opportunity to finish his elementary education. The
ratio changed in the third year to eight hours in the workshop and two in classwork.

Trade schools like this one arose elsewhere in France,
in Austria, and spread to northern Germany, Russia and the
United States but made little headway in Britain. Their method was to initiate the worker into the accepted way of practicing a trade. The initiation was thorough enough to qualify
the graduate to go out and make a living as a practitioner
with no further training. The type of supervision and equipment used sometimes made these schools costly to operate,
but the training itself proved to be one way to provide an effective substitute for apprenticeship. The other substitute,
to which we now turn attention, has greater relevance to the
history of library training, so we shall go into more detail.

2. Learning Generally Applicable Elements of Vocational Skill. When President John D. Runkle left Massachusetts Institute of Technology to attend the Centennial Exhibition in 1876, the question uppermost in his mind was whether he would find in Philadelphia any suggestions on how to
improve instruction in the industrial arts. He hoped he would.
The young Institute had pioneered in developing practical
methods of scientific and mechanical instruction but there was
still quite a gap between the training American enterprise demanded and the results being produced by the newly developing technical schools.

One way to close this gap would be to accept the trade
school as a model and operate industries and trades in schools
like M. I. T., but this would, as industries multiplied and grew
more complex, become too expensive. Another way would be
to reverse the procedure and provide the necessary practical
training in industrial establishments. The American Institute
of Mining Engineers was interested in this approach. A proposal in February, 1876, to organize schools in engineering
works where instruction could be correlated with workshop
and laboratory practice, caught on so well that arrangements
were made to explore the possibility at a joint meeting with
the American Society of Civil Engineers. This was done the
following June in Philadelphia, just when the Centennial was
opening. 3

Such was the state of affairs when a Russian exhibit
at the Centennial made a sensational contribution to technical
education. "Of the Russian exhibit as a whole," the New
York Tribune said on July 1, 1876, "it is not extravagant
praise to say that it is superb. " The judges of the exhibits
in Education and Science, among whom were Andrew D.
White and David Coit Gilman, wrote at length upon the work
of two technical schools which were responsible for the innovation: the St. Petersburg Practical Technical School and
the Imperial Technical School at Moscow. Their official report is liberally sprinkled with superlatives. The exhibit
was "unique. " It was "the most important representation
made by any state or nation. " It captured public interest
because it "presented a practical solution of a problem in
technical education which is everywhere recognized of the
very first importance, and yet which up to this time, has
only been half solved in any other country. "4 What was it
all about?

The system had originated in 1868 at the School in

Moscow,[5] which was under the direct patronage of their Imperial Majesties, Alexander II and Maria Alexandrovena.
This School trained mechanical builders, mechanical engineers
and technical engineers. It consisted ot two divisions, general and special, each division with a course covering three
years. The general division embraced instruction in religion,
the French and German languages, and all scientific subjects
previous knowledge of which was required of pupils in the special division--free hand drawing and linear drawing, descriptive geometry, general physics, zoology, botany, mineralogy,
chemistry, geodesy, analytical geometry, higher algebra, dif-
ferential and integral calculus, general mechanics, and drawing of machine parts. The three-year course in the special
division covered organic and analytical chemistry, metallurgy,
practical physics, mechanical and chemical technology, technology of wood and metals, analytical mechanics, construction
of machines, practical mechanics, railway construction, engineering and constructive art, projecting and estimating of
machines, works and mills, industrial statistics and bookkeeping. The School maintained, largely through student labor, shops which handled outside orders, and in so doing not
only showed students how to operate mechanical works on a
commercial basis but also provided them further workshop
experience while providing the School with part of its income.
Separate from these commercial works, the School maintained
an elaborate system of workshops organized solely for instruction in the "principles" of mechanic arts. Pupils were admitted to practice in the mechanical works only when they
had mastered, through practice in the instruction shops, the
elemental practices involved in the various phases of mechanic art such as turning, fitting, carpentering and forging.

Herein lay the revolutionary feature of what was so
soon to become known as "the Russian method." It was interpreted in the official report of the Centennial as follows:

> ... An account of the extraordinary representations
> of the great technical schools above mentioned ...
> must be indulged in such fullness ... as will
> clearly present the important lessons taught,
> namely, how to organize shopwork instruction so
> as to make it sufficiently thorough, economical
> or attractive, and how to connect such instruc-
> tion with the theoretical instruction given in the
> mechanical departments of technical schools. Here
> tofore, there has been much groping in this whole

field ... and much money has been wasted in vain
attempts to settle the principles that should govern
.... The schools at the two Russian capitols have
cut the knot by showing that the whole business of
practical instruction can be reduced to a comparatively few simple elements which, by pursuing a
systematic course--by taking the necessary steps in
proper order--may easily be mastered. ... They
have pointed out that in constructions of every sort,
certain typical forms are involved. ... Thus the
student has but to learn how to produce these few
forms in a most skillful manner in order to acquire
a mastery of the elements of practical mechanics.
The general principles laid down for the organization of shop-instruction are substantially these:
(1) There should be separateness of work for purposes of instruction from construction-work for purposes of business; (2) separateness of each general
class of work from every other; (3) equipment of
each shop so as to accommodate all who may be in-
structed by one teacher at one time; (4) systematic
graduation of the forms to be produced according to
skill required ... (5) if practicable, a construction
shop, where the elementary forms may be brought
into the combination required for practical use. 6

Melvil Dewey called the course which opened at Columbia in 1887 a "systematic apprenticeship." It is an expres-
sive description which fits the method introduced by the Russians. They referred to it as "a systematic method" of
teaching such practical arts as turning, carpentering, fitting
and forging. 7 They had hit upon the modern idea of job analysis, had broken down workshop practice into its elements,
sorted out the essential from the unnecessary and used the results to organize separate classes where these elements could
be taught thoroughly. This procedure made it possible for
the first time to drill young workmen in a body of skills common to various workshops, thus removing from apprenticeship
the whimsies and eccentricities peculiar to individual workmen.

Runkle applied to this process the illuminating name,
"alphabet of mechanism."8 The insight he sought to convey
was that good craftsmanship in various callings can be resolved into a relatively small number of elemental skills.
Once a beginner masters these, he is ready to go to work in
any shop in the field. Clearly the insight had important im-

plications for the future of the whole technical education movement. A single instructor could now teach an intricate vocational procedure or skill to a class of twenty to thirty apprentices as quickly as a master could teach it to a single apprentice, and the skilled teacher would probably outdo the master
in effectiveness. Furthermore, an apprenticeship school
could now expect to supply such training without prohibitive
costs. As President Runkle enthusiastically observed a few
weeks later when he recommended adoption of the Russian
method at M. I. T.: "It is not necessary for a school to operate a railroad to teach its civil engineers nor work a mine
to teach its mining engineers nor maintain a menagerie to
teach natural history."

     The meaning of teaching "principles" has been a re-
curring question throughout the history of education for librarians. It is instructive, therefore, to note the meaning
given it by the Russian method. The M. I. T. program as
reorganized in the fall of 1876 will tell us what we want to
know. M. I. T. had previously organized its training by vocations. It now substituted courses organized in terms of
"the principles of mechanic art." The resultant courses
were as follows: carpentering and joinery, wood-turning and
pattern-making (in woodwork); vise-work, forging, foundry-
work and machine tool-work (in iron work); designing, pat-
tern-weaving and dyeing (in textile manufacture).

     Of the several mechanic arts enumerated, vise-work
can be used as well as any to bring out the added flexibility
in training which the new method made possible. The elements of vise-work are: filing, chipping, sawing, scraping,
breast-drilling and tapping. But once having mastered them
all, the graduate was able to use vise-work in widely assorted types of production and construction--as in the work of
the blacksmith, tool-maker, gunsmith, die-sinker, iron-
mould-maker, locksmith, machinist, tinsmith, brass-finisher,
jeweller, maker of philosophical, nautical, musical and engineering instruments, etc. [9]

     The process was thus one of sorting out and mastering
those generally applicable elements of a vocation which, when
combined like letters of the alphabet, spell out vocational
competence.

Instruction in Useful Knowledge:
the Higher Technical School

Turning to the second category of programs, instruction in "useful knowledge" for working people took many
forms. 10 Four principal ways arose before, or in connection
with, the technical education movement to serve the needs of
lower grades of work: slanting of primary education for
workers' children toward industrial requirements; provision
of special classes for adult workmen who were interested in
advancement in local works or elsewhere; establishment of
schools or classes for developing in local employees the special skills required by the sponsoring industrial establishment; and establishment of private or state-supported schools
for the two-fold object of operating a trade and offering some
theoretical instruction as well.

Programs of the latter variety shade off into those of
technical schools designed to provide training for higher
grades of work. These higher technical schools--the early
models for U. S. "technical," "technological" and "polytechnic"
institutes--were developed in Germany. There the pattern of
education was influenced by a type of social stratification
which gave ordinary business and industrial workers of all
kinds status inferior to that of royalty, the military caste, in-
tellectuals, and others who made up the upper classes. Hence,
as the industrial revolution broadened the demand for the type
of master workman who could apply to the enterprise the best
available knowledge, the technical school, which has roots
going back to the 18th century and earlier, evolved as a companion and supplement to the university. The latter was, by
deepening tradition, dedicated to the pursuit of knowledge for
its own sake.

The differences between these two institutions, the university and the higher technical school, are now blurred, so
it is difficult to grasp the fact that the technical school originated, as did other forms of technical education, to get working people ready for their life's work. The literature makes
this view of the matter plain.

> For innumerable years [a 1745 statement reads] we
> men of learning have been able to think that we
> alone are the pillars of learning and that, outside
> our four faculties, sanity and reason are not to be
> found. We would retain honor enough if we were
> to cede one part, even the half of it, to our neigh-

bors who live in other classes (in commerce, trade,
agriculture and mechanic arts). And yet, amid all
the sums of money devoted to schools and academies,
they have received little or no attention. 11

This differs only in detail from the wording used in
describing similar schools which sprang up in the United
States in the years following the Civil War. An example of
this is provided by an article in the Forum, as late as 1891,
on "Technological Education in the United States." There was
by this time a tendency to use a term like "technological education" to cover all kinds of training which involved

in the first place, scientific laboratories of physics,
of chemistry and so on as well as field work in the
various natural sciences; in the second place, the
general drawing room, free hand and mechanical;
in the third place, the distinctly technical laboratories of engineering, of applied mechanics, analytical and industrial chemistry, architectural and
machine design, and the like, where principles find
their application and practice finds its foundation. 12

These forms of training were given an outward semblance of
identity, in spite of notable differences in aim, by the prevailing faculty psychology. The latter fostered the impression
that the most important thing about them was that they were,
one and all, "forms of training where the hand and the senses
play a part." From this standpoint, those colleges which
were in process of establishing scientific laboratories were
by definition becoming technical or technological institutions.
Looking past this artificial unity however we see, with this
writer in the Forum, that the college and the technological
institution were unlike in method and results. The colleges,
it is emphasized there, are less concerned with knowledge
which can be used for vocational purposes. In the technical
school, on the other hand, "the knowledge acquired is put to
immediate use." The writer goes on to say: "A technological school, then, is an institution of collegiate grade where
science is studied with reference to its application to productive and constructive industry." This emphasis on application
and vocational use recurs again and again, as one further
quotation will illustrate:

By a technical school I understand not one in which
the manipulation or routine of a trade is taught
[i.e., an apprenticeship school] but a school where

a lad receives general instruction in the principles
of applied science and special instruction in the application of these principles to the particular trade
he is following or which he is about to follow. [13]

Appraisal of the Technical Education Movement

The results were both positive and negative. Well before 1887, technical education had clearly demonstrated that
formal schooling could be used to produce results comparable
to old-style apprenticeship. Some methods produced even better results at less cost to master and apprentice alike. Second, there was a flexibility about technical education that
made it infinitely superior to apprenticeship as a means of
coping with new conditions in labor and industry. Changes in
the worker's world were creating a fluidity in kinds of jobs
which was modifying the whole pattern of daily work and the
kind of training required to do this work. The perfection of
a method so well adapted to the new situation was a major
contribution.

On the other side of the ledger, the movement failed
to distinguish between trades and professions. This is explained in part by the fact that technical education proved to
be a convenient weapon of change. It not only served vocations for which no special schooling had been organized before; it furthered a reaction against purely intellectual preparation in favor of practical training linked closely to working
conditions. Even the older learned professions were to benefit from the new emphasis, but the pendulum of reaction at
first swung quite wide, as the following colorful contribution
to Columbiana illustrates.

Richard T. Auchmuty, a prominent New Yorker and
friend of Melvil Dewey, founded the New York Trade School
in 1881, to give poor boys a chance to learn a trade "without
having to submit to the conditions imposed by the labor un-
ions of apprenticeship. " Auchmuty had no objection to apprenticeship but he believed the training period would have to
be cut down to keep skilled trades from being taken over by
European trained immigrants, and the Trade School was his
way of doing something about it. Using an adaptation of the
Russian Method, the school provided systematic training in
brick-laying, plastering, plumbing, carpentry, house and
sign painting, fresco painting, stone-cutting, blacksmith work,
and tailoring. There was no companion "construction" school,

as in Russia; it was, in the idiom of the time, an "instruction" school, pure and simple. Instruction consisted of four
months of intensive work in one trade and was designed to
produce skill comparable to an apprenticeship of three to four
years.

By 1890, the absence of cultural subjects had convinced
Auchmuty that the program, successful in all other respects,
should be moved to an academic environment. In December
of that year he formally offered the school, with its property
and endowment, to Columbia College. There was a string
attached: the Columbia trustees would have to continue this
very practical system of trade education unchanged. That
this step would take Columbia into a "new field," he realized;
but it was a step which he considered to be "in the line of
the work already undertaken by Columbia College in its professional and special schools."[14]

At this distance, it is less surprising that Columbia
turned down the offer than that it was made in the first place.
We must bear in mind that the present differentiation of professions from trades was yet to be made. Lines of demarca-
tion were in a state of flux. The following passage on the
importance of the new education to engineering is but one
example of many showing that Auchmuty's confusion on the
subject was not an isolated case:

> It has been found that a technical education and spe-
> cial preparation of the working-man, in the 'trades'
> represented by our 'profession,' are absolutely
> necessary ... to take the place of that system of
> apprenticeship which is now passing away.[15]

It was to be expected that the founders of the modern
library movement would start out with the language of their
times, so Dewey in 1879 uses "librarian's trade" and "librarian's profession" as interchangeable terms.[16]

The professions were not highly developed and were
influenced by the prevailing laws and customs of apprenticeship. Trades, on the other hand, were highly developed and
practical learning on the job had gained prestige through proud
national achievements in canal-building, road-building, and
mining. Since newer professions had to choose between "cultural" training of questionable relevance and increasingly well-
defined models of technical education, the gap was not easily
straddled by one who saw merits in both. Thomas H. Huxley
tried it in 1877, with the following ambiguous result:

> Technical education [he says], in the sense in which
> the term is ordinarily used and in which I am now
> employing it, means that sort of education which is
> specially adapted to the needs of men whose busi-
> ness in life is to pursue some kind of handicraft;
> it is, in fact, a fine Greco-Latin equivalent for
> what in good vernacular English would be called
> the teaching of handicrafts. [17]

He goes on to classify himself, an anatomist, as a
handicraftsman on the ground that his profession involves
among other things a certain manual dexterity--practical skill
acquired by training. Thereupon he divides production of
good craftsmanship, the mark of all finished handicraftsmen,
into two parts: (1) Preparatory instruction aimed at making
the mind as useful an instrument as possible, and (2) Workshop experience. This preparatory instruction, he observes,
has "nothing especially technical about it," and here we come
to his main point:

> Exactly so; that remark takes us straight to the
> heart of what I have to say, which is, that in my
> judgment the preparatory education of the handi-
> craftsman ought to have nothing of what is ordinari-
> ly understood by 'technical' about it. The workshop
> is the only real school for handicrafts.

Nature hailed the address as an eloquent expression
of the view "that, after all, the mind is the most important
instrument which the handicraftsman, whether he be a tinker
or a physicist, will ever be called upon to use, and that
therefore a technical education which teaches him to use a
lathe, or a tool, or a loom, before he has learned how to
use his mind, is not education at all."[18] The London Times,
on the other hand, found the speech instructive and amusing,
but confusing, and took Huxley to task for trying to reduce
the training of the handicraftsman and the professional man
to the same formula. Huxley's goal in dissecting a beetle,
the editorial concludes, is in reality different from that of
a workman who makes a watch. The distinction between the
two purposes, with all that it implies in educational methods
required to accomplish them, "is precisely that which distin-
guishes a handicraftsman from a professional man," and as
between the two "the anatomist's purpose requires a far higher intellectual education than ... the workman's."

If the technical education movement failed to grasp the

difference between trades and professions, it also failed to
grasp the difference between developing technicians and developing men and women who are fitted for the opportunities
and responsibilities of a free society. In 19th century European countries where the movement originated, the responsibilities of social and intellectual leadership devolved by long-
established tradition on a class separate from working people.
Not only was there no practical reason for educating the latter
for such responsibilities: any encouragement of the lower
classes to develop their minds was opposed by some as a
threat to stable government. America, on the other hand,
had no rulers except the people themselves. Self-government was conceived, not as an inherent capacity, but as a
possible achievement. In a narrow sense, the success of the
experiment might depend on exercising the right to vote, but
in reality it depended on discharging a variety of citizenship
responsibilities at a high level of enlightenment. Furthermore, self-government was part of a more inclusive way of
life which placed a high premium on developing the fullest
powers of the individual, maintaining a high standard of living, and promoting a standard of civilization befitting free
men. All these things called for education of an order which
forms and methods borrowed from the Old World proved in-
capable of providing.

    There is an epic quality about the vigor and imagina-
tion shown during the second quarter of the 19th century,
when the young republic set about relating lower and higher
education more closely to its aims and aspirations. By the
time the task was resumed after the Civil War, technical
education was no longer simply a means of providing a substitute for apprenticeship. It was an aggressive movement
which adopted the dichotomy of faculty psychology between
"head" training and "hand-and-eye" training to press its
claims against liberal education.

    The gradual accommodation of these two educational
philosophies to one another is illustrated by the experience
of Illinois where, in 1851, resolutions were adopted calling
for a university to meet "the felt wants of each and all the
industrial classes of our state."[19] In a few years, the Illinois drive branched out into a campaign to create "means
for the specific and higher education of the toiling masses of
the nation" as a whole. It was a campaign addressed to
"the industrial classes, including all cultivators of the soil,
artisans, mechanics, and merchants."[20] These efforts are
commonly credited with the initiation of the famous Morrill

Act, which laid the foundation for our land-grant colleges.
One of the first of these was the Illinois State Industrial University, which is now the University of Illinois. The latter,
when compared with the industrial school of 1867, offers students from families of all classes training for a much greater variety of callings, but there also have been even more
significant changes in spirit and purpose as the school has
adjusted its program to the way democracy treats its human
resources. Similar changes have occurred in some, but by
no means all, of the technical institutes which were founded
during the same post-war era of enthusiasm for technical education. Thus Massachusetts Institute of Technology, as an
example, remains a professional school but is now closer to
the idea of the modern university than to the technical education of that time.

        The rivalry which makes this one of the great eras of
debate on national educational policy was in some ways as intense in lower as in higher education. Reference has already
been made to Stetson whose Technical Education attacked the
public-school movement for weaknesses which he sought to
remedy by bringing it in line with the technical-education
movement. He and other advocates of the new cause scored
heavily with these arguments: (a) the public schools were
less effective in training the children of working people for
later life than was the education being used for this purpose
in other countries; (b) public schools give "head" training
whereas training for adult life, to be practical, should emphasize the training of "hand and eye"; (c) changes in American life were fundamental enough to justify thorough reconstruction of education anyway.

        These arguments were not lost on politicians, as an
address of 1883 by the Honorable William Walter Phelps,
U. S. Congressman from New Jersey, illustrates. The republic, he argued, can exist only so long as its citizens know
how to vote right and earn a living. To know how to vote
right, the young citizen must learn to read and write; to earn
a living, he must master the rudiments of industrial learning.
It is "the state's responsibility to give him both and there its
responsibility ends." There must not only be the public school
that teaches him to read and write, but there must be the industrial school that teaches him how to work; "or, what is
better and simpler, the one public school should have a division of time so that certain hours the children should be
taught to think and others to work."21

Acceptable adjustments followed two courses. One is described by M. A. Newell, President of the N. E. A. , State Superintendent of Education and Principal of the State Normal School of Maryland in an 1877 address on "Education and Labor":

> Do I think it possible to attach workshops to our public schools? [He asks]. Certainly not; but I do think it possible to have public workshops where boys can learn trades as well as public schools where they can learn letters. And just as we transfer the few from the state school to the state college, where they learn to be thinkers, I would transfer the many from the city school to the city workshop where they would learn to be workers. [22]

Less than a year later, the city of Baltimore endorsed this solution by founding a Manual Training School as a free public school. Similar schools appeared in Boston, Chicago, St. Louis, and other leading cities.

The other course was the inclusion of manual training in the regular program of the public school. One exhibition at Philadelphia in 1876 had shown the results of experiments in Massachusetts of teaching industrial arts, especially drawing, in the schools. The object was not so much to discover or develop special aptitudes as to balance "head training" with "the training of hand and eye. " The same idea was later to find forceful support in one of our educational classics, John Dewey's School and Society, published in 1899. Twenty years earlier, it was already being applauded by educators, among them John D. Runkle who argued persuasively that "to give hand instruction its full educational value it should be incorporated into the school course and pursued systematically in connection with cognate studies. " Both solutions, the separate workshop school and the inclusion of manual training courses in the public school, were lively topics in the 1880's. [23]

In Conclusion

The programs of technical education, which reached the crest of public approval in the United States between 1850 and 1887, fell into two main categories. One class consisted of the apprenticeship schools, which in turn could be subdivided into two classes. The first one, the trade school, trained the worker in the trade itself. The second involved

an analysis of the work processes of the trade or craft into
their basic elements, their ABC's. These elements of standard practice, taken together, constituted the underlying art
or know-how of the calling. Courses in the art were organized around these elemental techniques or skills. Often students would take them up seriatim, one being mastered before
going on to another. The name "apprenticeship school" is
appropriate because both types of training were more systematic than apprenticeship.

Another main category consisted of technical schools
and classes through which useful knowledge--i. e. , knowledge
having vocational application--was disseminated to working
people. This pattern was not as well defined as were the
apprenticeship schools because of differences in level and organization of instruction. These differences in turn were related to changing demands of a society which, in being in-
dustrialized, was making new and ever more fundamental
uses of organized scientific knowledge. The common function
of these schools was to give the more specialized type of
worker the kind of vocational preparation he required.

The great contribution of the technical education movement was to provide a workable substitute for apprenticeship.
Since this ancient system was being outmoded by the industrial revolution, something had to be done to fill the vacuum
and to provide training for new specialties which were springing up on all sides. How well working people's educational
needs would be met by a type of training which evolved mainly for trades and crafts was still to be tested by experience,
but that period offered no workable alternative. Another problem left to the future was what accommodations would occur
between a type of education which had been perfected for
workers in a class-conscious society and that suited to a society where all citizens share equally the responsibilities of
self-government and where the cultivation of human resources
is a primary goal.

Whatever the long-range problems, technical education
offered immediate results which changes in American life
made urgently desirable. In consequence, it attained phenomenal popularity and influence. It gave vigorous impulse
to the founding of land-grant colleges and state universities.
It explains the rapid growth of technical and technological institutes during the second half of the century and had much
to do with reform of the lower schools. It was within this
environment that librarians studied their problems and began
laying the foundations of modern library education.

REFERENCES

1. The article, "Apprenticeship and Education," in Monroe's
    Cyclopedia of Education (N. Y.: Macmillan, 1911.
    V. 1, p. 149-61) is one of the best secondary
    sources on this type of schooling available. The
    following from the section on France is worth quot-
    ing here:

    In France, more than in any other country, the ef-
    fort has been made to develop not only technical
    and art schools supplementary to apprenticeship but
    schools actually to perform the function and take the
    place of apprenticeship. From the first, the policy
    of the French people has been to effect these results
    mainly through public schools controlled by the cen-
    tral government.

2. Of the many contemporary sources on this school, per-
    haps the best brief, easily accessible source is:
    Great Britain. Royal Commission on Technical Edu-
    cation. Technical Instruction in France. Washing-
    ton: Government Printing Office, 1882. (U. S. Bur-
    eau of Education, Circular of Information, No. 6,
    1882.)

3. American Institute of Mining Engineers. Discussions on
    Technical Education at the Washington Meeting of
    the American Institute of Mining Engineers, Febru-
    ary 22 and 23, 1876, and at a Joint Meeting of the
    American Society of Civil Engineers and the Ameri-
    can Institute of Mining Engineers at Philadelphia
    on June 19 and 20, 1876. Easton, Pennsylvania:
    The Institute, 1876. See especially the address of
    President A. L. Holley, p. 7-23 and the discussion
    p. 24-43.

4. U. S. Centennial Commission. International Exhibition,
    1876. Reports and Awards, Group XXVIII, ed. by
    Francis A. Walker. Philadelphia: Lippincott, 1878,
    p. 161-162.

5. The description of the Russian exhibit in the report just
    cited (161-179) includes a full account of this school
    by its Director, Victor Della-Voss. See also Mas-
    sachusetts Institute of Technology. The Russian
    System of Shop-work Instruction for Engineers and

36   Library Education

Machinists. Boston: A. A. Kingman, 1876.

6. U. S. Centennial Commission, op. cit., p. 165-66.

7. Massachusetts Institute of Technology, op. cit., p. 16.

8. Massachusetts Institute of Technology. President's Report for the Year ending September 30, 1876. Boston: The Institute, 1877.

9. Rogers, William B. "Education by Hand," Harper's New Monthly Magazine, 58, 1879, 409-17.

10. To give some idea of the variety and number of technical schools which arose in the larger German cities in the nineteenth century, the Magistrate of the Berlin municipality had under his general supervision in 1899 the following: one weaving school, two handicraft schools, building schools with 267 pupils, work rooms and trade schools with an enrollment of 11,198 students who were qualifying themselves to be bricklayers, carpenters, joiners, shoemakers, painters, decorators, saddlers, upholsterers, blacksmiths, glaziers, chimney sweeps, wheelrights, basket-makers, bookbinders, gardeners, printers, tailors, confectioners, potters, photographers, plumbers, coopers, and barbers. In addition, there were four continuation schools for adult men, eighteen for boys, fifteen for girls, with a total enrollment in these schools of 18,487. Bertram, H. "The Continuation Schools in Berlin," in England. Ministry of Education. Special Reports on Educational Subjects, Vol. 9, 451-64.

11. Twentyman, A. E., op. cit., p. 466.

12. Tyler, H. W. Forum 12:18-27, 1891-92.

13. Alexander B. Shand quoted by Tyler in the article just cited.

14. I have drawn mainly on the following for information about Auchmuty's school: Auchmuty, Richard T. Confidential [Proposal] to the Trustees of Columbia College from Richard T. Auchmuty, December 1890 (Privately printed, 24 p.); and Combes, Edward. Report on Technical Education and Manual Training

at the Paris Universal Exhibition of 1889 and in Great Britain, France and the United States of America. Sydney: George Stephen Chapman, 1891. See p. 100-01, Appendix K, 226-32. For a sample discussion of associating technical education with universities, see Shaler, N. S. "Relations of Academic and Technical Instruction," Atlantic Monthly, 72, July-December, 1893, 259-68.

15. American Institute of Mining Engineers, op. cit., p. 45.

16. Library Journal 4:147.

17. Huxley, Thomas H. "Technical Education," Fortnightly Review, 29, 1878, 48-58. The explanation of technical education given by the early French report, cited elsewhere, deserves mention alongside Huxley's apt definition. Technical education is portrayed there as taking the place of apprenticeship and as capping off primary instruction by getting young workers ready to practice a trade (p. 16-18).

18. "Technical Education," Nature, A Weekly Illustrated Journal of Science 17:97-98.

19. U. S. Commissioner of Education. Report, with Circulars and Documents, 1867-68. Washington, D. C.: Government Printing Office, 1869, p. 305-06. See also James, Edmund J. The Origin of the Land-grant Act of 1862 (the Morrill Act) and Some Account of its Author, Jonathan B. Turner. Urbana-Champaign: University of Illinois Press, 1910. (University Studies, Vol. 4, No. 1).

20. Ibid.

21. Quoted in U. S. Bureau of Education. Education in the Industrial and Fine Arts in the United States. Part II. Industrial and manual training in public schools. Washington: Government Printing Office, 1892.

22. U. S. Bureau of Education, op. cit.

23. The annual report of the U. S. Commissioner of Labor for 1893 (Government Printing Office, 1893) is devoted entirely to industrial education in the United States and foreign countries. It makes the following

comparison: "The manual training school ... aims
at developing ... all the powers of the individual
.... The trade and technical schools on the other
hand aim at such special development as will give
a mastery of some particular craft. Unlike many
of the manual training schools none of those for
trade and technical training are parts of the public
school system. "

Chapter 3

ADOPTION OF THE APPRENTICESHIP
SCHOOL AS A MODEL

Melvil Dewey, founder of the first library school, conducted a preliminary class in the Columbia College Library
from 1884 to 1886 to try out the possibilities of organized
training. One of the students, Henry Watson Kent, later described Dewey as follows:

> What Dewey taught was not the love of books ...
> but how to administer a library and how to care for
> the needs of those who would know and use books
> .... He was not a great student or scholar nor a
> great bibliographer, but he was what might be called
> a great mechanician. He knew instinctively what
> was needed to make the library machine a good one.
> Dewey stood for the dignity of his profession, li-
> brarianship, and for the importance of the public
> library as second only to the public school....
> What the Columbia School taught me, what I had
> not known before, were the things that Dewey stood
> for and that ... I saw him accomplish. [1]

This is more than a characterization of a man. It
describes a new breed of librarian. Nobody polled opinions
in the 1880s; but had a poll been taken of American librarians
who best exemplified the contemporary ideal, Justin Winsor
of Harvard would probably have topped the list. Winsor's
first love, however, was scholarship: as his biographer puts
it, Winsor "found time" in his work on history and historical
bibliography to take active part in the American library movement. [2] Dewey grasped the fact that it was no longer enough
to treat librarianship as a side-job for first-rate minds or
as clerical work for factotums. He perceived that a new
profession was emerging; that the major problems were man-
agerial, as well as national rather than entirely local; that

39

the job called for dedicated full-time professionals; and that
all of this argued for an improved system of manpower development.

Dewey may have made the boldest break with the past,
but he was not the first to have the chance to do so.   A
century earlier, for example, when Gotthold E. Lessing became Librarian of the University of Wolfenbüttel, the German
nations presented a remarkable opportunity for planning future
library services, for devising uniform methods of library
organization, and training qualified library personnel, but the
opportunity was defaulted.[3]   Lessing was the logical one to
take the lead; but while he had a keen grasp of the importance
of the library to scholarship, he was not an imaginative administrator.   Continuing with his studies, he brought a certain distinction to the post of librarian, but treated it as a
side-job, being content to leave local library operations to
second-grade minds and to leave problems that took him beyond the front door of his own library to resolve themselves.
The progress of the American library movement owes a great
deal to the things that Dewey stood for and accomplished.
Library training was one of his earliest interests, and the nub
of the problem was to devise or discover a workable model
to use.

Early Discussions of Library Training

Perhaps the earliest discussion of special schooling
for librarians that we can safely say Dewey knew about is a
proposal by a German scholar that library economy, understood by him as a discipline concerned with handling a library
as an integral part of a larger academic organization, be
made a special study in the German university.   The account
opens with an oblique reference to the idea of a Professor of
Books, a phrase which Emerson had used in 1870[4] to dramatize the emergence of a new office or responsibility.   Emerson estimated that "the number of printed books extant may
easily exceed a million," and went on to demonstrate that he
who would read their hundreds of millions of pages must die
in the first alcoves of the library--even if he should read
from dawn until dark for sixty years.   No one else had made
it so clear that the ever-expanding record of the mind would
henceforth require the reader to follow some "rule" or "method" if he were to gain the best that books hold for him.   To
gain this, the ideal reader's guide would be those vanishing
masters "whose eyes sweep the whole horizon of learning";

but even if it stops short of perfection, as it must, guidance
of some kind, Emerson concluded, had become imperative.
It is this new and much-needed guidance function that he assigns to his Professor of Books.   In this way, Emerson's
essay on "Books" became an early contribution to the literature on library education.

        The German proposal just referred to was made by
F. Rullmann in a 28-page brochure published in 1874. [5]   The
1876 Report finds the type of instruction recommended there
better suited to the needs of American librarians than any
alternative in sight.   To quote from the Report:

> Considerable space has been devoted, under the title
> of Professorships of Books and Reading, to the dis-
> cussion of the question of a new college professor-
> ship the duties of which should be to teach what and
> how to read.   While this would meet the needs of
> college students, the much larger constituency of
> the public libraries would still remain, as now,
> generally dependent on the librarians for advice and
> direction.   Hence, it is clear that the librarian
> must soon be called upon to assume a distinct posi-
> tion, as something more than a mere custodian of
> books, and the scientific scope and value of his of-
> fice be recognized and estimated in a becoming man-
> ner.   To meet the demands that will be made on
> him he should be granted opportunities for instruc-
> tion in all the departments of library science. [6]

        The new branch of study as outlined by Rullmann was
to embrace: foreign languages; general history as well as
collateral studies such as paleography and diplomatics; "encyclopedia," with special regard to the structure of thought
comprehended by the major fields of learning; a history of
literature, with primary attention to books of greatest intrin-
sic importance and to books of special antiquarian interest;
the history of the manuscript, printing, and the booktrade;
the fine arts and book production; the history of library science; the management of libraries and archives; the world's
great libraries (bibliothecography); and practical instruction
in cataloging and classification.   In justification of the new
discipline, Rullmann drew attention to the difficulty of coping
with modern library problems without attacking them in this
manner.   German libraries, he observed, suffered from lack
of uniform codes of practice.   They relied on the costly habit
of solving local library problems with little understanding of

the experience of other libraries.   There was no common
body of professional thought.   University study was needed
to develop a generation of librarians equipped to deal with
all these fundamental matters.

The first issue of the Library Journal appeared, with
Dewey as Editor, in September, 1876.   An editorial statement
on "The Profession" stands alongside a review of "The Government Library Report. "   The reviewer points out that the
Report contains "a translation of Dr. Rullmann's tract advocating library science as a subject of special study in German
universities, " and adds:

> In line with the tract of Dr. Rullmann in the pref-
> ace, Mr. F. B. Perkins and Mr. William Mathews
> urge the establishment in the larger colleges and
> universities of chairs on 'books and reading, ' teach-
> ing not what to read, but how to read--the method-
> ology of handling printed knowledge.

A year later, in 1877, Dewey attended the International Library Conference in London as a member of the U. S.
delegation.   One session of this Conference was devoted to
the functions and qualifications of the chief executive of a library, and there Andrea Crestadoro spoke of Italian ideas on
the education of librarians:

> By a recent royal decree in Italy [the abbreviated
> record of his remarks states], it is ordered that
> in every national library [of which there were five]
> a chair of librarianship be established to teach and
> train students in bibliothecal sciences so as to quali-
> fy them for appointments as librarians. 7

Italy in the nineteenth century, proud of her ancient connections with letters and art, was among the pioneers of modern
library development.   A short-lived course of library instruction had been inaugurated at the University of Naples in 1865.
Four years later, in 1869, the minister of public instruction
had suggested a modest university course in library science.
A commission worked out what proved to be an over-ambitious
plan, which was incorporated in two decrees issued in January and March, 1876.   Covering various aspects of library
administration, these new regulations outlined a two-year
course of study leading to a diploma, to be handled by two
officials and open to members of the staff of the Vittoria
Emanuel Library at Rome as well as to students from the out-

side. Drawing liberally on the best thought of other European countries, the projected course of study embraced instruction in the following subjects: the history and external conditions relating to books, both in early and in later times; elementary knowledge of how to define and classify the sciences and the most fundamental works in each field; the origin and varieties of handwriting; the invention and history of printing; the state of the booktrade; the proper arrangement of a library, the administration of its internal machinery and its relations with the public; the formation of catalogues; the most important works on bibliography; some knowledge of the working machinery, endowments and actual condition of the principal libraries of Europe and their history; and the elements of paleography.[8]

The whole experience illustrated the difficulty of decreeing major professional developments into existence. The plan does not appear to have been put into effect in any of the five national libraries. Presumably, the short interval before the 1877 Conference did not allow enough time to reveal this outcome.

Charles H. Robarts, of All Souls' College, spoke of educating librarians in an address on "University Libraries as National Institutions."[9] Referring to Carlyle's oft-quoted remark that a true university is a collection of books, Robarts dwelled on the fact that the "extraordinary multiplication of books" was not only enriching the intellectual resources of universities but was also transforming the role of the library and the librarian. Library collections had been large enough for quite a long time to require some kind of organization, and librarians had grown accustomed to thinking that their responsibility ended there. In reality, the "mechanical assistance" afforded by organizing a collection was no longer enough. Changing conditions, he argued, were making it increasingly desirable to provide readers an opportunity to consult "living and intelligent guides." He approved of the American idea of appointing professors of books because it would help modernize the role of the library and the librarian:

> Assistants qualified in that special knowledge which has been termed Bibliothekswissenschaft are more essential to a great university library; and amongst the advantages of the development of university libraries we may hope for the rise of a school of highly trained students in bibliographical knowledge.

In the discussion period, one British speaker, who

enthusiastically endorsed Robarts' position, emphasized the
propriety of university sponsorship of such work and hoped
that the outcome would be a "school of librarians." Justin
Winsor gave the idea further support, saying,

> There is no calculating the good capable of coming
> from a body of educated fellows of an Oxford Col-
> lege devoting themselves to the science of library
> management. It is a fortuitous and fortunate com-
> bination of forces such as the world has never seen
> and from its consummation, I think we may safely
> date a new departure and an elevating outcome.

Winsor held a position in this 1877 Conference second only
to that of John Winter Jones, Librarian of the British Museum. He was presiding at this session and made his remarks
from the chair.

It was a historic discussion. It caught the outlines of
what the builders of the new era were to achieve and showed
that laissez-faire procedures in library training were being
re-examined on both sides of the Atlantic.

Dewey was then 25. When seven years later he proposed the establishment of a library school, the opposition
was led by William F. Poole and Mellen Chamberlain, librarians respectively of the Chicago and Boston public libraries.
Chamberlain argued against ALA encouragement of the scheme
on the ground that it would be "hasty." He was answered by
Samuel S. Green, whose argument on the other side produced
what is perhaps the best summary on record of these early
American discussions of library training:

> I remember [he says] that the matter of trying to
> have facilities provided for training and educating
> persons wishing to become librarians was talked
> over at length by the gentlemen and ladies who went
> to the Conference of Librarians in London, in 1877.
> They held long conversations on shipboard regarding
> the subject and it was generally considered very im-
> portant that such facilities should be somewhere
> provided. 10

Harvard was the place that seemed indicated to Green. On
their return, he pressed Winsor to take the lead in organizing
a program of general and special training there:

> Why should there not be instruction given at Har-
> vard in library work and economy and the best re-
> sources of the country be thus utilized to give the
> general culture and special training needed by li-
> brarians?[11]

Reluctance on grounds of haste had little justification except
in the minds of newcomers like Chamberlain, for as Green
pointed out, special training for librarians "has been frequently discussed at meetings of this Association; if not publicly, certainly in the conversation of librarians attending
them, and by librarians when they have met on other occa-
sions than those meetings."

In Britain the 1877 Conference was followed in 1878
by W. E. A. Axon's plea for professorships of bibliography.
The main thing universities do, he asserted, is what the university did for Carlyle and what Emerson holds up to them
to do: they qualify the student to read in various fields and
tongues and they set forth clearly the vistas of reading which
are open to him. Viewed in this light, the crowning accomplishment of the university might be said to be the development of "good readers," and it is this responsibility which
Axon assigns his professors of bibliography. As this assignment is spelled out, it is narrowed to the job of developing
good "methods of literary investigation"--a rough equivalent
of "bibliographical methods"--since for him bibliography
meant the grammar of literary investigation. Specifically,
instruction in bibliography is broken down into the following
subjects: the literary record of the mind or what Axon calls
the history of literature in its concrete form; the arts involved in producing these literary materials (paleography,
typography, paper-making and book-binding); systems of clas-
sifying knowledge: principles of library organization and management; and memory aids.[12]

Justin Winsor's position at Harvard was cited in the
discussion following Axon's paper as an illustration of the way
an Emersonian professorship of books and reading should be
set up. That is, it should always be connected with a great
library where the professor would be "accessible for consultation on particular books and on courses of reading." This
would be a means of avoiding any tendency for the professorship "to degenerate into a mere glorification of typographical
antiquarianism."

Friedrich A. Ebert's The Education of the Librarian,

published in 1820, had been widely read on the continent but
his views were not fully presented to the English-speaking
world until 1881. [13]   The role of the librarian in building collections of books had led Ebert to conclude that the former's
work presupposes, more than anything else, a discriminating
sense of history.   He must see to it that his library stands
above the present and he will fail in this if he is preoccupied
with what is local and for today.   The preparatory studies
Ebert prescribed for the librarian included: Greek, Latin,
French, Italian, English, History, the history of literature
and bibliography, diplomatics, the arts involved in book production and "encyclopedia" in the 18th century meaning of the
term.   Building on this foundation, the prospective librarian
would then go on to develop competence in what today would
be called the principles of cataloging and classification derived from a comparative study of actual catalogues and
schemes of classification.

Another development in the period prior to the organization of a library training program at Columbia was the announcement of an elective course in bibliography, taught by
Raymond C. Davis, Librarian of the University of Michigan,
a member of the American Library Association and one of
the first outside lecturers to be brought to Columbia to speak
to the students after the library school was opened.   Davis's
course was offered for several years beginning in 1879-80,
the year Michigan introduced the elective system.   It carried
no credit until 1882-83, when formal credit was authorized
and the course was expanded.   Lectures to aid readers in
the use of the library and to familiarize them with recent
books were given on Monday evenings during October.   The
second semester was devoted to lectures on "historical, material and intellectual bibliography. "[14]

Also in 1879, Library Journal carried an announcement from the French Ministry of Public Instruction that candidates for library posts in French universities would be
placed on probation for two years and would have to pass a
professional examination.   The candidates were required to
write a dissertation in bibliography and to classify fifteen
works representing different subject fields as well as different periods in the history of printing. [15]

At its annual meeting in 1880, the Library Association
of the United Kingdom resolved unanimously

That it is desirable that the Council of this Associa-

tion should consider how library assistants may
best be aided in their training in the general principles of their profession.

A committee studied how this could best be done, concluded
that the training of library assistants could be made an ex-
tremely useful feature of the new Association, and recommended at the annual meeting in 1881 that the Association
grant certificates of proficiency, first class and second class,
to those who passed specially prepared examinations. To
qualify for a second-class certificate the candidate would have
to show a reading knowledge sufficient for cataloging of at
least two languages other than English, have at least a year
of practical experience in a library and pass examinations in
five subjects as follows: (a) English literature of the last
hundred years, (b) one other European literature, (c) principles of the classification of knowledge, (d) elements of bibliography, including cataloging, and (e) library management.
To qualify for a first-class certificate, the second rung in
the ladder, he would have to show competence in a third
foreign language, have another year of practical experience
in a library, pass advanced examinations in these five subjects, and, in addition, pass an examination in general literary history.

This proposal, rejected when first presented in 1881,
was adopted unanimously in 1882 and the first examinations
were given in 1885. 16 It had been assumed that courses in
bibliography and librarianship would be required to aid candidates in preparing for these examinations, but no such courses
materialized before the early vitality of the movement had
spent itself. These pioneers in the years following 1877 were
ahead of their time: library training did not gain firm footing in Britain till well in the twentieth century. But the Library Association succeeded in laying a good foundation for
a system of examinations under national auspices, and this
continues to be a feature of professional training and status.

Early Stages of Dewey's Thought

In the Columbia University Libraries is a Dewey manu-
script written probably in 1876. The original title, "The
American Library Journal," has been changed by striking out
"Journal" and writing "Association" above it in a strong hand.
Minor changes have been made in the text to suit the thought
to the new title. Dewey was active in creating both of these

organs, and the manuscript in this form indicates that to him
the main purpose of each was to serve as an educational
channel through which the younger and less experienced librarians were to benefit from the experience of recognized library
leaders.

> What the librarian ought to be and what we have
> faith he will be some day, is ... well illustrated
> in our best equipped and best taught schools.   Need-
> ed appliances, text books, and reference books are
> at hand.   The thousand details connected with those
> appliances, with the school room, its methods and
> rules, have all been settled by the combined judg-
> ment and experience of the profession, focalized
> and put before all its members in its journals.
> Such a teacher, when he begins his work, is able
> to stand on the shoulders of all his predecessors,
> profiting by all their experience....   A number of
> the leading librarians took council [sic] as to what
> should be done.   The first great need was clearly
> a means of communication between the scattered
> members of the profession.

When the American Library Journal became a reality,
it carried in the mast-head a quotation from Justin Winsor
intended to emphasize the new organ's educational role:

> We have no schools of bibliographical and biblio-
> thecal training ... and the demand may perhaps
> never warrant their establishment; but every librar-
> ian with a fair experience can afford inestimable
> instruction to another in its novitiate; and there
> have been no duties of my office to which I have
> given more hearty attention than those that have led
> to the granting of what we could from our experi-
> ence to the representatives of other libraries...

Dewey's first published remarks on special training for librarians appeared in 1879 in an article entitled "Apprenticeship of Librarians."[17]   The library school he originated a
few years later is commonly assumed to mark a change-over
from apprenticeship to professional education, but this is a
careless interpretation of the problem as it presented itself
at the close of the 1870's.   In the clearest assessment of the
situation made by anyone up to that time, Dewey observed
that "there has not been even a system of apprenticeship."
This is no criticism: apprenticeship was established only in

the older vocations and was losing ground by the time newer
vocations like librarianship were ready to absorb trained personnel. It is a statement that faces up to the fact that provisions for library training would have to start from scratch
and that advances would have to be made one attainable step
at a time.   Starting the ALA and the Library Journal were
such attainable steps, but these and other informal substitutes
for systematic training were seen to be insufficient to support
a vigorous library movement:

> The form that seems most probable [as the next
> step, he goes on to say] is that certain librarians
> will take assistants for the special purpose of train-
> ing them to take charge of other institutions.
> These assistants will give their services ... with-
> out other compensation than the instruction given
> and the opportunities for practice under trained
> supervision.

Dewey was a realist who would not overlook the inertia of
ideas inherited from the past.   The most articulate spokesman for conservative ideas as to how librarians ought to be
trained was William F. Poole.   In a criticism of Dewey in
1883, Poole summed up his attitude as follows:

> I have entertained the idea that practical work in
> a library, based on a good previous education in
> the schools, was the only proper way to train good
> librarians. [18]

The implication here is: there is not now a system of apprenticeship, true; but a move toward such a system would
be better than schooling of the kind Dewey was advocating.
It was a position that was in line with accepted tradition in
vocational training generally and was typical of library thought
of that day.   Thus Justin Winsor, for years the dominant
figure in the American library world, joined considerately in
discussing the possibility of university-sponsored instruction
for librarians in 1877 but seems personally to have adhered
to the view that practical experience in a good library "is the
best preparation for librarianship. " Joseph Borome has
shown that this was his view in 1891 and produces an illuminating reply to an inquiry made by a university president on
behalf of a young man who wished to become a librarian.   It
reads in part as follows:

> There are schools where instruction is given for

this career, the principal of which is the library
school at Albany.... Instruction is given in these
schools for pay, and it is questionable whether such
opportunities have not some of the characteristics
of a necessary makeshift. These schools have
grown up and fill a want because the larger libraries could not afford to undergo the distraction of
instructing novices, except so far as it becomes
necessary for filling vacancies in their own staffs.[19]

But if Dewey's 1879 article remained close to prevailing library thought, it marked an advance beyond the kind of
haphazard training which was obtained merely through paid
employment. The influence of the technical-education movement, then nearing the height of fashion in American thought,
was plainly in evidence. Indeed the originality of this article lay in the fact that it is the first consistent application
to librarianship of the central concept of technical education
--special training of a vocational nature for each special kind
of everyday work:

We hear a great deal [the article says] of the importance of having trained librarians.... We need
a training school for preparation for the special
work. The village schoolmistress is provided with
normal schools by the hundred where the best methods of teaching are taught. Physicians, lawyers,
preachers, yes, even our cooks have special schools
for special training. But the librarian, whose profession has been so much exalted, must learn his
trade by his own experiments and experience.

Pointing out that no one teacher could spread himself over
specialties which differ as much as bibliography and library
economy, Dewey goes on to observe that "as in all training
schools, different men must take in charge different branches."
He concludes with the observation that the librarian's training
school must be attached to the shop--a good-sized, well managed library. "A large variety of books are needed in the
work; the pupils must see all the work doing from day to day
in all its details; they must have practice in doing each part
of it under careful supervision."

Dewey went to Columbia in 1883 with the understanding
that he would receive full support in developing a special
training program in the new Library there. Following is an
outline of the more formal aspects of the program which he
submitted to President Barnard and the Trustees:[20]

1. <u>Practical Bibliography</u>: To teach what author and treatise is wanted. Another way to say it is that the study of bibliography would take in what books there are in a given area, their comparative merits and how to use them.

2. <u>Books</u>: To teach what edition is best to buy or borrow, wherever there is a choice of editions.

3. <u>Reading</u>: To teach how to get from the book what is wanted, and no more, most quickly and most easily.

4. <u>Literary Methods</u>: To teach how to remember, record, classify, arrange, index, and in this way make most available for future use, what the books contain.

This outline deals with subjects which are similar to ideas discussed earlier in the chapter. It is fairly obvious too that the proposal in this form was pointed, or could be pointed, toward rounding out the education of college-bred men, whether they planned to be librarians or not. The 1883 proposal had three other principal features:

First, there was a highly practical auxiliary part of the program not covered by the above outline, which introduced more technical training in two ways. Non-resident lecturers were to be engaged to give series of lectures on technical aspects of special departments of library work. In addition, all students were to have supervised practice in library work. This work was to differ from the experience gained from ordinary paid employment in that the beginner would be rotated through all departments and get first-hand experience in each one. Nothing was said at this point about how long this work experience would be, whether it was to take place in a single library or whether it was to be given before, after or concurrently, with the lectures. All this was to come later.

Second, the work covered by the four-point outline above sums up the duties to be assigned to a new position in the Columbia faculty--a Professorship of Bibliography. This is the side of the proposal which was stressed in the first published account of it. The reason the emphasis falls here is explained no doubt by the fact that Dewey was asking a major institution to create a post for which there was no precedent. He was obligated to be fairly specific about responsibilities which would justify the innovation.

Third, the practical part of the program stays close

to the thought of the 1879 article but the Professorship of
Bibliography stays just as close to the discussions of bibliographical knowledge and guidance summarized earlier in the
chapter.   The notion of a Professorship of Bibliography was
short-lived, as we shall see.   Why it was added or why the
center of emphasis shifts from practical training in 1879 to
bibliographical instruction in 1883 is not clear unless it was
to take account of the contributions of others who were interested in the venture.   It is worth observing in this connection that President Barnard, at one point, looked upon the
projected program as one designed primarily to give "instruction in books and how to use them."   As late as May 30,
1886, Ainsworth Spofford, the Librarian of Congress, was
answering an inquiry of Barnard's in these terms:

> The central idea in a training school for librarians
> should be (as it seems to me) to teach thorough and
> accurate research.... If a university can do noth-
> ing else for a student, it should teach him to ex-
> haust all sources of information before accepting a
> result.   I hail with much satisfaction your decision
> to add an optional course in bibliography to the cur-
> riculum of your university. [21]

John W. Burgess, founder of the first of the graduate
faculties of Columbia (Political Science), was in the early
1880s exerting counter-pressure against technical education.
He was calling for higher education to avoid the temptation
to connect itself directly with the practice of some profession,
urging instead that professional students be encouraged "to
branch out into cognate and auxiliary studies [and] lift their
professions out of the condition of a mere technique into the
position of a true science."[22]   It was Burgess, a friend of
Dewey's from their days together at Amherst, who seems to
have had most to do with the transfer of the imaginative
young librarian to Columbia.   From this fact no less than
from his generally vigorous role in remaking Columbia into
a university, it would not be surprising to find Burgess working with Dewey and Barnard on blueprints for the new course
at some point along the way.

Whatever the explanation, the 1883 proposal was open-
ended and less a unified program than a melange of incon-
gruous elements.   The principal achievement between then
and 1887 was a greater internal cohesion of elements.   The
program unveiled at the opening in 1887, while still open-
ended, held together better.   Dewey's creative powers were

by then reaching their peak and the conception of a School of
Library Economy, the name finally decided upon, bears the
strong impress of his interests. A circular of information
dated 1884 had stated:

> The Board [of Trustees] have intentionally avoided
> deciding details, hoping that suggestions ... of ex-
> perienced librarians ... and ... the needs of those
> hoping to attend it, together with the practical ex-
> perience gained from teaching meanwhile two pre-
> liminary classes, will make clear what is really
> needed. 23

The circular for 1886-87 describes the program which
ripened under these influences. It is modeled after practical
experience and is headed up by a Professor of Library Economy. Unity of purpose and a transparent clarity in organization are achieved by sloughing off most of the functions identified with the Professorship of Bibliography and returning to
the educational philosophy first set forth in the 1879 article.

Main Features of the School of Library Economy

The program of the new School can be summed up under two headings. First, it ruled out all "cognate and auxiliary studies" of the kind advocated by Burgess and sought to
limit its scope to technical education:

> Though bearing a similar name, [the School of Li-
> brary Economy] differs widely from other schools
> in its objects and methods.... It confines itself
> strictly to its peculiar work, and makes no attempt
> to give general culture or make up deficiencies of
> earlier education.... The library school is not like
> an agricultural college, which gives a general liter-
> ary or scientific course with more or less agricul-
> ture included or kept in view as a possible occupa-
> tion. This school is rather a short and purely
> technical course.... 24

Second, the program was, in the language of the survey made in chapter two, that of an apprenticeship school.
It was designed to produce the same kind of competence as
apprenticeship by using more systematic methods:

> Not only are the limits of subjects studied closely

drawn, but in their treatment the school is more a
systematic apprenticeship in which every effort is
made to advance the learner rapidly rather than to
serve the master's interests by keeping him as a
pupil without salary as long as possible. Its methods have almost nothing of the usual textbook and
recitation.... It is proposed to condense the instruction into a single quarter and to give ... a
two-year apprenticeship. [25]

The director and six other part-time members of the
library staff formally opened the School of Library Economy
to twenty students on January 5, 1887. The plan combined
lectures, instruction and an apprenticeship under fluid arrangements which changed rapidly during the early years.
Terminology even underwent some change, as the case of
"instruction" illustrates. To give practical library work educational significance, the supervisor was expected to take an
active interest in and responsibility for the growth of the student working under him. The new attitude was the leaven
used to transform library employment into apprentice "instruction," and that has indeed gone on leavening the whole of
personnel administration in the 20th century. The term "instruction" acquired a specialized meaning as a name for the
kind of supervised practice work done for learning purposes
which the School introduced. "Instruction" included lectures,
some of which were conferences or conversations rather than
formal addresses, [26] and other teacher-directed activities such
as seminars, which did not involve learning by doing.

Lectures and the new practice-instruction were combined in more or less equal proportions to make up the program of the three-months lecture term. The practice-instruction headed up in a daily three-hour period of practice work
under supervision. The lectures as described in the 1886-87
circular fell into five courses, organized partly by subject,
partly by who gave them. The "Course in Library Economy"
was given by the director and members of the library staff.
Reviews and examinations were based on it. The "Course in
Bibliography" was intended to survey, with the aid of the College Faculty, the major departments of knowledge, each professor or subject specialist giving one or more lectures on
the bibliography of his subject. "Lectures by Specialists" in
binding, printing, publishing, bookselling, mechanical equipment, etc., soon merged into a fourth course, "Advice from
Leading Librarians," to be called "Extra" (and later on "Outside") lectures. A fifth course, "College Lectures," was a

sort of accessory or dividend; it included campus and down-
town lectures which although not part of the students' work
were thought to be "specially adapted to their needs." At-
tendance was voluntary.

The course by outside experts was conceived in 1886-
87 as "a series of lectures entirely independent of the course
of instruction and embodying whatever they [leading librarians]
think will be most helpful as their message to beginners...."
But as early as April 21, 1883, Samuel S. Green, "the first
regularly appointed [non-resident] lecturer in the School,"
was thinking of these contributions in somewhat different
terms. In a letter to Dewey of that date, he wrote:

> I should say that if I were to give instruction to
> students it should be on methods of making a li-
> brary of real benefit to the industries, schools and
> institutions of towns and cities. Short courses by
> persons in their specialties would be the plan would
> it not?

The initial series of lectures was hardly set up before
Dewey was referring to it as "the main course."27 It was
extravagant praise, but what Green had called "short courses"
quickly became a useful and popular feature of the School.
The weakness of the literature made it impossible to have
access to the best thought and experience of the profession in
any other way.

The four subjects assigned the Professor of Bibliography in 1883 were not included in the 1886-87 program. The
same subjects, however, appear under "Library Lectures" in
the section of the circular devoted to the College Library.
Their purpose as described there corresponds to what nowadays would be called instruction in the use of the library.
Various instruction aids were utilized in producing an effective program of technical education, but through it all there
was the purpose of obtaining the results produced by practical
experience. Practical training, wrote Dewey,

> ... is the end sought and any means that promise
> to make more efficient librarians will be tried....
> Lectures and reading alone will not achieve the best
> results in training librarians without the seminars,
> problems, study of various libraries in successful
> operation and chiefly actual work in a library.28

He goes on to say elsewhere: "However excellent may be the
results from the lectures, instruction, seminars, problems
and visits, the main reliance must be on experience. "

In Conclusion

        The School of Library Economy arose in 1887 in re-
sponse to accelerating demands for qualified library personnel.   It was a product of contemporary ideas on library
training and of the insights of Melvil Dewey.   None of Dewey's
contemporaries read the meaning of changing library personnel requirements as clearly as he.   Ideas then current on
how to train librarians fell into a few general patterns.   The
oldest originated in European libraries where the preservation and use of intellectual materials had exerted a strong influence on personnel requirements.   During the formative
period of Dewey's thinking, European ideas on library training laid stress on these elements: "encyclopedia" (the history and organization of learning), foreign languages, historical bibliography, other auxiliary disciplines which support
literary and historical scholarship, and what we would today
call classification and cataloging.

        Another idea was of contemporary origin.   It showed
a sensitiveness to changes arising from accelerated production of books, from the spread of literacy, etc. , all of which
affected the service potential of libraries.   It led to proposals
for training in what some called books and reading, others
called guidance of readers and still others called bibliography.
Whom the training was for, was left vague.   All these suggestions proved a little too airy to be used in organizing
courses for the training of librarians, although Dewey made
a passing attempt to do so.   A third approach to library
training was a planless pattern, being the haphazard practice
then used by all librarians, European and American.   It
amounted to no formal training whatsoever, not even a system of apprenticeship in the stricter meaning of that term.
Training there was, of course, but it was the product of working one's own way up the ladder, and was left to chance and
individual enterprise.

        The School of Library Economy struck out on a path
different from all of these.   Dewey considered the training
favored in Europe as "too antiquarian. "   The only thing he
took from this source was instruction in the history of books
and libraries, which was not added until a later date.   His

first proposal to the Columbia Trustees made a place for guidance in books and reading, but this was later dropped out of the professional program and became the basis of instruction in the use of the library.

In spirit and purpose, the final program of the School of Library Economy was closest to the "planless" training then in vogue among libraries. Dewey sought the same sort of results, but was bent on producing them more systematically and in less time. At least two ways to do this were open. One was to fall in with those who dwelled vaguely on the cliché that the best training ground is a well-managed library. The job then would be to use the better libraries and organize a bona fide system of apprenticeship. The other way was to take over the methods of technical education, which was demonstrating in one field after another that schooling could be used to produce the very kind of results that were generally desired in librarianship. Dewey chose the latter course. Like technical education in other fields, the new School signified a break with those who favored apprenticeship over schooling of any kind; but unlike those schools which offered general education, the School of Library Economy offered only "a purely technical course." While this meant producing the same results in terms of training that came from haphazard experience, the school set out to do the job more effectively and in less time by planning the training as "a systematic apprenticeship."

REFERENCES

1. Kent, Henry Watson. What I Am Pleased to Call My Education, ed. by Lois Leighton Comings. New York: The Grolier Club, 1949, pp. 15, 16, 17.

2. See James Truslow Adams's Biographical Sketch of Winsor in the Dictionary of American Biography.

3. Hessel, Alfred. A History of Libraries; trans. with supplementary material by Reuben Peiss. Washington, D. C.: Scarecrow Press, 1950.

4. See the "Essay on Books" in his Society and Solitude. Boston: Fields, Osgood & Co., 1870.

5. Library Economy considered from the standpoint of a

58   Library Education

common organization among libraries: Library Science as a Special University Study in Germany,
Freiburg in Bavaria, 1874. The title of the original: Die Bibliothekseinrichtungskunde zum Theile
einer gemeinsamen Organisation: Die Bibliotheks-
wissenschaft als solche einem besonderen Universi-
tätsstudium in Deutschland unterworfen.

6. U. S. Bureau of Education. Public Libraries in the
United States of America; Their History, Condition
and Management; Special Report. Pt. I. Washington: Government Printing Office, 1876, p. xxiii-
xxvi.

7. Conference of Librarians, London, 1877. Transactions
and Proceedings. London: Printed at the Chiswick
press by C. Whittington, 1878.

8. Bolzani, Count Ugo. "On the Regulations of Italian Public Libraries," Library Journal 4:183-87, June 30,
1879.

9. Conference of Librarians, London, 1877, op. cit.

10. Library Journal 8:290, 293, September-October, 1883.

11. S. S. Green to Winsor, Nov. 1877. Quoted by Joseph
A. Borome in his doctoral dissertation, "The Life
and Letters of Justice Winsor." Columbia University, 1950.

12. Axon, W. E. A. "Professorships of Bibliography."
Library Association of the United Kingdom. Trans-
actions and Proceedings, 1878. London: Chiswick
Press, 1879, pp. 104-07.

13. Brace, W. F. A. "Ebert's View of a Librarian's Education." Library Association of the United Kingdom.
Monthly Notes. Vol. 2, 1881, 30-36. The account
in the text limits itself to sources so clearly in
Dewey's path that it would be difficult to suppose
he failed to come across them. Since one of the
earliest of these sources, the 1876 Report of the
Bureau of Education, presents Germany as a land
where the importance of providing "opportunities for
instruction in all the departments of library science
... is beginning to be realized," a separate para-
graph is in order about developments there.

'The first and so far the only professorship in the
auxiliary sciences of librarianship in Prussia [Dr.
Johann Leche wrote in 1901, "ALA Proc.," Library
Journal 26: Conf. no., p. 199] was founded in 1886
in Göttingen,' but according to Milkau the idea of
a library school goes back to Ebert and Schrettinger.
Ebert's views are summarized in the text. Schrettinger, the first to advocate special training for librarians, wrote the first manual of library science
and hoped to see it used in some well-managed library to aid in training librarians. Rullmann looked
upon his plea for a common organization among libraries and for special study of library science in
universities simply as an extension of the ideas
which Schrettinger had expressed nearly half a century earlier. The Austrian under-secretary of
state, Baron Von Helfert, issued an order in 1858
to work out requirements for candidates for library
service based on examinations which presupposed
both general education and special preliminary library training; but the project was too far ahead of
its time to succeed. A Munich edict of 1864 regu-
lating admission to the Imperial Court and State
Library picked up the idea of examinations and
specified requirements which made it possible for
appointment without meeting formal requirements
for a university degree. The Institute of Austrian
Historical Research when reorganized in 1874 included in its statues a provision that it should serve
as a 'seminar' for archival and library personnel,
but it produced more archivists than librarians.
Frederick T. Althoff's appointment as Kultur-Minis-
ter of Prussia in 1882 marked the beginning of a
new phase of German librarianship. He considered
the education of librarians as a significant and integral part of the total planning of German library
development. He took an active interest in establishing in Göttingen the aforementioned professorship, which was held for many years by Carl
Dziatzko.

14. See the official announcements of the University for the
years mentioned.

15. Library Journal 4:460, December, 1879.

16. See the proceedings of the Association. One of the most

important general statements for library training to
appear in England during these years was a section
in: Tedder, Henry R. "Librarianship as a Profession." Library Association of the United Kingdom. Transactions and Proceedings, 1882. London: Chiswick Press, 1884, pp. 163-72.

17. Library Journal 4:147-48, May 31, 1879.

18. Library Journal 8:288, September-October, 1883.

19. This letter is quoted in full in Public Libraries 29:14-
15, January, 1924, but my attention was first
called to it by Dr. Borome's research.

20. Library Journal 8:285-91, September-October, 1883.

21. Unpublished manuscript in the Columbia University Libraries.

22. Burgess, John W. The American University. When
Shall It Be? Where Shall It Be? An essay.
Boston: Ginn, 1884.

23. Columbia College Library. School of Library Economy.
Circular of Information, 1884.

24. Columbia College Library. School of Library Economy.
Circular of Information 1886-87.

25. Ibid., pp. 26-27.

26. Columbia College Library. School of Library Economy.
Circular of Information, 1887-88, p. 35.

27. Library Journal 12:78, January-February, 1887.

28. Columbia College Library. School of Library Economy,
Circular of Information, 1886-87, p. 33.

Chapter 4

MATURING OF THE TRAINING PROGRAM:
A CASE STUDY

The opening of the School of Library Economy marks
the dawn of modern education for librarianship. This chapter and the next deal with the period extending from 1887 to
1920, or thereabouts, during which the first wave of creative
work was spending itself.

Preview of the Forming
of the American Library School

This span of twenty-five to thirty years is notable both
for what was done and left undone. One accomplishment was
to revolutionize the character of training. Up to the establishment of the School of Library Economy, there had been
no formal training at all, nothing but such fortuitous training
as an employee could pick up in his own library. It was not
all easy sailing for the library schools; they had to cope with
some skepticism and resistance at the outset, and with considerable competition later on; but the idea of systematic
preparation that they stood for was quickly accepted.

Another outcome was the triumph of the middle course
which Dewey decided on in forming the first school. Its frank
orientation toward technical education brought opposition from
one side; its reliance on systematic instruction in place of
having beginners learn library work entirely by doing it brought
opposition from the other side. The public at large, however,
and certainly the great majority of librarians, reacted much
as they were doing to the more general technical-education
movement and welcomed technical instruction as a workable
means of accelerating production of trained librarians.

But the period also produced its share of inconclusive

61

results and problems. For example, the switch from a do-
nothing attitude to acceptance of active responsibility for library training might be taken to imply a ready triumph of the
library school. The fact is that this was a period of experimentation and the library school was only one of the institutional forms tried out. It gained and held first place in professional respect, but the head of one school estimated as of
1917[1] that competing agencies were turning out two to three
times as many librarians each year as the library schools
were.

        Closely related was the halting start made toward co-
ordinating programs of education and training. A national
committee on library training served usefully as a clearinghouse of information and sounding board of professional opinion, but when the time seemed ripe to vest it with authority
to lead the way in developing an accreditation program, the
profession balked. It was thus a period which, although prolific in number and kind of training programs, failed to create a channel through which the profession as a whole could
effectively participate in shaping educational policy. To make
matters worse, these programs conformed to no pattern as to
length, sponsorship, facilities, entrance requirements or size
and quality of staff. The state of disorganization was being
described as chaotic well before 1920. But in spite of all
this, the era stands out for what it did to put the library
movement on a professional footing.

        So much for a preview of the period which gave spe-
cial education for librarians its initial cast. In this chapter,
attention is centered on the maturing of a workable training
program to replace the old laissez-faire practice of haphazard training which modern library needs were sweeping aside
as no longer practicable.

        The original school did not stand alone long; and if in
establishing it Dewey made librarians his debtor for all time,
the conversion of the Columbia experiment into a national
movement had to be the work, not of one man, but of the
profession and the general public. The various plans for organizing professional training that were tried out will be examined in the next chapter, but for reasons of concreteness
and brevity, it is fitting to start with a short case study of
the central course which the education of librarians traversed
during the years, 1887-1920.

        The first library school, the parent of all the schools

that followed, is the logical one to use for this purpose.   It
remained securely in the forefront of progress, and served
as the model to copy.   Its work is well documented, and it
was favored during the malleable first decade in being able
to work so closely with the American Library Association
that it was sometimes referred to, even in print, as the official school of the Association.

Evolution of the Albany Library School

At the close of the winter quarter, March 30, 1889,
the Columbia Library School[2] transferred to the New York
State Library, "together with its faculty, books, pamphlets,
illustrative collections and all the special matter accumulated
for its use," and resumed work on April 10.   Here, under
friendly auspices, it flourished until 1926 as the New York
State Library School (referred to hereafter as the Albany
School, its popular name), then returned to Columbia where
it merged with the Library School of the New York Public
Library to form the School of Library Service.   In one of
the best characterizations of progress for the whole period,
Dewey wrote in 1888 that "The instruction constantly improves
by the introduction of new methods and the systematizing of
details."[3]   In general, improvements piled up rapidly at one
end of the period and sloped off at the other, so the early
years will require the most attention.

The First Generation, 1884-1905.   The essentials of
technical education began to be applied to librarianship when
nine "pupil assistants" went to work in the Columbia Library
in 1884 as members of the first of the two classes that were
used to try out the possibilities of formal schooling.   The
combination of "lectures and actual library work" emphasized
library work: classwork was limited to late afternoons twice
a week when students heard a lecture and discussed what they
were doing.   One of the main developments of the next decade
was a rapid increase in formal classwork.   In 1887, the two-
year combination was envisaged as a three-months lecture
term, with the amount and kind of instruction for the much
longer apprentice period left indeterminate.   The arrangements permitted students to conclude their training in "some
other well-managed library," but this was an option never
exercised and soon forgotten.

The second year the lecture term was lengthened by
adding an eight-weeks preparatory term of classwork in cata-

loging and classification. The trend continued the following
year, the last at Columbia, when the calendar was for the
first time lined up with the regular academic year. The
transfer to Albany was the occasion for re-examination and
further change. Following is a resumé of the program as
outlined for the Regents:

> Junior year. Cataloging, shelf listing, accessioning
> and elementary library economy scheduled for the
> first twelve weeks, October to Christmas; dictionary
> cataloging in January; classification in February;
> library economy, March and April; apprenticeship
> work in the State Library and visits to other librar-
> ies, May and June; vacation, July through Septem-
> ber. In the first five months, students were to
> receive one lecture a day; in March and April,
> three lectures a day. The rest of the student's
> time during these seven months was given over to
> work under supervision of members of the library
> staff who had responsibility for instruction.
>
> Senior year. The nine months, October to June,
> included three lines of activity: (1) one hour of
> classwork daily, a seminar or a lecture; (2) two
> hours of supervised work in the State Library; and
> (3) classwork in special subjects. The seminar on
> reading came on Monday. Lectures the same hour
> on successive days each week were devoted to bib-
> liography, cataloging, classification and library
> economy. The classwork covered much the same
> ground as the lectures but followed a different time-
> table. The first five months of the year were de-
> voted to classification, library economy, cataloging
> and dictionary cataloging in that order. The four
> remaining months were divided equally between li-
> brary economy and library work. [4]

It is a blueprint that shows firmer commitment to
formal schooling. Subjects are fitted into a timetable. Class-
centered activity as a method of organizing the learning experience continued to gain on learning library work simply
by doing it. There was more organized instruction and the
supervised practice moved farther toward being class-centered
"laboratory work" under specially assigned personnel. The
blueprint, promptly endorsed by the Regents, was spelled out
in a modern-style curriculum in 1891-92, [5] a date which seals
the commitment of this, the parent school, to formal classwork as a method of organizing the learner's experience.

The next revision occurred in 1901, with several of
the changes noted below occurring in between. Following are
the subjects included as of 1901-02, [6] the ones dating back as
far as 1891 being enclosed in quotation marks:

> 'Elementary and advanced cataloging, ' 'elementary
> and advanced dictionary cataloging, ' 'elementary
> and advanced classification, ' 'elementary and ad-
> vanced bibliography, ' 'reference work, ' selection of
> books, 'accession department work, ' bookbinding,
> 'shelf department work, ' 'loan department, ' 'library
> buildings, ' 'founding and government of libraries, '
> administrative, supervisory and State commission
> work, 'history of libraries, ' history of printing, li-
> brary editing and printing, indexing, 'original bib-
> liography' and visits.

It would take more space than it is worth to make this
summary complete by noting minor material on printed forms,
appliances and other details of library method and equipment
which is comparable for both years, 1891 and 1901. A few
things that were being tried out in 1891 dropped out of sight
before 1901: Reading and literary methods, Library bookkeeping, Library language lessons, Libraries on special subjects
("law, medicine, theology, art, music, science, etc. "), a
Reading seminar and a thesis.

The Regents established in 1889 the degrees of bache-
lor (B. L. S.), master (M. L. S.) and doctor (D. L. S.) of library
science. The honorary D. L. S. [7] appears never to have been
conferred. The B. L. S. was offered as late as 1901 for "two
years of college work and two years technical work in the library school, " but stood primarily for the two years of specialized study. The thesis requirement was soon left to the
M. L. S. , awarded to those holding the lower degree who, in
addition, completed not less than five years of professional
work as the faculty prescribed and presented a satisfactory
thesis, bibliography or catalogue. As for "Libraries on special subjects, " Dewey reported in 1898 that the faculty had
agreed upon a rotating treatment of law, medical, engineering and other special libraries. [8] The object was to insure
access to instruction in a given specialty once every three
years, but the 1901 revision gives no indication that the plan
was carried out.

The reading seminar provided an opportunity to read
and discuss current books. Originated in 1889 by Salome
Cutler Fairchild, it quickly grew into central importance for

both years, covering foreign as well as American works after
1893. Five years later, the seminar evolved into the new
course, "Selection of books," which in addition took over material on book-buying from the course on accession department work. "Administrative, supervisory and state commission work" was announced in 1901 as the area which the
School expected to make its leading specialty. It took account
of suggestions from the field respecting the importance of library administration and the propriety of having the school
give more attention to the higher branches of library science.

Three other courses were added before 1905: advanced
reference work, public documents and typewriting. The course
on documents resulted from expanding material on the subject
covered in shelf department work. When instruction in typewriting was added in 1903, use of the library hand in cataloging was made optional. Instruction in handwriting dated from
1884.

Taking our bearings as the program neared the end of
its second decade, we can extend Dewey's observation of 1881
and say that steady improvements continued to be made in
method and organization. All along the way, but especially
in the early years, the training program moved steadily away
from the methods of apprenticeship toward the type of apprenticeship schooling which the 19th century had perfected as an
improvement upon apprenticeship. There were other improvements. The three pieces which had been the heart of the
training program from the start were: the work which headed
up under the Professor of Library Economy (library economy,
practical bibliography, cataloging and classification); the "extra lectures" by outside specialists, mainly librarians; and the
practical work done by students under supervision. The affiliated lectures by scholars in the College made a place of sorts
for themselves, but it was a place apart; it would strain the
truth to say they ever became indigenous to "a purely technical course." This dropped out at Albany, making it possible to build a more harmonious whole out of the three remaining segments.

The location at Albany, when considered from the
angle of developing a technical course, was itself an improvement. The advantages were brought out by a standing committee on the Library School which the ALA created in 1889
to assist in promoting the objects of the School. In its first
report (1890), the committee weighed whether the School had
gained or lost by the move. The conclusion, which Dewey

echoed in a statement of his own:[9] a loss so far as opportunities for visiting libraries, printing and publishing houses
and binderies are concerned, but this was easy to repair by
devoting a week to visits in other cities. The new location,
on the other hand, removed "the constant temptation" to spend
time on things outside the library field.

> It is better ... not to attempt to listen to or make
> notes on lectures or subjects not in direct line of
> library work while taking the School course, and
> it is therefore a gain to be in a city like Albany
> which is not under the constant stimulus of metro-
> politan life and thought.[10]

Dewey concluded his long term as Director in 1905.
By then, the School was operating smoothly, its character
well-defined, its future assured. This happy state of health
and growing usefulness owes much to Dewey's perception of
what immediate training needs were most pressing. But related factors played their part too. To the ALA, a stead-
fast friend and ally, Dewey was able in 1898 to report support from the State at a level which put the School's faculty,
physical facilities and operating budget in a class to itself.
The annual report for that year, the first separately published,[11] listed a faculty of eleven including part-time mem-
bers--which number rose to twelve in 1901. The growth
from eight members in 1889 was accompanied by intangibles
of experience and continuity. Three of the twelve (Dewey,
Mrs. Fairchild and Walter Biscoe) had been with the School
since 1887; four others (Florence Woodworth, Ada Jones,
Dunkin Johnston and May Seymour) since the earliest days at
Albany. The Library Museum housed "the most complete
[collection] ever made" of books, photographs, appliances and
other visual and demonstration aids.

It was a time when librarians, paced by Dewey, were
standardizing procedures and their labors produced the
School's first textbooks. "Indispensable in making dictionary
catalogs: the standard authority, often spoken of as the 'cataloger's bible',"[12] is the way an Albany publication referred
to Cutter's Rules for a Dictionary Catalog shortly after the
appearance of the 1889 edition. Originally published in 1876,
it went through two other smaller editions as well as five re-
printings by 1903. The ALA furthered the standardization
movement by publishing its Condensed Rules for an Author and
Title Catalog in 1883. Dewey launched a new journal, Library
Notes, in 1886 to disseminate ideas on library methods and

published in the second number a modified set of cataloging
rules of his own. He republished this code in 1890 under
the same covers with two other codes, "Library School Accession Book Rules" and "Library School Shelflist Rules. "
The resultant work, entitled Library School Rules, liberally
illustrated to aid the student, saw intensive use as an elementary textbook. The 42-page precursor of the Decimal
Classification and Relative Index, published in 1876, had by
the end of the century, when it went into a weightier sixth
edition, taken its place as another one of the professional
classics. Other teaching aids were published in a bulletin
series which the School inaugurated in 1891: Johnston's
Selected Reference Books (1899), Biscoe's Selected Subject
Bibliographies (1899), his Selected National Bibliographies
(1900), and a catch-all, Lecture Outlines and Problems (1902).
The last-named made available for the first time outlines developed in most of the older courses not served by the other
textbooks named. The five alumni lectures in 1905 by James
I. Wyer on U. S. government publications were revised and
published in the same series in 1906.

        Admission requirements were high. The enrollment
in 1897-98 of 30 students from ten states and two foreign
countries was representative, being near capacity. Women
predominated. By insisting, as he did from the start, that
they be admitted, Dewey had flung open a career opportunity
at a time when most professions were still closed to women,
and as a result the library profession enjoyed an exceptional
advantage in recruiting able students. Entrance examinations
emphasizing history, literature and general information were
supplemented by letters from references and interviews where
possible. Many of the students were college graduates. Of
the 267 students in all who had matriculated by 1898, a total
of 160 had been to college, 117 having graduated. The colleges they came from were of high quality: Wellesley contributed 19 graduates, Smith 14, Cornell 13, Vassar 11,
Michigan 10. Harvard led the men's colleges with eight.
Fifty-six other colleges from Mt. Holyoke to Heidelberg and
Yale were represented. With homespun but telling imagery
("If there is to be good grist, you must put good grain into
the hopper"), Dewey repeatedly emphasized the importance of
careful recruiting and the good grain thus selected produced
more of its kind. Following an assiduously cultivated trend,
the School in 1902 went the rest of the way and began to require a college degree for admission. It was at the time an
achievement which few schools serving any profession could
match.

Out in the field the prestige of the School grew as capable young graduates showed their abilities and the idea of systematic training caught on. An alumni association was created in 1894, a standing committee to give counsel and support in 1900. The ALA committee on the Library School and its successors, rarely critical and always cooperative, rendered service of utmost value. These were not the only channels of communication. There were the reports in Library Journal, the School's own extensive publishing program, and a steady procession of visiting lecturers. There were thirty-eight of these in 1887, fourteen in 1897-98, seventeen in 1900-01. Part of the over-all decline in number of lecturers is explained by the vogue of the short course of two to ten lectures after the first year. [13] In 1900-01, nine of the seventeen lecturers delivered but one lecture. Cutter, on the other hand, delivered ten. Caroline Hewins delivered three on children's work; S. B. Griswold two on law librarianship. William E. Foster's five lectures were on reference work, library service to schools and browsing collections of choice titles--areas he had pioneered at Providence. At least seven of the seventeen, including all of the above named, could be described in Dewey's phrase as "regular non-resident lecturers" who visited the School repeatedly. Cutter's annual pilgrimage was a highlight for the Deweys, the staff and the students from 1887 until his death in 1903.

This visiting lecture program served three purposes. One often spoken of was inspiration--the opportunity to see and hear the great and near-great. A second was the furtherance of mutual understanding. Every inch the promoter, Dewey once observed that the doubters and critics "are wholly converted when they 'come and see'. "[14] Perhaps there is a promotional ring in this, but the fact stands that he kept his sawdust trail well worn by the tread of converts. The third purpose throws interesting light on the beginnings of library-school faculties. During the lecture term, the student's day at first went something like this: three hours a day for lectures and seminars, with about the same amount of time under "teachers" whose job was to help the School do "the most practical of all work"--that is, "to [supervise and] revise carefully the individual work of each member of the class. "[15]

Visiting lecturers, in other words, and especially those who gave short courses on their specialties, corresponded roughly to clinical professors in present-day medical faculties. There was a difference in rank and function. The non-

resident "faculty" of the School, along with the Professor of
Library Economy, ranked with the College Faculty and bore,
as they did in the College, chief responsibility for the character and substance of instruction. The rest of the "faculty"
were resident librarians, usually of less stature and certainly
lower in rank. In all, 160 lectures were presented in 1887.
The non-resident practitioners gave 72, leaving 88 to be given
by the Professor of Library Economy, the College Faculty and
others including a few "literary names." The responsibilities
of local teachers grew with the shift to class-work: "a teacher who has been in daily contact with the class and is familiar with all its previous work and needs can help them more
than a comparative stranger of greater ability and knowledge
in that special topic."[16] There was, however, no altering
of status to match this altering of function and no additions
to the resident staff from the ranks of strangers of greater
stature and broader experience.

       If this way lies a failure, nearby lies a brilliant tri-
umph. The launching of a library school was opposed by
some who observed how libraries differed in their methods
and who reasoned that employees trained only in methods
Dewey knew and favored would not do. Cataloging and classification were the chief areas of concern. To counter this,
Dewey had his impressive group of non-resident lecturers
and stressed "comparative study of methods." The School
received no publicity that first year more telling than the
statement by one of its first students, Mary Wright Plummer,
before the ALA conference of 1887. It was a convincing report, full of high praise except at one point:

            There has been expressed by several of the class
            in my hearing, a doubt whether it is best for the
            school to attempt to teach more than one system
            of cataloging.... In school parlance, we found
            ourselves 'mixed up' by the different methods taught,
            so that when we came to be apprentices we had to
            relearn some things in order to do our work cor-
            rectly.[17]

Dewey stuck to his commitment while library methods each
year became more uniform, in public libraries especially.
Meanwhile, the standardizing process was quietly but effectively resolving the issue of studying one method vs. comparing them all. Years passed. Then one day, after Dewey's time, the profession awoke to the fact that the more
basic methods of American libraries had been substantially

standardized and that training in generally-accepted methods
no longer meant training for this library or that, but for general library work. From that day on the library school's
preeminence over rival methods of training librarians was to
go unchallenged.

The Second Generation, 1905-1926. The Albany School
began listing its courses in 1906 under four headings--admin-
istrative, bibliographic, technical and practice work. The
use of classifications which were similar, if not identical, became the general rule among formal training agencies shortly
thereafter. The turn of the century had brought a spate of
criticism--of the adequacy of the goals and results of technical education, of too much stress on cataloging and classification and too little on administration, community relations,
bibliography. Resources were not available to make radical
changes in staff or program. The Albany School considered
any such measures unnecessary. To it, as to the majority
of librarians, the criticism seemed to be due chiefly to ignorance of what the schools were doing or to unsound ideas
as to what sort of training librarians needed. The fourfold
scheme nominally gave "technical work" a new and narrowed
significance, and gave added dignity to administrative and
bibliographical work. It was a simple step which did much
to further accord among librarians, but was more a re-label-
ing process than a break with the philosophy of technical education. A little was added, a little taken away; but the substance, methods and aims of the courses continued to be
much the same as before.

This feat of tact owes much to the imagination and
finesse of Edwin Hatfield Anderson, Director from January
1, 1906 to June 1, 1908. A product of the School, Anderson was in hearty accord with its educational philosophy; but
having risen to eminence in one enterprising center (Pittsburgh) and soon to be attracted to another (New York), which
was already challenging Boston as the library capital, he was
among the young Turks who were calling not for less attention to library mechanics but for more to methods of making
the public library a vital force in the life of the community.
We accordingly find him, while at Albany, bending all efforts
to strengthen methods of conducting "public libraries both
large and small and especially to emphasize the broader and
more general phases of their management which call for executive and administrative ability.... "[18] The outside lectures,
replanned with this aim in mind, began to be bracketed with
other courses on administration: a full-length course on

children's work was organized, study of library buildings re-
emphasized, and a senior elective on the administration of
large libraries introduced--all in a few months.

        Anderson also extended the elective system. The first
half-dozen years after 1887, practice work took up about half
of the student's time--600 to 800 hours a year. The requirement for juniors dwindled to about 100 hours by 1905, with
seniors doing about twice that much and the faculty increasingly convinced that classwork had more "educative value"
than the apprentice work. The elective system had been introduced in 1898 to let seniors do some practice work in the
field where their chief interest lay. The extension of the
privilege in 1906 permitted seniors to choose 100 hours from
a total of 350 in specified areas, some involving practice
work only, others lectures as well. Classwork up to this
point had been the same for all students, so this small step
away from an inelastic program was an important move toward making electives or planned options a central element
of the library school program.

        By 1908, when Anderson left to take charge of the
New York Public Library, the education of librarians had become something of a specialty in its own right and James I.
Wyer, who succeeded him, was already an acknowledged expert in the field. He was a dedicated alumnus who had
learned at first hand the internal workings of libraries of different types and had since 1906 been learning the workings
of the School as Vice Director. During Wyer's long tenure,
which lasted till the School returned to Columbia in 1926, the
now specialized task of perfecting the organization and methods of the instruction program went on from where the first
generation had left off. Changes significant enough to report
to the public fell off in number and consisted mostly of adding
electives to meet manpower needs in new areas. New courses
included: Law or legislative reference work, announced in
1910 but deferred to 1912; The library in the community, for
public librarians, 1911; Library extension, 1913; High school
libraries and Business library administration, both 1917.

        Joining in the silver anniversary commemoration of
the founding of the School, Anderson recalled in 1912 how
difficult it had been to find a job (salary: $50 a month)
back in 1891, when "it was not necessarily an advantage to
have had library school training."[19] "When I see today [he
went on] how the libraries are competing for the output of the
library schools, I realize how conditions have changed in

twenty-one years.   The demand for school-trained people is
now greater than the supply. "

The great divide between the earlier and the later part
of the period 1887-1920, is the change in the public's attitude
toward school training.   It brought with it a change of mood
in library schools.   Members of the second generation, the
first to be professionally trained, had believed in the promise
of the innovation enough to cast their own future in the balance with it.   They had watched the scales teeter a bit, then
dip decisively in their favor.   What more natural under these
circumstances than to consider the job in their time as largely
one of taking the system handed on to them and serving the
demands which public approval was now bringing in heart-
warming fashion?   The later reports of the Albany School reflect this mood of gratitude and responsible stewardship.
The dominant tendency was to proceed "along well-tried lines,"
making only such changes as seemed "necessary to keep the
school work in harmony with the needs of modern libraries. "

A disastrous fire on March 29, 1911 swept away the
School's quarters, equipment and records.   Alumni and
friends rallied magnificently to insure the School's future.
Recovery from this energy-draining blow was followed by
World War I.   Outwardly, therefore, it was a time of turbulence and readjustment.   It was, however, a time of in-
ward calm and confidence so far as the instruction program
was concerned.   The work for 1913-14, for example, was
"a year of quiet progress," the year 1918-19 "uneventful,"
and 1922-23 "a period of undisturbed progress. "

It is a picture of happy relations for a record period
with the dominant library forces of the time, and the stability gained by the program under such agreeable conditions
can be seen by the comparison below.   The subjects named
are those listed in the official announcement for 1922-23.   If
the subject was also listed in 1906-07 it is enclosed in quotation marks.   Subjects listed in 1922 but not 1906 are followed by a single figure, the credit weight of the course in
1922.   Subjects in quotation marks are followed by two figures: the first represents credit in 1906, the second in 1922.
It was necessary to adjust the published figures for 1906 to
make comparison of the two years possible.   With the aid of
the faculty during his first months in office, Anderson com-
puted the amount of time students put in on each course, including class meetings as well as preparation.   The only
weighting given a course then was this total of hours a student

spent on it. Internal evidence indicates that one point of
credit under the 1922 system corresponds to about 25 hours
of the Anderson totals of 1906. Accordingly the ratio of 25
to 1, carried to the first decimal, was used in transposing
the original figures for 1906 into those found below. Minor
variations in title, scope, etc., are disregarded. Following
are the requirements for the Junior year:

ADMINISTRATIVE SUBJECTS: "Administration of small libraries" 1, 0.5; "American library history" 0.4, 0.5; "Library buildings" 0.4, 1; "Library work with children" 0.4,
0.5; "Library visit" 3.4, 3.5; "Seminar" 1.2, 2; total 8, 8.
BIBLIOGRAPHIC SUBJECTS: "Bibliography" 3.8, 4; "Reference work" 5, 5; Selection of books 15.2, 12; total 24, 21.
TECHNICAL SUBJECTS: "Bookbinding" 0.6, 1.5; "Cataloging"
11.4, 7; "Classification" 3, 3; "Loan work" 1.1, 1; "Notes
and samples" 2, 2; "Order and accession" 1.4, 1.5; "Printing" 0.6, 1.5; Shelf work 1, 0.5; Subject headings 3; total
21, 21. PRACTICE WORK 4, 8. Grand total for junior
year: 57, 58.

And for the Senior year, the following:

ADMINISTRATIVE SUBJECTS: Administration of large libraries 5; "Library visit" 3.4, 3.5; "Seminar" 1.4, 3.5;
total 5.3, 12. BIBLIOGRAPHIC SUBJECTS: "Government
documents" 1.8, 2; History of books and foreign libraries
0.8, 1; Selection of books 13.2, 12; [Original] "Bibliography"
8, 8; total 26.8, 23. TECHNICAL SUBJECTS: "Classification" 2.4, 3; total 10.4, 3. PRACTICE WORK 4.6, 8.
Grand total for seniors exclusive of electives 47.6, 46.
Electives 4, 8.

ELECTIVES FOR SENIORS (from which an additional
4 credits were selected in 1906, an additional 8 in 1922):
"Bibliographic practice" 1, 1-2; "Cataloging" 4, 4; "Indexing"
0.8, 2; "Reference or reference practice" 2.6, 5; Library
extension 2; Library survey 8; Original bibliography 8; School
libraries 4; Law library and legislative reference practice 2-
4. Total electives 14, 39.

Required work counted in totals above for 1906 but not
otherwise listed (because not offered in 1922): Outside lectures, 1 credit (i.e., 25 hours) for each of the two years;
and for seniors--Subject bibliography, 3; Cataloging, 6; Notes
and samples, 2. Electives for 1906 similarly counted above:
Administration of large libraries, 1; Library buildings, 1.6.

While library schools gained a measure of stability, even of power, during the later years of the period there were problems aplenty. In terms of the Albany experience, none was more insistent than how to adapt a purely technical course to newer specialties of growing importance--school libraries, special libraries, etc. The logic of the model seemed to call for a separate course for each specialty, but in that case, where was the proliferation to end? Wyer, in announcing "Law and legislative reference work" in 1910, warned that the School could not go the limit and offer a new course for each type of library work which might have its own "peculiar problems." Somewhere, he admonished--and it was the first time the point was made--this "minute subdivision of courses" would, if pursued, get out of hand. [20]

In view of the growing number of positions in special-subject libraries, he saw two possible solutions. One was to recruit subject specialists and give them the usual technical library training. Such recruiting would be difficult and probably unwarranted, he believed, because of salaries and no less because the clientele needs, even in special fields, tended to be too general to make subject training decisively important. All this underlined the importance of the alternative possibility suggested--the use of technically trained librarians who, with encouragement, could develop on the job the subject competence necessary to handle the more specialized demands. Experience was cited to show that the generalists who were going out from library schools could and did develop this competence on the job, given the time to do it.

In a 1917 paper on "Library School Courses for Business Libraries," Josephine A. Rathbone, another outstanding Albany graduate who left her imprint on the education of librarians, gave what may be the classic formulation of the attitude toward special librarianship during the twilight when library schools first met the problem and could not yet see it clearly. [21] Her thesis was that, "insofar as business libraries are libraries--that is, organized collections of books and other printed material--the library school course trains for the work of collecting and organizing such libraries." The library school was able to do this because it had, so to speak, deciphered the ABC's of how to do such jobs: it imparts "a technique, a method of work, that can be used in any kind of library," and in so doing develops "a kind of mental training" or skill in digging out, organizing and presenting information scattered through many sources--all with

a minimum loss of time and energy. Her survey of one-year
library schools showed general agreement that the course
was already so full that nothing more could be added. As
for the two-year schools, Illinois had a special course for
seniors; Albany announced one that year, 1917; and the New
York Public was considering one. Thus our period closes
with specialization in libraries increasing, with demands for
trained librarians outstripping the supply, with educational
problems getting more complex, and all library schools
oriented toward those libraries which supported professional
training best and benefited from it most. This left the newer specialties like library service to business in a position
of second priority, as Wyer's reply to Miss Rathbone brought
out:

> There is clearly an increasing demand for library
> school students for business places. We are not
> able to fill the demand. We do not try very hard
> to do so; we haven't enough students to fill the real
> library places that ask our help.

Other library schools have already found their way into the discussion, a signal of the fact that as we move away
from the 1880's, it is the library school as an institution
rather than a single library school, that we must understand.
It is time to broaden the story with a word about major issues that arose in this period.

Areas of Conflict

Is Technical Education Enough? There was uneasiness
in the minds of some over whether the educational interests
of the library profession were safe and secure under the aegis
of technical education. Doubts were most prevalent in scholarly libraries and centers of higher learning. Ernest Cushing
Richardson, Librarian of Princeton, found much to commend
on visiting the Albany School on behalf of the ALA in 1890,
but urged an eventual broadening of the program to cover
more branches of library science in which those who aspired
to go to the top would need grounding. On the negative side,
his fundamental criticism, voiced with cordiality and restraint,
was that the aim was overly narrow and the method of attack
ill-suited for great depth: there was specifically a lopsided
emphasis on library economy; and in handling a subject having the compass of bibliography, the School was given to
"teaching method without science, praxis before principle."22

Wm. I. Fletcher, Librarian of Amherst, conceded in his charming little volume, Public Libraries in America, 23 that librarianship had as of 1894 not gained recognition as a learned profession but held up responsibility for book collections and their use as a highly challenging one intellectually and socially. Dr. K. Peitsch, Assistant Librarian of the Newberry Library, who later joined the faculty of the University of Chicago, agreed, but thought the road to recognition as a learned profession might be a long one because the proportion of learned librarians was so small. This he was sure would change, "but I do not expect the solution to come from the library schools whose work in other respects however I am not disposed to criticize at a time when libraries are bursting from the ground like mushrooms."24

Charles Welch, Librarian of the Corporation of London, Guildhall, raised doubts at the Second International Conference of 1897 which had repercussions on this side of the Atlantic. The central problem in organizing suitable training for librarians, he felt, lay in properly relating university training of a high order (including bibliographical study) to the practical training of the library itself. The ideal as he saw it: let a well-educated lad go to work in a library at 15; help him grow on the job; send him to the university for his degree after four years of experience, and there combine professional training with university work. He looked upon the systematic training being offered by "schools of library economy" as at best a "subsidiary aid," a limitation which, if not inherent, was accentuated by the way it was organized. For the training was being offered the student in advance of any library experience as a base to build on, thus fostering the illusion of being able to qualify for library work without sound experience and reducing the usefulness the training would have if it were preceded by experience. 25

Not much is known about a short-lived course in library science launched by Columbian (now George Washington) University in October, 1897, except that it was set up as one of the professional programs in the scientific school of the University and was manned by a group of distinguished bibliographers--Ainsworth R. Spofford, who served as Director; H. Carrington Bolton, of the Smithsonian; Henderson Presnell, U.S. Bureau of Education; and William Parker Cutter, U.S. Department of Agriculture. 26 A prime mover in the original undertaking, Cutter went a step farther in 1904 and proposed that the President and the Trustees of the University establish a library school of a new type. Here is a digest of the proposal:

Failure of library schools to produce librarians of
higher grade. Existing library schools were much
alike, the Albany School being the parent of them
all. They were chiefly concerned with popular circulating libraries where methods were pretty well
standardized. The library schools were doing a
good job of supplying libraries of this type with
subordinate assistants--catalogers, children's librarians, loan-desk librarians, etc. College and research libraries had proportionately more work of
higher grade. The Albany-School plan of developing expert knowledge of methods was not enough
here. 'The school-trained library assistant or librarian of the day is doing work little higher in
grade than that of the grammar school; the high
school, college and university grade of librarian is
not coming from the library school. '

Two lines of work a library school of a higher type
would conduct. The undergraduate training in library methods would correspond to the best in existing one-year courses. The higher training: a two-
year course at the graduate level, one year on 'library administration (organization, physical facilities, library personnel, readers and services, professional literature, professional organization and
training); a second on knowledge, description and
use of books. '27

Cutter took charge of the Forbes Library in Northamp-
ton shortly afterwards, and nothing came of the proposal.
Whether this proposal grew out of the Washington experiment
cannot be said with certainty, but it bears a close resemblance to the better-known views of Aksel G. S. Josephson,
an Albany graduate of fertile mind whose numerous professional contributions range from the original turn he gave the
cataloging policy of the newly-formed John Crerar Library to
the founding of the Bibliographical Society of Chicago. Josephson cautioned library schools about a mistake in policy he
thought they were making: their formula for raising standards
was to raise entrance requirements but to keep the quality of
instruction on the same plane.

If the standard of entrance requirements be thus
continually raised without a corresponding progress
in the instruction, the faculties of the schools may
someday be confronted with the fact that the step

from the college to the library school will not be
regarded by the students as a step upward. 28

The first year of technical work in library schools he
believed could be allowed to stand unchanged. In place of a
second year of much the same thing, he proposed a year at
least of more specialized professional study to be integrated
with other university work, the combination to lead to the
M. A. or Ph. D.   Something of this order was needed, he
argued, --"something that a library school or a training class
cannot give, " if libraries were to attain their fullest usefulness.   For the library "is part of, and ought to be the center of the intellectual life of the community, " to which readers come for information about resources, methods of study
and investigation.   "To answer such questions mere knowledge
of methods is not enough, not even if combined with the general culture which is the result of college studies; solid
scholarship consciously adapted to the special aims of libraries is required. "

One component of the higher program advocated would
be bibliography: the history, methodology, organization, in-
terrelationship and literature of subject fields; the classification of knowledge accompanied by study of various classification systems; cataloging; bibliography and reference, to re-
word his "bibliographical reportories, " and "the use and
handling of books as literary aids;" history of libraries and
bookselling; paleography and archives.   The other component,
library administration, would exclude "minor topics of library
economy, " but would include methods of library administration,
history of library and other material aimed at giving "an intelligent view of library work as a whole. "

Again in 1901, Richardson reported on visits to library
schools made on behalf of the ALA. He found the students
first-rate; found greater similarity in courses and methods
than he had anticipated ("there are few good things in the matter of practical training taken up with one which are not soon
adopted by the rest"); inspiring teachers; deep interest in
keeping the curriculum attuned to the real needs of the profession; and "a growing sympathy with the historical and larger aspect of things. "   Looking ahead, he supported the idea
of distinguishing between technical education and professional
education of a higher order. He would like to see Drexel
and Pratt, for example, undertake nothing more than "the
technical training which gets right down to the business of
making selected, bright students just as familiar with library

technology as can be done in a year's time: the proper work,
as I should judge, of an institute school. " On the other hand
he would like to see "second year courses ... developed into
high character courses sustained in only a few schools but
there sustained on a high level. "29

If this was the weather to port, what was it like to
starboard?

In 1887 Dewey wrote of a formal proposal to encourage
the best students to spend longer than two years on their
preparation. 30 It presupposed a fellowship-scholarship program, and would cap off the three-year program with a Master's (M. L. S.) degree:

> This expanded program would include considerable
> work in languages and comparative literature as
> well as the advanced work in bibliography and li-
> brary economy. One of the marked successes of
> the last year has been the bibliografical lectures
> by various professors of the university. This fea-
> ture is to be very largely extended hereafter, so
> that bibliografy will receive as full treatment as
> library economy and perhaps justify a change of
> name from the limited Library Economy to the gen-
> eric name Library Science, covering bibliografy,
> cataloging, classification and the group of topics
> connected with library management known as library
> economy. When the School was named, it was
> thought best to begin with only the technical part
> and wait till the demand of the public justified
> broadening the scope to cover library science. 30

The tone, the subject matter singled out, the deliber-
ate contrast between library economy and library science--
all point toward an orientation broader than technical education. It was an intention that is further documented by a
manuscript in the Columbia archives--a draft of a new section
of the university statutes drawn up in the standard form used
in other sections where the powers and responsibilities of the
several faculties are defined. The text envisages a "School
of Library Science" to consist of the President, the Dean or
Director, and the officers who give instruction; admission to
be limited to "graduates of literary colleges" and others who
qualified by special examination; the degrees to be B. L. S. ,
M. L. S. , D. L. S. --exactly as authorized by the Regents after
the move to Albany except that the thesis requirement for the
three-year M. S. was more specific.

President Barnard submitted the proposal to the Trustees May 2, 1887. Handwriting on the document, identified as that of Bernard Beekman, Clerk of the Trustees, states that it was on this date referred to the Committee on Courses and Statutes--and there the official record falls silent. No further action along this line was taken except the special course of forty lectures offered by professors in the College, 1887-89, as a companion to the course on the bibliography of their respective subjects. The new course must have been a difficult one to teach, for it was to provide the student with "a comprehensive and comparative view of the leading literature of the world" as well as the knowledge needed "to answer wisely the questions he is likely to be asked in various departments."[31] Library language lessons were added at the same time, but here no pretense was made at basic instruction, the aim being quick mastery of frequently-used foreign technical terms.

As if in furtherance of the 1887 move from the limited Library Economy to Library Science, and as if to meet the 1890 Richardson criticism of this limitation, it was announced in the 1891 Handbook that the course at Albany would cover library science in its broadest sense. Then a remarkable thing happened:

> Library science [this 1891 Handbook continues] is interpreted in its broadest sense as including all the special training needed to select, buy, arrange, catalogue, index, and administer any library in the best and most economical way.

This is the identical definition that was used over and over for "library economy" during the years when a purely technical course was first crystallizing.[32]

The reaffirmation of library economy was complete. The new Handbook, using again and again the original language of 1884-87 publications, presents anew and in detail the philosophy and organization of a technical course which confines itself to its special work. Dewey seems never to have wavered from this position thereafter. In 1901, when criticism of technical education swirled to its peak, he reiterated that the School offered only a technical course. He saw the issue as one of "practical vs. historical and antiquarian" interests. Taking the offensive on this issue, he conceded that subjects supporting the historical and antiquarian were touched on but lightly and that it might in theory

appear better to stress them more, but contended that the
School's first obligation was to the libraries which were asking it for trained help and that surely it would be more directly valuable to graduates and libraries both, to concentrate
on the thousand practical details which make for efficient and
economical service. 33

This is the shape in which the issue was left--a conviction on one hand that technical education was not enough,
and a conviction on the other that a program which met the
felt needs of libraries so successfully was good enough.

Library-training vs. Library-school Training. The
ALA in 1887 formally expressed gratification at the first
year's workings of the School of Library Economy. 34 It was
a gesture made historic by the fact that it originated with
William F. Poole as President and with Mellen Chamberlain
as Chairman of the Committee on Resolutions. These two
men, it will be remembered, were the leading critics of special schooling for librarians at the Conference of 1883 where
Poole made one of the most cogent statements on record of
the idea that library work is an art which can be learned
best by doing it. He pointed to the Boston Public, the Boston Athenaeum and other well-managed libraries as centers
where such learning was already going on, adding that the
best way to meet the expanding demand for persons learned
in the art would be to get these larger libraries to take the
logical next step and accept responsibility for giving persons
of good previous education a chance to work in them at no
cost to the library except the opportunity to learn. If the
Columbia proposal involved this procedure--and Dewey in the
discussion period stressed that it did--Poole was for it, he
said, but he was opposed to any suggestion of learning library work the academic way by "giving systematic instruction by means of lectures. "

The issue persisted. Harking back to 1883, an ALA
committee undertook in 1894 to find out how feasible it would
be to enter the profession by the route Poole favored. Of
the libraries whose size and circumstances could be supposed
to offer facilities suitable for professional training, 100 were
canvassed and 80 replied. Only seven, all in large cities,
were willing to take apprentices. 35

The year following the Welch paper at the Second International Conference, the old problem again became an issue when a debate was scheduled at the Chautauqua Confer-

ence (1898) on the merits of "apprenticeship as a means of
library training. "[36] Defining apprenticeship as training in
library work by doing library work, William I. Fletcher,
Librarian of Amherst and advocate of special schooling,
agreed that apprenticeship had much to be said in its favor.
Moreover, it had back of it the sanction of all those successful merchants and Lord High Admirals who had learned the
details of their jobs from the ground up.   In candor, however, some things had to be said on the other side: the apprentice has to spend many hours and days doing over and
over work in which there is no longer any real educational
value.   This is unsystematic and wasteful. He accordingly
settled on the more systematic method as the better of the
two:

> ... there can be no more reason for commending
> the apprentice system as superior to the technical
> school system in library work than in other occupa-
> tions. We now believe in giving the boys who are
> to be electricians as well as those who are to be
> ministers the best general and then the best tech-
> nical training available. Nonetheless must 'appren-
> ticeship' as a means of library training, fine as its
> results have been in the past, yield the palm to the
> more philosophical and more truly effective system
> of the library school.

Reuben G. Thwaites, Secretary and Superintendent of
the Wisconsin State Historical Society, agreed with his op-
ponent that the beginner receives training that is more systematic and that he tends on this account to make more
rapid progress in a library school.   But this advantage, he
argued, was offset by lack of direct contact with the public,
by the remoteness of general instruction from local conditions
and by mistaking a diploma as the mark of a finished librarian.   He conceded that the apprentice could be and often was
neglected or exploited, but went on to say that under a good
chief, the beginner would get better all-around training, at
least for that particular library, than he would get at a library school.   He concluded that some combination of the two
would be better than either method pursued singly--a contention that supported the "training class."

John Cotton Dana, reporting at the Montreal Conference (1900) on behalf of the ALA Committee on Library
Schools, made a stirring plea for professional endorsement
and support of any and every effort to further the training

of library workers--in library schools and training classes
or out. 37 It is the classic presentation of this point of view
in library literature.

The argument started from the phenomenal shift in
professional sentiment that Dana had witnessed since the
1880s. Then, the question was whether preparation for library work could be obtained in library school; now the question in the minds of library school people, he feared, was
whether training for library work could be obtained anywhere
else. Dana was emphatic that it could, and arraigned the
schools for preempting, or tending to preempt, library
training, saying that every library should be a library school.
He went further. Suppose a chief librarian--he hypothesized
--were given a choice between two people equally well qualified when recruited, but the first had worked two years in a
library like the one where the opening existed, whereas the
second had spent two years in a library school and no time
as an assistant. Speaking as one who had operated an early
apprentice class, Dana believed the librarian would choose
the library training over the library-school training: he felt
doubly sure of his ground if the library training, instead of
being haphazard, had been organized as a genuine apprenticeship permitting all-round work in the several departments of
library activity and giving the apprentice a chance to observe
the operation of the system as a whole. As for enhancing
the reputation of librarianship as a profession, the outcome
in Dana's mind hinged, not on the way in which the technical
training was dispensed, but on success in recruiting persons
who, by native ability and previous education, were equipped
for achievement eminent enough to command public recognition.

It was a hard-hitting report that went unchallenged in
the discussion that followed. From the middle-ground position of technical education, Dewey was able to assume that
there was from the library-school standpoint no quarrel over
the purpose and results of training and he passed over the
question put so forcefully by Dana about the merits of alternative methods--library training vs. library-school training--
in producing these much-needed results. He turned instead
to another significant point in the Dana report and dwelled
on the fact that the growth toward higher entrance requirements at Albany was in line with the committee-held conviction that the way to get competence of a high order was to
recruit it. No course, he conceded, could do more than bring
out individual qualities:

> If a man is born of poor fibre, of poor fibre he
> will remain. You can polish agate; you can polish
> mahogany; but you can't polish a pumpkin--and if a
> third-rate man comes to a library school ... he
> will be a third-rate librarian to the end of the chap-
> ter. 38

Still, the issue would not go away.

The peak of national debate was reached in 1905.
That year, the Portland Conference featured a comparison of
the merits of library and library-school training. 39 The
spokesman for the library schools was well chosen--Mary
Wright Plummer, who went on from the 1887 conference
where we met her, to lead two library schools to positions
of front rank. She spent most of her paper on the importance of native ability and a good education as emphasized
by Dana and Dewey in 1900, following this with a significant
distinction between the librarian of the higher order and the
ordinary library employee. Her central thesis was that library-school training is an aid to workers of both orders
but is planned primarily for library workers of the lower
order:

> Panizzis and Pooles and Winsors are not and never
> will be wholly produced by library schools, though
> library schools may contribute to their training.
> Such eminent examples are born librarians. The
> born librarian will not need a school to teach him
> principles of classification ... he will evolve sys-
> tems of classification and cataloging, and methods
> of administration without ever going near a school,
> and the school will adopt his principles and meth-
> ods and learn from him. But there will not be
> many of him, and there will be thousands of library
> employees and it is for these that our schools are
> at present intended.

Frederick M. Crunden, Librarian of the St. Louis
Public Library, spoke for training in the local library. His
central contention, similar to Dana's in 1900, was that American librarians had swung from one extreme (early opposition
to library-school training), only to find themselves at another
where their position was equally indefensible. He remembered
himself--erroneously, it would appear from the 1883 record--
as the only librarian who had spoken out confidently in favor
of the original experiment at Columbia. Library schooling

had meanwhile made a lasting place for itself as one method
of producing results of the kind the profession was united in
desiring. It would, however, be a mistake, he argued, to
look upon the library school as the only method capable of
producing these results:

> I agree [he says], that trained service is necessary
> to the successful conduct of a library. I hold, how-
> ever--and I think that experience compels agree-
> ment, though it seems to be made something of an
> issue--that this training can be attained as well,
> though not as quickly or pleasantly, by practical
> work in a library as by a course in a library
> school.

Every library, he went on to say, can and should be "a
training school for librarians." With Miss Plummer, he
agreed that this special training, by whatever method received, plays a role of secondary, if not tertiary, importance
in the life of the profession. His ranking of the prerequisites of high accomplishment were: native ability or fitness
for library work 45 per cent, a good liberal education 40
per cent and special technical or professional training 15
per cent.

In the discussion following, Dewey drew a picture of
the training structure which he saw emerging. It would embrace professional meetings, professional journals, state-
employed library visitors to encourage and direct the growth
of those in charge of small libraries, brief institutes, summer schools, library courses in normal schools for teacher-
librarians and, at the summit, the library schools. It was
an answer--though only an oblique one--to Crunden in which
no reference was made to local-library training.

George Herbert Putnam, Librarian of Congress, observed in a brilliant impromptu summary that Miss Plummer
and Mr. Crunden, in seeking positions which would leave
room for the other fellow, had united to produce a compromise that threw the whole case away. For the essence of
what each one had said in different ways was that specific and
systematic training was, after all, not really necessary. He
went on to picture the impact on the public: advocacy of special training by the academically-inclined had been countered
by strong dissent from the other side and that both parties
had laid stress, amid great applause, upon qualities that have
nothing to do with specific and systematic training--traits indeed that cannot even be cultivated or bettered by it.

In Conclusion

The first burst of creative effort in forming the American library school spent itself during the third of the century extending roughly from 1887 to 1920. To obtain an understanding of the cast given professional library training during this plastic period, we have concentrated on the experience of the first library school, in the belief that what is thereby lost in generality is offset by gaining a picture with sharper focus. The Albany School won the accolade of "mother of library schools." Enthusiastic graduates went out to establish new library schools, and the inbreeding helps explain why it was copied so extensively. One informed observer, surveying the scene as of 1909, summed it up by saying that "the schedule [of courses] of each new school has been based, line by line, upon that of the older schools, with unimportant variations."[40] Using the Albany experience as a guide, the following are seen to be the main lines of progress:

Formal training came to stay. The idea of library-school training caught on so rapidly that, within a few years, all opposition melted away or found expression in some competitive type of training. Nobody defended any longer the old style haphazard training.

Continued adherence to technical education. The period ends as it began with the use of the apprenticeship school as the accepted educational model. The Albany experience discloses three reasons for this. First was the climate of popular support. The great majority of librarians, like the public at large, reacted favorably to the results produced by technical education. Second, there was a minority who were convinced that schools of library economy were not suitable instruments for developing members of a learned profession --that library schools were "teaching method without science, praxis before principle"; but the trouble with these critics was that they came up with no constructive alternative. Third was Dewey's pragmatic attitude. In response to criticism, he sought a conciliatory way out, but gave up. Unwilling to swap off a program that was conceded to be successful, he reiterated the School's commitment to library economy on the ground that its first obligation was to the libraries which were turning to it for trained help. That was in 1901. Thereafter the acceptability of the model was not seriously challenged.

Program development within the framework of technical

88   Library Education

education.   Classwork soon showed a decisive superiority
over apprenticeship practices as a method of organizing the
learning experience.   The development of teaching aids for
use in classwork strengthened library literature.   Dependence
on short courses by non-resident experts yielded, as the literature developed, to a better-organized curriculum in charge
of resident faculty members who made teaching their career.
Students of superior ability were recruited.   An early problem of aim and scope of program was solved by relocating
the School outside an academic center, and courses were
developed in stricter harmony with the idea of a purely technical course.   Courses as well as placement records show
a dominent interest in public libraries; but so far as was consistent with this interest, genuine effort was made to serve
libraries of other types as well.   The content of the program
improved as experience showed what was most practical to
further the library movement.   All the while formal schooling
was setting up a chain reaction of its own.   The more the
profession was taken over by librarians trained to apply uniform practices, the more generally accepted these methods
became; and as library practices became uniform, it became
the more feasible to offer training in accepted practice which
would fit the needs of any local library.

     While the usefulness and the prestige of library schools
steadily increased, they did not have the field to themselves.
It is time to turn our attention to the other half of the story
of 1887-1920--to the several institutional forms which were
tried out as means of furthering the preparation of library
workers.

                            REFERENCES

1.   Root, Azariah S.   "The Library School of the Future,"
        ALA B. 11:157-60, Mar. 1917.

2.   Use of this name after 1887 suggests that it came to be
        preferred to the official name.

3.   LJ 13:96-97, Mar.-Apr. 1888.

4.   New York State Library, Albany.   Annual report for the
        year ending Sept. 30, 1889.   p. xxxiii.

5.   New York State Library, Albany.   Bulletin.   Library
        School, no. 1.   Handbook, 1891-92.   Aug., 1891.
        p. 30-42.

6. New York State Library, Albany. <u>Bulletin. Library
    School, no. 9.</u> Handbook of New York State Li-
    brary School. Sept. , 1901. (Bulletin 66), p. 394-
    403.

7. <u>Handbook</u> 1891-92, p. 4.

8. "ALA Proc. ," <u>LJ</u> 23: Conf. no. , Aug. , 1898, p. 134.

9. <u>Handbook,</u> 1891-92, p. 6-7.

10. "ALA Proc. ," <u>LJ</u> 15: Conf. no. , Dec. , 1890, p. 91.

11. N. Y. State Library, Albany. <u>Annual Report of Library
    School, 1898.</u> (Library School no. 3, Apr. 1899).
    Contains a record of where all preceding reports in
    the series are to be found.

12. See the Cutter bibliography in Dewey's <u>Library School
    Rules.</u>

13. No other school made as full use of the short course as
    Albany. The Illinois announcement of 1907-08, for
    example, observes that "There are so few textbooks
    on library economy that instruction is given almost
    altogether by lecture and laboratory methods"; but
    lists only its strong, regular faculty. It is easier
    to illustrate than describe accurately the use of
    semi-regular staff members because of different
    ways of listing them. Thus in 1905-06, Pratt lists
    with the regular faculty William Warner Bishop (for
    history of classical studies), then at Princeton, and
    James C. Egbert, Professor of Roman Archaeology
    and Epigraphy at Columbia, as part of the regular
    faculty. Egbert taught paleography to advanced stu-
    dents at Pratt for several years. Wisconsin illus-
    trates quite different arrangements. The faculty
    was divided into two groups: six from the Wiscon-
    sin Library Commission; six from cooperating insti-
    tutions. Fourteen additional lectures were listed
    as of 1907-08, ten from the University. They
    were given regular responsibilities, mainly for sub-
    ject bibliography, and included men of the stature
    of Frederick Jackson Turner (bibliography of Amer-
    ican history) and Richard T. Ely (bibliography of
    political economy).

14. <u>LJ</u> 12:169, Apr. 1887.

15. LJ 13:97, Mar.-Apr. 1888.

16. Columbia College Library. Fifth Annual Report ... and
     Second Annual Report of ... the School of Library
     Economy, June 30, 1888, p. 25.

17. "The Columbia College School of Library Economy from
     a student's standpoint," LJ 12:363-63, Sept. -Oct.
     1887.

18. N.Y. State Library. Annual Rept. of New York State
     Library School, 1906 (Bulletin 115; Library School
     24).

19. N.Y. State Library School. The First Quarter Century
     of the New York State Library School, 1887-1912.
     Albany, N.Y. State Education Dept.: N.Y. State
     Library School, 1912, p. 45.

20. N.Y. State Library. Annual Rept. of New York State
     Library School, 1910. (Library School 29; Educa-
     tion Dept. Bulletin no. 484.) p. 24.

21. "Library School Courses as Training for Business Li-
     brarians," Sp. Libs. 8:133-35, Nov. 1917.

22. "ALA Proc.," LJ 15: Conf. no., Dec. 1890, pp. 93-95.

23. Boston, Robert Bros., 1894. (Columbian Knowledge
     Series, no. 2).

24. Zentralblatt für Bibliothekswesen 12:134-36, Feb.-Mar.
     1895.

25. Welch, Chas. "Training of Librarians," in Internation-
     al Library Conference, 2d, London, July 13-16,
     1897. Transactions and Proceedings. London,
     1898, p. 31-33.

26. LJ 22:708, Nov. 1897.

27. Cutter, Wm. Parker. Suggestions for a School of Bib-
     liology at Columbian University. Washington:
     Printed as manuscript, 1904.

28. The Josephson summary is based on two of his papers:
     "Preparation for Librarianship," LJ 25:226-28, May

1900; "A Postgraduate School of Bibliography," ALA Proc. LJ 26: Conf. no., Aug. 1901, pp. 197-99.

29. "Report of the ALA Committee on Library Training," LJ 26:685-86, Sept. 1901.

30. Library Notes 1:268-70, Mar. 1887.

31. See the Circulars of Information for 1887-89.

32. First use known to the writer: "The School of Library Economy interprets Library Economy in its broadest sense, as including all the special training needed to select, buy, arrange, catalogue, index, and administer in the best and most economical way and collection of books, pam   or serials." Columbia College Library.   School of Library Economy. Circular of Information, 1884.

33. Handbook, Sept. 1901, p. 379.

34. LJ 12:449, Aug.-Sept. 1887.

35. LJ 19: Conf. no., Dec. 1894, p. 119.

36. LJ 23: Conf. no., Aug. 1898, pp. 83-84.

37. LJ 25: Conf. no., Aug. 1900, pp. 83-86.

38. Ibid., p. 112.

39. LJ 30: Conf. no., Sept. 1905, pp. 164-76.

40. ALAB 3:427-36, Sept. 1909.

Chapter 5

COMPETING PLANS OF ORGANIZATION

Hannah Packard James presented before the Second international library conference in 1897 the best review of American education of librarians that the closing years of the 19th century afford.[1] She describes four institutional forms into which library training was branching out, taking care to note that they were all rooted in the movement to provide special training for special work. Albany stood alone in the class at the top, the library school; it was an established part of the University of the State of New York, closely affiliated with the ALA, and was pointing its work toward "advanced positions in the different departments of library work." Next came the "high-grade training classes" at Pratt, Drexel and Armour Institute. These took account of the fact that the high entrance requirements of "the library school" ruled out many who, while unable to meet them, were yet fitted by nature and education to do admirable work as assistants or as heads of smaller libraries, and, with experience, to advance to more important positions. The Armour Institute program had recently been transferred to the University of Illinois. There, the basic education of students was to be further strengthened: the technical work was being placed in the junior and senior years, leaving the first two for the regular college course. "Lower" training classes which operated more along the historic lines of apprenticeship constituted Miss James' third class and summer schools her fourth. The latter should not be confused with summer sessions which nowadays form a regular part of all-year programs.

We shall follow a 1909 classification which is briefer than Miss James' and discuss these training agencies under three headings instead of four: summer library schools, apprentice and training classes, and library schools. This 1909 statement,[2] prepared by an ALA Committee to inform the public about available training facilities, mentions correspondence courses also, but these are omitted from the account to be given here.

Summer Library Schools

The popular summer school movement originated with an experiment at Amherst College begun in 1891 by William I. Fletcher.[3] It was a short, intensive course intended mainly for persons already engaged in library work, mostly as librarians of small libraries. For four hours a day for five five-day weeks (later six), students worked under the direct tutelage of Fletcher. The course consisted of lectures and supervised practice, largely of the kind that Dewey originated and called laboratory work. Fletcher was adept at leading his students to the best library practices of the day through critical comparative study, the object of which was not simply to familiarize them with procedures they would use but to develop judgment as to why they were the best.

A one-man undertaking, the school closed in 1905, as Fletcher neared retirement, but it served as a model which others copied with varying modifications. The University of Wisconsin, urged by the State Library Commission, started a similar six-week course in 1895.[4] It covered much the same ground but placed less stress on critical and comparative study. The course progressed by following in logical order the handling of the book--from the time it entered the accession book until it was classified, cataloged, loaned, repaired and rebound. These "theoretical lectures" (using "theory," as it was customarily used by technical educationists to comprise the principles which have to be mastered to gain proficiency in an art or craft) were supplemented by three to five hours of supervised work each day. The Albany School followed suit in 1896.[5] Salome Cutler Fairchild justified the shorter course as the best means of dealing realistically with educational needs of a transition period; but she also stressed the importance of the more thorough course, which required 76 weeks.[6] The summer work consisted of: simple cataloging, classification, accessioning, shelflisting, loan systems, and some elementary work in bibliography and library economy.[7]

The ALA Committee on Library Training listed twelve summer schools as of 1920: Albany, Colorado Agricultural College, Columbia, Illinois, Indiana Public Library Commission, Iowa State University, University of Michigan, Minnesota

State Board of Education, University of North Carolina, Pennsylvania Free Library Commission, Simmons and Wisconsin
Free Library Commission. 8   The length of course was generally six weeks, with a range from four to eight; for entrance, high-school graduation; for staff, one instructor for
every eight to twelve students, with a staff of four as the
average.   The American Library Annual for 1916-17 had
listed twenty-two short courses. 9   The smaller number in
1920 is accounted for partly by exclusion from the later report of extension and other courses which did not conform to
the typical summer school pattern, partly also by a loss in
popularity never regained after World War I--except for a
few years in the late 1920s and early 1930s when library development outstripped the supply of trained librarians.

The principal difficulties of the summer school were
human ones.   Its greatest service lay in providing training
that dealt as thoroughly as the time allowed with the essentials
of running a small library.   Its natural clientele were those
who were tied to their communities by bonds not loosened by
their library interests.   For those who were to use their
small-library experience as a stepping stone to higher responsibility elsewhere, the summer school turned out to be either
a cheap substitute for or costly preliminary to more extensive
training.   By 1920 these difficulties were creating confusion.
Four of the twelve summer schools were conducted by state
library commissions, seven by colleges, only three by regular library schools.   The courses of the library commissions
were designed for workers already in service.   A follow-up
system was being perfected: some commissions withheld
final certification of work in the course until state library
visitors were able to report favorably on the student's performance on the job.   Colleges, universities and library
schools had no such follow-up system.   They were drifting
along with different practices but the drift was toward a
strictly pre-service program, sometimes correlated with, but
more often in competition with, the one and two-year library
schools.

Two courses were open to summer schools to avoid
this competition.   One was to go out of existence, as some
did.   Another was to expand into a full-fledged library school.
The most unusual metamorphosis of the latter sort was the
summer school of the famous Chautauqua Assembly. 10   Drawing as many summer schools did on the best educational tal-
ent in the field, this school launched a typical six-week course
of lectures and practical work in 1901 with Dewey as general

director and Mary E. Hazeltine, Librarian at nearby James-
town, as resident director.   Mary E. Downey, succeeding to
the resident directorship in 1906, noticed that quite a few
students migrated from one summer school to another in
search of additional preparation.   This sparked the idea of a
year's program to be completed in four summers, and the
renamed Chautauqua Summer School for Librarians was the
result.   The plan went into effect in 1918 with the addition
of a second quarter of work, and the first class (four students) was graduated in 1920.   It flourished throughout the
1920s and then was swept away by the changing fortunes of
the Assembly, new trends in education for librarianship, and
the depression.

Apprentice and Training Classes

        Late nineteenth century experience in library training
shows creative imagination as well as the confusion that is
to be expected from experimenting with something new.   A
normal school in Colorado, plagued by arrears in cataloging,
enlisted the aid of students, gave them in return some supervised experience in organizing a library, and, flushed with
enthusiasm over the results, announced a training class of
sorts.   Another class was announced when a public librarian
in Pennsylvania organized a weekly staff meeting and gave
her three loan desk assistants a "seminar" in the use of the
reference collection and the card catalog.   In 1901, John Cotton Dana took stock of the library training that was going on
in forty-two leading libraries[11] and found that:

          Many librarians were training assistants in local
          library routines: 43 per cent frequently changed
          assistants from one department to another, if only
          temporarily, to familiarize them with all depart-
          ments; 12 per cent encouraged assistants, at a
          time when libraries were just beginning to be de-
          partmentalized, to take responsibility for special
          lines of work.

          A much larger number, 48 per cent, were giving
          their assistants 'training in library work aside from
          routine duties. '

Here is the breakdown of practices as Dana presents them:
weekly, monthly, or quarterly class or staff meetings, 43
per cent; the use of bulletins or other measures to inform

the staff about changes in method, new plans, etc. , 32 per
cent; provision for assistants to attend library meetings without loss of pay, 21 per cent; use of staff suggestions in book-
buying, 21 per cent; encouragement of staff reading, 12 per
cent; public recognition of individuals for special accomplishment, 12 per cent.

Dana, already farther away than some from the practice of letting assistants "work their way up" without help,
had caught hold of the modern idea that helping members
of the staff grow while on the job is one of the responsibilities of good library administration, but obviously things
were getting confused. Were all measures to encourage professional growth on the job and all organized professional instruction to be lumped together indifferently, and if not, how
were they to be sorted out from one another? Electra Col-
lins Doren, one of the first to try to clear up the confusion,
suggested a distinction between "informal training" and "special training" as follows:

> Experience in library routine in any or all depart-
> ments of work in one library [she says] is not
> 'special training' ... neither should the listening
> to lectures on library subjects or mere class, club
> or seminar discussion of library methods be called
> training. A course in library science may be more
> or less comprehensive and detailed according as it
> is intended to be elementary, secondary or higher
> instruction, but in no case is it training in a spe-
> cial sense unless the subjects in the course are
> made to cover a definite field, and there is re-
> peated drill in developing principles and applying
> them to specific problems set for the student to
> solve within a given time. Inspection and correc-
> tion of his work by the instructor, practice and
> test for the student until he has mastered the dif-
> ficulties and can really do a given amount of work in
> a given time according to a definite standard of
> thoroughness, accuracy and form, constitute special
> training. 12

She had another object in this paper, which was to
stress the need of establishing a more harmonious relationship between different styles and shades of special training.
The results can be restated briefly under three headings.
First, all special training is "systematic training"--a learning experience that is organized to accomplish results speci-

fied in advance. Second, special training was as of 1898
being built around the work of a class. This was in line
with a trend already noticed while discussing the development
of the library school: apprenticeship as a model for organizing the learning experience was dying out in favor of class-
centered activities in charge of a teacher. The reason for
this was well brought out by Katherine L. Sharp when she explained the growth of laboratory work at Illinois:

> This term [laboratory work] for practical work has
> been adopted since the connection of the school with
> the university. Formerly this work was done at
> pleasure during the day, and it was of a very mis-
> cellaneous character. This lacked system, and did
> not give satisfactory results.... Now regular lab-
> oratory hours are assigned; definite work is dis-
> tributed beforehand, and an instructor is in charge;
> tardiness or absence from laboratory is as serious
> as from a recitation. [13]

Third, there were, according to Miss Doren, two classes of
special training agencies, but they differed more in organization and level of work than in aim or principle. Albany,
Pratt, Drexel, and Illinois comprised one class; summer
schools, training classes, extension and correspondence courses
the other. The first-class institutions offered "higher technical training"; the other class "elementary training. " They
all covered essentially the same subjects, one providing a
more comprehensive treatment than the other.

One of the best examples of "elementary training" as
here described was set up by Miss Doren herself. [14] She
had entered the service of the Dayton Public Library in 1879,
rising through the ranks to the post of Librarian in 1896.
The experience had given her first-hand knowledge of the in-
effectiveness as well as of the human waste involved in the
old system of haphazard training through employment. She
forthwith reorganized the library. The main thing achieved
by this was to make library training--in her own enlightened
phrase--a responsibility of library management. All positions on the Library force were classified according to seven
grades:

> (a) Chief executive; (b) Head cataloger; (c) Account-
> ant assistant [Librarian emeritus] and Catalog as-
> sistant; (d) 'Medium clerical work': delinquents'
> accounts, inventory and shelf list, accession entry

and withdrawal, alphabeting and filing catalog
cards, order, clerical and copy work; (e) 'Minor
clerical work': charging and discharging books,
borrowers' records and accounts, filing book-slips
and borrowers' cards; (f) 'Student' or 'substitute'
assistant service; and (g) 'Messenger service': all
mechanical work upon books, including reshelving,
dusting, mending, collating, labeling, embossing,
etc.

Esther Crawford, a capable young Albany graduate, took
charge of the newly-approved Catalog Department and Training Class. The class was "for the systematic training" of
assistants below third grade in rank as well as of a staff of
substitutes drawn from resident candidates for employment.
The student was admitted to work for one to two calendar
years with three-months probation at the outset to test fitness
to go on. He gave one hour of service to the Library in return for each hour of class work, except in cataloging where
the rate was three hours for each hour of class work. Graduates of the Training Class were not promised a position but
were promised preferential consideration in the order of
merit shown by performance record. Meanwhile the student,
after three months training, was eligible for service in grade
six (as student substitute) or grade seven (as messenger).
The pay scale, while hardly impressive, was in line with
practice elsewhere: for service beyond the time used to
recompense the library for instruction, 6 cents an hour as
messenger, 10 cents as student substitute. After six months,
the pay began to move towards an 18 cents ceiling for substitute work, with no mention of the messenger, whose road to
fortune obviously lay in rising to the rank of substitute.

     The class opened in the fall of 1896 with an enroll-
ment of seventeen, including three library assistants and
four younger high school students who entered for brief messenger training only. Together they worked 1,507 hours the
first year to compensate for instruction, were paid for an
additional 5,754 hours of "extra service." Seven received
certificates for successfully completing the year and some of
these moved up rapidly. Ten years later, one was Head
Cataloger, another Head of the Loan Department, a third in
charge of School Library and Children's Work; a fourth Head
of the Reference and Shelf Department.

     The course of instruction was laid out to cover two
years of nine months each. "It was not designed to be a

library school, its immediate function being the organization
and future development of this Library alone, through the
means available from local sources.   When that shall have
been in some degree accomplished, its purpose may be considered as fulfilled. "   The subjects taught were:[15]

> First year: rules and regulations for borrowers,
> shelf care and inventory, the library hand, note-
> taking, and frequently used abbreviations, book rou-
> tines (preparation for the shelves, order work and
> preliminary accession), book numbers, application
> of the Dewey Classification to filing of trade miscel-
> lany, seminar (current events, book lists and eval-
> uation), loan work, accession work, binding work,
> and alphabeting.

> Second year: lectures and problems in the use of
> reference books, review of the principles of acces-
> sion work and further experience in accessioning,
> elements of the Decimal Classification, and diction-
> ary cataloging.

The resemblance to the early program of the library
school is readily apparent--a combination of lectures and
practical experience designed to initiate the beginner into accepted library practices.   Beginning with the simpler routines,
"the instruction was arranged to follow exactly upon the lines
and within the limits of the regular work of the library, lecture and test practice work always preceding experience in
the performance of the real work. "   The essential difference
from the library school was: local methods were codified
and used as the basis of instruction with "no instruction in
comparative methods given except as used incidentally by way
of illustrating the subject under consideration. "

The model for the class at Dayton was the Los Angeles
training class.   Popular interest in this pioneer class (of
which more later) led Adelaide R. Hasse to give a full account of it in 1895 in a series of how-to-do it articles entitled "The training of library employees. "[16]   "Plainly, " she
said in language that helped give these classes their name,
"they are nothing more or less than the old-fashioned apprentice system, with a competitive examination before admission
and another when the required term of apprenticeship has
been completed. "

Conflicting use of "Apprentice class" and "training

class" brings up the question whether there was a difference
between them that amounted to anything. The question has
to be answered both ways, so varied were the meanings given
the terms; but there were underlying reasons for all this confusion and it will be useful to see what they were. The apprentice class and the training class were alike in being de-
partures from the laissez-faire tradition. They were alike
in always being geared closely to the local library, in recruiting heavily from local residents and in being attentive to
training for positions of lower rank. "Training class" was
used generally to include apprentice classes, but when used
more narrowly as the opposite number of "apprentice class,"
it meant a form of training that was higher in some particu-
lar--in entrance requirements, for example, or length of
course or number and qualifications of teachers. The point
is well illustrated by Faith E. Smith, director for many
years of the Chicago Public Library Training Class who, in
one of the best papers of the period on the subject, [17] differentiates the two as follows: "The training class of the large
library is an evolution from the apprentice class. It signifies more formal and extended instruction than did the apprentice class...."

     It can be put this way. Experimentation following the
19th century break with haphazard training methods ran the
gamut from library schools down to outright apprenticeship,
with the objectives of technical education consistently serving
as the lodestar and standard of the whole training system.

     Time and again haphazard training through employ-
ment is referred to in the literature as apprenticeship, but
it did not deserve the name. As the idea of systematic training caught on, bona fide apprenticeships were organized.
They involved no formal class instruction: the unpaid learner was rotated through various departments so he could learn
library work by doing it--always, of course, under the supervision of some "master of the craft."

     But most libraries which developed local training pro-
grams went directly from the haphazard system to apprentice
classes. Technical education was a new way of producing
results of the kind apprenticeship had been producing for gen-
erations. The library apprentice class was a blend inspired
by alert librarians who, in the vein of Thwaites at Chautauqua
Conference, sought the benefits of both systems by combining
the old and the new.

The revolutionary feature of technical education was, as we have seen, the introduction of schooling--a method of organizing the learning experience so that whole classes could work together. It was a feature which gave special education for librarians its most distinctive turn, and it was this feature that was combined with time-tried methods of apprenticeship to produce the typical apprentice class.

The experience of 1887-1920 with apprentice and training classes thus confirmed the insight of the originators of the apprenticeship school that formal schooling--systematic classwork under a good teacher--produces similar results more efficiently than the ancient methods of apprenticeship.

What sort of a future did all this portend for a flourishing crop of apprentice and training classes? Some were to evolve into full-fledged library schools. Others evolved into competitors of library schools. The risingstar of the latter did not mean that all the advantages were on their side. The ALA Committee on Library Administration reported at the Bretton Woods Conference (1909) on the use of apprentices. [18] Libraries standing at extremes in size were about equally divided between those that did and did not take apprentices. But 109 of the 187 libraries reporting fell in the middle group (10,000 to 50,000 volumes); 66 of these (61 per cent) regularly took apprentices, 34 did not, three took them only when new assistants were needed. A follow-up in 1911 showed comparable results. Standards varied significantly on entrance requirements, length of course, proportion of formal instruction, etc. Chief advantages cited in favor of the practice were: the library could afford such training (which usually entailed no cost except staff time), but could not afford other "trained help"; it provided more thorough knowledge of prospective employees; provided more effective initiation into local library methods; and capitalized on the contacts and community interests of local residents who wanted to work.

The competition gained vigor from criticism of library schools. These criticisms tended to revolve around four themes. Some librarians were critical because library school training was priced so high that their libraries could operate on a lower salary budget by training their own staff, especially for the lower positions. Second, the isolation of library schools interfered with gearing the training to the needs of the local library, and teachers with limited practical experience further reduced the direct applicability of school

training.   Third, library schools made up for this isolation
as best as they could by teaching comparative methods, but
this approach was too theoretical.   It left the student not
trained in the methods of any particular library as well as
he would be by an apprentice class.   Even the respected advantages of formal instruction did not escape criticism.   No
one phrased it better than Clarence Sherman[19] who in a debate in 1932 defended training classes on the ground that the
educational principles and practices they relied upon were the
match, if, indeed, not superior to the "mass instruction, at
arm's length from direct application, " that library schools
relied upon.

       The struggle between the library school and the train-
ing class, while mainly the profession's affair, was public
enough for anyone to take sides who cared to do so.   Shortly
after one ALA conference where the education of librarians
was a headline topic, a Chicago editor received a circular
about the Springfield (Massachusetts) Training Class and
plunged into the discussion with the following:

          The library training class is doing good work.
          The education and 'breaking in' of apprentices by
          this practical method, where the public library is
          large enough to afford the requisite facilities and
          is also in constant need of new recruits to its
          working force, cannot be too highly commended.
          As compared with that admirable institution, the
          library school, there is a saving of time and ex-
          pense to the learner and an avoidance of that some-
          times excessive devotion to theory which a two or
          three years' course at Albany might conceivably en-
          courage in some zealous students.   Local conditions
          and local needs are also better learned in the li-
          brary training class, and greater surety of immedi-
          ate employment at the end of the course may some-
          times be counted on. [20]

Then follows a description of the Springfield Training class:
a nine-months course, 43 hours a week, one month's instruction and practice in each of the library's departments.

       The newer training classes edged ahead of apprentice
classes in popular favor as they edged closer to library
schools.   While by nature they veered toward being competitors, much effort was exerted by training-class directors to define for them a supporting role.   The California State Library

experience is representative.   In 1911, the Library asked for
an increased appropriation with the understanding that if the
increase were granted, the library would conduct "a library
class on more liberal lines than its former apprentice classes,
though not aspiring to the dignity of a library school."[21]
Here the training class is placed at a midpoint on the scale.
Higher up than elementary classes like the one at Dayton, it
made its bid for status, not as a competitor of the library
school, but as a sort of junior partner.   This is the conception that was back of a prolonged but unsuccessful effort to
integrate training classes, along with library schools, into a
graded national system of training agencies.   The move
reached its peak at the Asbury Conference (1917) where the
Professional Training Section, taking up a subject that had
been sidetracked since 1905, considered the following proposal
for standardizing the work of these higher classes.[22]

> Applicants: at least 18 years of age, a high school
> education or equivalent, an entrance examination
> less advanced than for entrance to library schools.

> Organization: the course to consist of 1000 hours
> of work to be divided equally between classwork and
> practical work in different departments; to last six
> to eight months; no paid work; to be in charge of a
> full-time person, a graduate of a library school.

> Instruction: details to be left to individual libraries
> but to include the fundamentals of library technique.
> Suggested subjects followed closely those taught in
> library schools, with the addition of general litera-
> ture, history or art; the library profession; the li-
> brary movement; and citizenship training--all intend-
> ed to broaden the student's outlook.

Jessie Welles, an extension specialist and library
school instructor, as Chairman of the Section, recommended
that librarians and library schools accept these or similar
standards as a means of putting "secondary education" in library work on permanent footing.   The analogy was for many
years a popular one, but it masked a misleading argument.
Such plausible-sounding secondary education for librarians,
the friends of library schools pointed out, amounted to building up apprentice classes into second-rate facsimiles of the
better library schools.   As one speaker at the Asbury Park
Conference put it during a comparison of training classes and
library schools, the library training class when it copies the

manners of a professional library school "is only a makeshift, however necessary, however valuable.... More than this, it is a menace as well, for it turns out people who believe themselves trained when they are merely prepared for real training. "

Library Schools

      The three styles of training we are considering--summer schools, training classes, library schools--show notable differences from one another in method, organization, type of student recruited, etc. , but our survey has revealed a kinship that is equally notable: all three were generated by much the same theory as to how to educate librarians; all responded to the same sort of environment; and all sought to produce results strikingly similar when allowance is made for differences in length of program, in calibre of students, etc.

      Early library literature documents this kinship in a variety of ways. Prior to the James paper, in which the point is well made, Library Journal began running a regular column of news in 1893 on "Library schools and training classes," a feature which was continued to 1913. The same year, 1893, George Watson Cole, addressing the New York Library Club at a meeting at Columbia, made the point more specific:

            When the members of the pioneer class of the Library School met for their first lecture in this room they were told and fully believed that they were about to attend the only school of its kind in the world. In the short space of six years, five similar schools have been started in different parts of the country. They are located respectively at the Pratt Institute in Brooklyn, the Drexel Institute in Philadelphia, the Armour Institute in Chicago, the Free Public Library at Los Angeles, California, and at Amherst College, where Mr. Fletcher has opened a summer school for teaching library methods. [23]

Some of Dewey's writings showed full awareness of the kinship. An example is the following from an annual report in 1892.

Last year [he says] attention was called to the library training class at Pratt Institute in Brooklyn,
conducted by one of the early graduates of the
School. This year a similar class has been opened
by the Drexel Institute in Philadelphia, where Miss
Alice B. Kroeger of the class of 1891 and Miss
Bessie R. Macky of the class of 1892 are librarian
and assistant. In Los Angeles, California, there
is a class which follows the general methods of the
School. It seems to the faculty wisest that this
system of branch schools or of classes more or
less closely affiliated to the original School should
care for the increasing numbers who wish instruction and for whom we have no room.... 24

The profile along which training programs ranged themselves shows a gradual movement away from the ancient methods of apprenticeship to something "higher." What was left
unsaid above and now requires emphasis is that library
schools generally, following the trail blazed by the School of
Library Economy, started out on the same base and traversed
the same upward course. If their star rose faster and higher, it was because of features which won out in the competition for professional acceptance. What were these features?

While the progress of library schools is rooted in
Dewey's choice of apprenticeship schooling as a middle road,
the progressive use of formal instruction in training classes
made it impossible to go on treating this feature as the private possession of library schools when it came time to set
national standards of excellence. Accordingly, the standards
prescribed for membership in the Association of American
Library Schools[25] by its original constitution dealt with minimum essentials for sound professional education, with emphasis on points believed to account for the peculiar excellence
of the schools. These standards were: (1) a minimum faculty of two full-time members (or the equivalent in part-time
staff), at least two of whom had studied a year in library
school; (2) a program of training for general library work
(as distinguished from training for work in a particular library) which extended over at least one academic year; and
(3) provision that students should have had as a minimum a
high-school education.

There were six library schools which met these standards: the Albany School; Pratt Institute Library School, founded in 1890; the University of Illinois Library School, founded

at Armor Institute of Technology in 1893 and transferred to
Urbana in 1897; Simmons College Library School (1902); University of Wisconsin Library School (1906); and Syracuse University Library School (1908).   The library schools of Western Reserve University (1904) and the New York Public Library (1911) came in with the understanding that they would
meet these standards.   At the organization meeting, minor
revisions as to staff were added so as to include the two
other members of the original roundtable, the Carnegie library schools at Pittsburgh (1901) and Atlanta (1905).   Three
other schools were admitted toward the close of our period
--the Library School of the Los Angeles Public Library (1918),
the University of Washington Library School (1919), and the
Library School of the St. Louis Public Library (1921).

     While there were other library schools, these taken
together sum up much of the best experience of this period.
The library school triumphed because of two factors: its
course of study was longer and more thorough than the summer school's; its training was not, like the training class,
geared to a particular library.   Aside from these factors the
lines blurred, although library schools tended to have larger
full-time faculties, higher entrance standards, and (if an exception is made of the summer schools) the most degree-
granting institutions among their sponsors.

     The life histories of these thirteen schools likewise
emphasize the fact that the several training agencies were
all variants of the same educational model.   Three originated
as library schools: Albany, Atlanta and Simmons.   The
work at Columbia in 1884-86 resembles that of apprentice
classes of a later date, and its example could hardly have
been lost on those who perfected this style of training; but
these "preliminary classes," as they were called, were really a trial run used to perfect technical schooling in a new
field.   The Southern Library School, [26] established as a regional center with a Carnegie grant, opened in 1905 with students from four states.   Its name changed to Library School,
Carnegie Library of Atlanta in 1907, and another grant the
same year put it on permanent footing.   Except for the regional emphasis on recruiting, its one-year program was not
much different from the better training classes in other large
public libraries like Brooklyn and Chicago.   Simmons was
founded to provide education for women in fields in which they
could earn an independent livelihood: education for librarianship was one of the branches of study from the outset.   No
basic innovations as to courses were made, but the work was

taken over four years, along with other college courses:
Illinois began in 1903 to require three years of college for
admission to professional courses for librarians, then advanced to graduate footing in 1911. Simmons adopted the
three plus one plan for its four-year program in the early
1920s, but set a precedent of another kind as early as 1905-
06 when it started offering a condensed "one-year program"
to graduates of approved colleges. It appears to have been
the first of the fifth-year programs to be offered by an academic institution. Albany was on a graduate footing earlier,
but it had a two-year program.

        Three others of the thirteen grew out of summer
schools: Wisconsin (1895), Western Reserve (1898) and
Washington (1905). The summer school in Cleveland originated at the Public Library under the enterprising leadership
of William H. Brett. Esther Crawford of Dayton, in direct
charge until the school was reorganized in 1904 and made a
regular professional school of Western Reserve, was succeeded by her chief, Electra Doren. Brett served as Dean
till his death in 1918. In line with a popular early procedure,
Western Reserve at first allotted solid blocks of time to different subjects--such as public documents, library records
and elementary classification, loan systems, binding and repair of books. The two principal advantages of this were:
practice work could be tied in more closely with instruction
and more practical use could be made of non-resident specialists.

        The seven remaining schools originated as training
classes. The earliest record of the work at Pratt is an un-
dated brochure, probably of 1893, which is headed, The Pratt
Institute Free Library Training Classes. It carefully dis-
tinguishes the work at Pratt from "that of the Library School
at Albany, which is the official school of the American Library Association. " Essentially the same subjects were covered as at Albany: the difference lay (1) in limiting the
training to methods used in the local library, and (2) in planning the work for librarians of small libraries and assistants
in larger ones. The original aim to train for the local staff
was changed the first year. Other changes were soon remaking the training class into one of the nation's ranking library
schools. Cultural subjects dropped out. New technical subjects were added--twenty-one in the first twelve years. From
the beginning, subjects received parallel treatment instead of
being studied in solid periods. A regular faculty, chosen for
aptitude in teaching, was organized in 1895. Shortly afterward,

in 1896, the original one-year course of lectures and practical work was expanded to two years.

The work of energetic leaders under conditions that invited creativity, these schools show fascinating variety in origin and development. Frank W. Gunsaulus challenged civic-
minded Chicagoans with "what I would do if I had a million
dollars," and advised from his pulpit that he would himself
build an institute for technical training where the poorest boy
could have an opportunity equal to the richest.[27] When Philip
B. Armour came forward to pick up the gauntlet, it was not
surprising that apprentice training was included as a feature
of the new institute library, for Gunsaulus' enthusiasm for
books and libraries was legendary. What was more remarkable was the choice of Katherine Sharp to take charge of the
work. A gifted and dedicated educator, she was soon laying
farsighted plans for a school which has consistently maintained a position of educational leadership.

Syracuse, setting an early example of academic recognition, elected its Librarian, M. J. Sibley, instructor in library economy in 1892.[28] Undergraduate instruction in the
use of the library, which Sibley inaugurated, evolved first into a two-year training class and then, by gradual steps, into
a full-fledged library school.

Billings and, following him, Anderson capitalized on
opportunities afforded by the New York Public Library for
specialization but, to avoid exploiting students (first in the
training class, then the library school), they made liberal
arrangements for "paid work." All concerned were happy
until 1915, when "paid work" suddenly loomed as a roadblock
to membership in the AALS. By this date, library schools
were moving toward having their credentials stand for formal
course work--a policy which tended to reduce practice work
as a formal degree requirement.

Edwin H. Anderson's annual report at Pittsburgh in
1901 showed the Carnegie Library striding ahead in the new
field of service to children and told about "a training class
for children's work" set up October 1, 1900, to meet the demand for qualified librarians. With a two-year program of
lectures and apprentice work, its standards were first-rate
from the outset, and in its special field it was in a class to
itself. A course in School library work was added in 1915;
another for General library work in 1918.

The St. Louis Public Library, starting with a one-
month apprentice class (1905) which evolved into a strong
training class (1910), changed to a library school of "standard grade" in 1917. One of the announced reasons: "the
only nearby schools are in universities."[29] Circumstances
suggest another reason. Probably the fullest comparison of
library schools and training classes ever held had taken place
at the Asbury Conference the preceding year.[30] Harriet P.
Sawyer, head of instruction at St. Louis, spoke for the training classes and she made a strong case for then. She conceded that training classes varied considerably in quality, de-
pending on the resources of the sponsoring library, then argued that a half dozen or more libraries maintained programs
of a quality that compared favorably with the best of the
schools. She dealt with specific points of excellence: courses
similar and in charge of persons with comparable training;
school-terms as long and some even longer; parallel entrance
requirements; practice work about the same except that some
training classes were in library systems which offered opportunities superior to those within reach of some library
schools; comparable equipment, access to outside lectures,
opportunities to visit other libraries, etc. In short, the
training class and the library school were described as identical in aim ("to provide trained workers") and the methods
were enough alike that success depended less on whether the
graduate came from one or the other than on matters of per-
sonality and devotion to the work.

Five years later St. Louis qualified for membership
in the AALS, with no evident change of attitude and with
Miss Sawyer still in charge. The tide of professional sentiment was, however, running in favor of the library school,
and St. Louis swung around with the current.

The story of the Los Angeles class illustrates the process by which apprentice classes evolved into library schools.
To gain admittance to that original class in 1891 which was to
be "copied throughout the country,"[31] six students took a simple entrance examination; went to work without pay three hours
a day for six months, moving from one department to another;
passed a final examination and became eligible for substitute
work. No promise of permanent employment was given but
vacancies were filled only from candidates who qualified in
this way.

Straight use of the apprenticeship method--or "under-

study" method to use another of the Library's phrases--was
superseded in 1892 when classwork was inaugurated. The
new feature fitted easily into the apprentice routine: heads
of departments as it came their turn gave "lessons in comparative methods," followed by a term of practical application. Instruction covered handwriting, typewriting, proofread-
ing, and library printing, book selection, ordering, accessioning, shelf-listing, classification (Dewey and Cutter taught,
other systems explained), reference work, indexing and loan
systems. A second term of six months was devoted to cataloging and library administration, the one based on Cutter's
rules, the other on library reports and professional literature.

     For twenty years and more, the main object of the
class was to provide recruits for the local library staff, but
similarity in standards and practices made it a valuable if
limited source of supply for other libraries of the region.
This outside demand grew, so in 1914 it was announced that
better facilities afforded by a new building "make it possible
to accept a limited number of students wishing to prepare for
library work elsewhere," and the name was changed to
"Training School of the Los Angeles Public Library." This
is the way the program stood at the time:

> For admission, preferred age range, 18-30; high
> school education or equivalent, with college educa-
> tion recommended; simple entrance examination in
> literature, history, current events, art, music,
> modern social problems. Two-months probation.
> Practice work four days a week, four hours a day.
> Special lectures and visits.

Courses were laid out under the four headings below. Quotation marks signify subjects offered with practically no
change from 1914 to 1918, the year the Training School was
admitted to membership in the AALS. The figure following
the subject signifies the number of lectures or periods in
1914; the second figure, if two, the number in 1918. Periods
were fifty-five minutes in 1918, the length not specified in
1914.

Bibliographical and Critical Courses. Survey of literature,
25; Book selection, 10; Bibliography of special subjects, 15;
"Publishing houses," 4, 10; "Trade bibliography," 4, 6;
"Book buying and ordering," 5, 6; "Reference work," 23, 45;
"Work with children," 15, 30; "Public documents," 12, 10;
"Periodicals," 6, 10.

Technical courses. "Cataloging," 20, 40; "Classification,"
18, 30; "Accession department," 6, 6; "Shelf list" and "inventory," 3, 3; "Binding and repair," 7, 7; Miscellaneous, 5.

Administrative courses. "Library administration," 6, 17;
"Departmental routine," 9, 9; "Loan administration," 16, 8.

Miscellaneous courses. History of books and libraries, 5;
"Current events," 16, 10; "Current library literature," 8,
16; Library extension and legislation, 3.

The 1918 curriculum kept the fourfold classification of
courses, but replaced "miscellaneous courses" with "special
courses" (county, school and children's work, the latter giving greater emphasis to children's literature). The total
number of periods had increased from 229 to 440, the school-
year from eight to nine months, full-time personnel from two
to four. The stated requirement of practical work dropped
to 282 hours from around 550, but the extra "exercise work"
required to support additional class work makes exact comparison impossible. On the whole, the program became more
thorough, better organized, more carefully manned.

No subject was dropped between 1914 and 1918 except
Library extension and legislation. New courses added were:
County libraries, School libraries, The library movement,
and Original work involving preparation of a thesis or bibliography; Evaluation of fiction; [Subject] Bibliography; History of
books and printing; Subject headings; Recent literature; Library buildings, and Registration [or borrowers and related
problems not covered in Loan administration]. New material
was incorporated into some courses which in name showed
little change, while others were more extensively reorganized.
The outstanding example of reorganization was book selection.
Helen Haines in 1918 pulled together material from four
courses (book selection, survey of literature, bibliography of
special subjects, evaluation of fiction, the latter a course
she had pioneered) into a single course. Entitled "Book selection," this was probably the least technical course so
named in the country. It was designed to cultivate the critical capacity which the librarian at his best uses in judging
books and, more particularly, to familiarize the student with
writers and books, their scope, qualities and values in several much-used classes of literature (fiction, biography, history, travel, sociology, and religion) and with selection
sources and aids in these fields and attention to the principles involved in discriminating selection. The rest of the

Comprehensive Survey of Literature went into the new course,
Recent Literature, which took in literature, especially modern poetry, drama and essays, fine arts, science and industrial arts.

   When the school year was lengthened to nine months
in 1915 it was announced that "practically all the subjects
taught in any one year library school course" were going to
be offered.   The AALS was being organized and the following
year, the Training School applied for membership.

   What happened next is illuminating.   James I. Wyer,
director of the Albany School, made an inspection and reported favorably, but it took time for the Association to get
a meeting of minds as to what to do.   "We are not quite
positive," the Chairman of the Executive Committee reported
on December 30, 1916, "that they are so much ahead of some
of the fine training classes in the country, and we are not
prepared to ask you to admit them at once."   One well-informed member, more emphatic, thought the Los Angeles
School was "a most excellent training apprentice school,"
nothing more, and that if it were admitted, the training class
at the Brooklyn Public Library, as an example, should be
admitted too.   It was agreed that the standards prescribed
by the constitution were met in some respects, more than
met in others, but the majority demurred for three reasons.
One was the lack of full-time personnel.   As of 1916, the
work was in the hands of 16 people, of whom all were part-
time except a full-time principal and one reviser.   Second,
the courses were adequate to qualify students for general
library work, but there was a more technical point on which
Los Angeles fell below standard.   The class drew students
only from California and placed them all there; many, if not
most, in the local library.   Third, the constitution prescribed
a full year of professional and technical work: the Los Angeles course of study included "perhaps too much on the academic side, courses in literature and things of that kind rather than the full amount of professional and technical work."
While the school might have claimed that the courses in literature were technical, Los Angeles was weak in book selection, and perhaps in administration as well, as compared
with other schools.

   A waiting period was agreed upon to give the applicants "a chance to change conditions that do not meet approval or to submit further evidence."   The full-time staff was
promptly increased from two to four.   The proportion of

"Technical and Administrative work" was increased also.
Whereas the total number of "periods" of instruction increased
92 per cent between 1914 and 1918, the increase for Technical courses was 166 per cent, for Administrative courses
just over 100 per cent. This revised program included new
subjects, heavier stress on old ones, skillful reorganization
and rearrangement--all aimed at proving that schooling of
high quality had replaced apprenticeship. The school, however, continued to pioneer literature courses which looked to
some like a break with technical education. The Association
found the "further evidence" convincing, and the Training class
became the first institution to be added to the original list of
ten members. Soon thereafter its name was changed to Library School, Los Angeles Public Library.

Beginning of a Coordinated System of Training

        We have before us the picture of a divided house with
an ill-coordinated set of institutions resulting from different
views as to how to train librarians. There was another consequence to be noted. Outside of local interest and experimentation of the kind described in the foregoing pages, librarians relied on nothing but discussion to guide them to a national policy on library training, and as time wore on the
need of an organized channel through which to assert the profession's interests in this matter gained increasing attention.
Here, division within the ranks made itself felt again; for differences of viewpoint tended to frustrate the building of machinery to support national planning. The formation of the
ALA Committee on the Library School in 1889 was the first
step toward such machinery. 32   The Committee's responsibilities grew as it became the Committee on the Library
School and Training Classes (1895), then the Committee on
Library Schools (1896). Proceedings of the Chautauqua Conference (1898) show that the profession was awakening to the
significance of personnel development in all its aspects and
was drifting toward impartial encouragement of any and every
style of training that promised improved performance on the
part of library workers. After the Dana report of 1900, this
mood hardened into ALA policy and the Committee on Library
Schools was reconstituted as the Committee on Library Training.

        The reorganized committee was directed, in accord-
ance with its own recommendations, to visit the various
schools and training classes, report its findings, and present

such recommendations as it saw fit.   It was the first time
any committee had been empowered to endorse or withhold
endorsement of training programs in the name of the library
profession.   The trouble was that a profession which encouraged any and all kinds of training really had no clear standards of organization to use in forming favorable or unfavor-
able judgments.   Meanwhile, the multiplication of programs
of assorted lengths and pretensions made the problem of national coordination ever more pressing.

Dewey had been the first to say that something would
have to be done about those who were "climbing on the bandwagon and dragging their feet. "   Under a sharply worded
title, "Library schools of doubtful value,"[33] he warned in
1902 that the whole cause of special training was being
jeopardized by a misguided zeal which was producing one library school after another in institutions where only the
skimpiest attention was being given to the competence of those
placed in charge or to other prerequisites of high-quality
work.   If the institutions themselves failed to check this tendency, he went on, it might be necessary for the ALA to interest itself in the matter or for the schools that maintained
high standards to form a separate organization.

The Committee's report at the Portland Conference
(1905) was the first and only attempt to set standards for
assorted training programs all the way from apprentice
classes to correspondence courses.   The Committee did not
succeed in agreeing even among themselves and asked to be
discharged.   Streamlined to include only winter and summer
schools, the report,[34] with the following provisions, was approved in 1906:

1.   Winter schools [library schools and training classes]

Entrance requirements.   Three years beyond high
school or an entrance examination in history, literature, language and economics.

Instruction.   At least a third of the instructors to
have been trained in a recognized library school; the same
proportion to be experienced in other libraries than the one
connected with the school; some of the instructors to have library duties; one instructor for every 10 students doing laboratory work; and at least a sixth of the student's time to
be given to practical library work under supervision.

Tests and credentials. A certificate or diploma at the end of the course certifying satisfactory completion of all requirements, including tests, but not certifying fitness for library work.

Subjects to be taught. Decimal and expansive classification, classed and dictionary cataloging, library economy (accession work, shelf-listing, loan systems, supplies and statistics, order work, building and rebuilding), lectures and problems in reference work, trade bibliography and book selection.

2. Summer Schools

Entrance requirements. A paid position as librarian or assistant or a definite written appointment to a position.

Instruction. At least one instructor trained in a recognized library school; at least two instructors with experience in other libraries than the one connected with the school; one instructor to every fifteen students; at least a fourth of the student's time to be given to practical library work under supervision.

Tests and credentials. A pass-card stating the subjects studied, with a plain statement that the course completed was a summer course.

Subjects to be taught. Same as in winter schools except omission of expansive cataloging and classed cataloging.

Embodying as they did the best judgment of a representative committee, these recommendations had wide influence, but they were enforceable by no authority except professional sentiment. In 1908, the Committee, still led by Miss Plummer who had drafted the original standards report in 1905, asked the ALA to decide whether to initiate accreditation by authorizing preparation of a formally approved list of training agencies. The Council refused, declaring that it adhered "to its established precedent of taking no action looking toward any expression of opinion on library schools."[35] Meanwhile, in 1907, the ten library schools enumerated above had organized a round-table for discussion of problems of common interest. It fell to this informal organization to do what it could to control a situation which by then was being described as chaotic.[36] The AALS was the result. Membership was based on carefully considered criteria and served

as a form of accreditation open to any agency capable of
qualifying. Adoption of the 1912 constitution therefore was
the first successful step toward observance of formal standards.

In Conclusion

The object of the chapter is to review problems and
progress of the period of 1883-1920. The outstanding developments were the following:

Acceptance of training as a professional responsibility.
William F. Poole's defense of "the idea that practical work
in a good library based on a good previous education" as "the
only way to train good librarians" has led to the supposition
that a system of apprenticeship was in operation then, but
this is a mistake. A system of apprenticeship implies that
somebody assumes responsibility for training the beginner,
but as of the 1880s, training was not considered the business
of the library employer or anybody else. The new employee
was paid to do some job that he was qualified to do, and
progress up the ladder depended on how fast he caught on to
the rest of the work of the library through haphazard contact
with it. By the time of the Second International Library Conference in 1897, all this had changed. There were critics
of library schools, but there was agreement on all sides
that organized training in one form or another was necessary. [37]
Indeed, the pendulum swung to the other extreme and the prevailing attitude became one of encouraging any and every style
of training that seemed to hold promise of improving the
performance of library workers on the job.

Stabilizing the organization of library training. In
the absence of any national guidelines to follow, there was
some inevitable floundering. How broad was the concept of
training? Did it for example embrace the training of student
assistants? What role should library management be expected to play in the overall task of library training? Should
the profession have a voice in approving training programs
or pursue a hands-off policy in the matter?

In a major decision early in the twentieth century, the
American Library Association, acting on behalf of the profession, adopted a hands-off policy and left it to open competition to determine what forms of training should survive.
In a singularly short time, the competition narrowed to library

schools, apprentice and training classes, and summer schools.
The service of the library school was so well received that
its place at the top of the system was never seriously threatened. The summer school proved unsurpassed as a means
of providing intensive practical training in how to operate a
small library. The apprentice class proved to be an unsurpassed means of training new employees in the work of the
local library where a larger staff was required. As time
passed, the apprentice class yielded ground to the training
class, a hybrid that geared training to the practical needs of
the local library but increasingly emulated the library school.
When the dust settled from the flurry of early experimentation, it was these agencies that had established themselves
as components of the training system.

Establishing standards of excellence. By 1920, the
tide of interest among professions in relating their education
and training to theoretical learning was rapidly advancing,
but library schools were handicapped in falling in with this
trend. This chapter suggests two reasons why. To begin
with, the stability that was achieved was a stability among
rivals. It was difficult for library schools, in the absence
of nationally approved standards of excellence, to consider
raising their standards much higher. Rephrasing Gresham's
law, low training standards of rival agencies tended to drag
all standards down to their level.

A second handicap is treated more fully in the next
chapter--the grip which the unwritten standards of technical
education had gained on the library imagination, and continued
to gain with each annual crop of alumni. Division of opinion
within library ranks, there was--but the rank and file stood
firmly together on the crucial matter of aims and results to
be sought through training. Here the chief point at issue, as
we have seen, was a subsidiary one: can these results be
achieved more easily and effectively through some form of
apprenticeship schooling or through some more overt form of
apprenticeship?

REFERENCES

1. "Special Training for Library Work," in International
     Library Conference, 2nd, London, July 13-16, 1897.
     Transactions and Proceedings. London, 1898, pp.
     34-39.

2.   Plummer, Mary W.   "Training for Librarianship,"
     Wisconsin Library Bulletin 5:45-49, June 1909.

3.   The account of training agencies given in this chapter
     is based mainly on official sources such as an-
     nouncements and reports; attention in these notes is
     also drawn to additional sources used which are not
     so easily located from information supplied in the
     text, as in this instance: Fletcher, W. I.   "The
     Summer School Class at Amherst, Massachusetts,"
     ALA Proc., LJ 23: Conf. No., August 1898, pp.
     67-68.

4.   Ibid., p. 67.

5.   Ibid., pp. 66-67.   See also Dewey's announcement:
     Public Libraries 1:26, May 1896.

6.   Dewey's announcement just cited puts the figure at 80
     weeks.

7.   N. Y. State Library, Albany.   Annual Report of Library
     School, 1898, p. 138.   (Library School No. 3,
     April 1899).

8.   ALAB 14:284-89, July 1920.

9.   American Library Annual, 1916-17.   New York: Bowker,
     1917, pp. 285-322.

10. In addition to official announcements, see: LJ 26:220-21,
     April 1901; 697-98, September 1901.   Downey,
     Mary E.   "The Chautauqua School for Librarians,"
     LJ 47:455-57, May 15, 1922.

11. "Library Training in 42 Libraries," Public Libraries
     5:533, November 1901.

12. Public Libraries 4:3-8, January 1899.

13. "ALA Proc.," LJ 23: Conf. No., August 1898, pp. 63-
     66.

14. The account is based on annual reports of the Dayton
     Public Library and Museum, especially the report
     for September 1, 1896 to August 31, 1897.

15. Op. cit., pp. 10-11.

16. LJ 20:202-03, 239-41, 272-73, 303-05, June-September
     1895.

17. "The Theory of the Training Class in the Large Library,"
     ALAB 5:268-71, July 1911.

18. ALAB 3:203-15, September 1909.

19. "The Training Class Is Not Passing," ALAB 27:26-31,
     January 1933.

20. Dial 47:35-36, July 16, 1909.

21. Sutliff, Mary L. "Library Training in California,"
     ALAB 5:263-68, July 1911.

22. Welles, Jessie. "Secondary Education in Library Work,"
     ALAB 11:148-53, July 1917.

23. LJ 18:194-95, June 1893.

24. N. Y. State Library, Albany, Annual Report for the Year
     ending September 30, 1892, p. 42.

25. Information about the AALS including verbatim quotations
     from proceedings is based on its official Report of
     Meetings.

26. Information about individual schools and training classes
     is occasionally drawn from secondary sources but
     is based mainly on official announcements published
     separately or in LJ's regular department, "Library
     schools and training classes."

27. Robertson, David A. "Frank Wakely Gunsaulus," Dic-
     tionary of American Biography. N. Y.: Scribner,
     1932. V. 8, p. 52-54.

28. Sibley, M. J. "Syracuse University--Library Economy
     Department," Public Libraries 11:262-63, May 1906.

29. Bostwick, Arthur E. "St. Louis Library School," Pub-
     lic Libraries 23:14-15, January 1918.

30. "Comparison of the Curricula of Library Schools and

Public Library Training Classes," <u>ALAB</u> 10:185-94, July 1916.

31. Sutliff, Mary L. , <u>op</u>. <u>cit</u>. See also the annual reports of the Library, esp. the 13th (1891) and 14th (1892). The phrase quoted is taken from the following sentence in the Library's annual report for the year ending November 30, 1906: "This library was the first in America to introduce (16 years ago) the Training class which has been copied throughout the country. " p. 10. The rest of the account of these Los Angeles developments is based on: the announcements, annual reports and AALS Report of Meetings.

32. "ALA Proc. , " <u>LJ</u> 14: Conf. No. , May-June 1889, p. 278. The later steps in the evolution of the Committee are likewise reported in ALA Proceedings.

33. Public Libraries 7:119-20, March 1902.

34. "ALA Proc. ," <u>LJ</u> 31: Conf. No. , August 1906, pp. 175-77.

35. <u>ALAB</u> 2:409-10, September 1908. <u>LJ</u> 33:287, July 1908.

36. Elliott, Julia E. "Library Conditions which Confront Library Schools," <u>ALAB</u> 3:427-36, Sept. 1909.

37. The opening sentence of a series of articles originally published in the Wisconsin Library Bulletin, which was popular enough to be published in book form by the ALA, reads: "Positions on the library staff should not be given to untrained persons. " Wisconsin, Univ. Library School. <u>An Apprentice Course for Small Libraries; outlines of lessons, with suggestions for practice, work, study and required reading.</u> Chicago: ALA Published Board, 1917, p. 7.

Chapter 6

THE SWAY OF UNWRITTEN STANDARDS

The concluding chapters are concerned with developments between the close of the first World War and the adoption of the 1951 national standards of library education. They deal with a second period of change that compares in importance with the first, and this chapter is a bridge between the two periods.

If one asks why it was necessary to turn around and start changing a pattern of education that had so recently gained stability, it is because the twentieth century had set library manpower requirements on a collision course with standards born of nineteenth century solutions. The 12,276,964 volumes or thereabouts which comprised the nation's library resources as of 1876 were scattered among fewer than 4,000 libraries with an average of around 3,334 volumes each. The Library of Congress had 300,000 volumes; Harvard 277,650; Yale 104,200; but on the whole libraries were quite small by modern standards. Only 12 libraries had more than 60,000 volumes. Columbia, for example, had only 34,790. And on the average these libraries were growing at a snail's pace of 287 volumes a year. [1]

By 1920, all this had changed. A new growth rate and spiralling book collections manifested deeper changes: an enrichment of cultural resources, new involvements in research, aggressive development of specialized manpower in older and wholly new fields, and unprecedented use of improved information sources of all sorts. Here and there research library collections began rivaling the strength of Old World libraries. Special and school libraries were still running into complacency and resistance, but were making headway. And the great expanding system of public libraries, unsurpassed in vigor and progressiveness, was creating manpower requirements of a new order.

121

A thesis in what follows is that the program of library education which grew up in simpler times around apprenticeship schooling was no match for these changes, but there is a corollary that lies at the heart of this chapter. We begin with a word about tradition and how it affects innovation or change. "Tradition" refers to an accepted way of thinking that one generation hands on to another. Nietzsche anticipated later scientific findings when he observed that accepted ways of thought gain veneration with age, weighing, as one writer puts it, like an Alp on the minds of all living. Because it bears heavily on the thinking of those to whom it is handed on, tradition impedes change. Engels gave this side of the matter a near cosmic sweep, calling tradition the vis inertiae, the inertia force of history.

It was more common earlier than now to think of educational standards mainly in terms of certain measurable externalities that are essential to orderly management of education: the kind of sponsorship an educational program enjoys, adequacy of financing, size of staff, admission requirements, degree of national coordination, and the like. [2] We are soon to see that no generation after Dewey's displayed greater interest in library education than that of the 1920s and 1930s; but outside of the Graduate Library School of the University of Chicago, of which more is to be said later, the major investment of time and money at the start of the second period went more into these externalities of educational management than into improving the educational process itself. This being the case, invisible norms of thought handed down by the preceding generation were left to weigh as an inertia force on library education. During the '20s and '30s there was undoubtedly an interest in seeing them changed; but it failed to surface into national action. The adoption later of the 1951 standards is accordingly used as the terminus of this study: the action climaxed a national movement from within the schools themselves to bring this unexamined substructure of educational thought more in line with modern academic thought and practice.

This is the direction in which the discussion is to move, but we are getting ahead of the story. Our job in this chapter is not to sort out durable contributions from perishable ones, although some of this will be done: it is to probe more deeply into the thinking of the prewar generation (as we shall call the pioneers of the first period) to see what major conclusions gripped their imagination and had most to do with the educational tradition which they created and handed on.

I. HISTORICAL AND THEORETICAL FOUNDATIONS

Alfred N. Whitehead reminds us that great ideas often
make their entrance in strange guises and with unseemly al-
liances. Professional education of librarians was a new idea
whose moment had come, but certain ideas which it entered
with appear strange or unseemly or both at a distance.

The Nature of Library Economy

The ALA Glossary of terms defines library economy
as the practical application of library science to the founding
and administration of libraries. It is a misleading definition
which reads back into the nineteenth century a comprehension
of the nature of science that had to wait until the reign of
library economy was overturned. One gets closer to the contemporary meaning of library economy by writing "library"
into Noah Webster's old nineteenth century definition of "economy," thereby making it read as follows: Library economy
is the "management, regulation and government of the [library]
household ... or the system of rules and regulations which
control it. " This places the emphasis where it belongs, on
normative as distinguished from scientific principles--on the
accepted methods, rules or standards that serve, or ought to
serve, as norms for running a library.

A glance at contemporary literature confirms this
usage. Of the early summaries of library economy, none
surpasses that of Charles A. Nelson, of the old Astor Library. It appears in the Annual Cyclopedia for 1886 (v. 11,
n. s. , pp. 474-478). He couples the origin of the "new science," as its founders called it, with the growing consciousness of library conditions and needs which the U.S. Bureau
of Education began fostering shortly after the Civil War. The
bureau's annual reports, beginning in 1870, published such library statistics as were available. These reports called attention to and supported the groundswell of popular interest in
the subject. "Unexampled increase" of libraries had followed
and the Bureau found itself besieged with inquiries on how to
establish and operate them. Having stumbled on to this need,
the Bureau undertook to do something about it by publishing
the well-known Centennial report on "public" libraries, significantly subtitled "Their history, condition and management. "[3]
The object was to report on "the development and growth of
the library interest ... and it was also thought best 'that the
result should be accompanied by the suggestions and conclu-

sions of librarians and others, whose ability and experience
enable them to speak with authority on library subjects'. "

        Librarians of a later period use the 1876 report large-
ly as a statistical source without thinking of this deeper purpose; but as Nelson goes on to say, the report is notable because it "formulated for the first time the principles of the
new science of library economy.... This special report supplied to all librarians of the country a text-book of methods
and appliances for library management and administration, in
which some of the most eminent of their number gave the results of their experience and best thought, and it also revealed to most of them the possibilities of making their profession second to none in its educating power upon the people. " By way of bringing the 1876 report up to date, Nelson
cites major contributions by leading authorities of the 1880s
(Cutter, Winsor, Poole, Dewey and others), and prominent
in his list are such titles as: "Rules for making a dictionary
catalogue"; "Library building"; "The organization and management of public libraries"; "Works of reference for libraries";
"Binding and preservation of books": and "College library
administration. "

        The gist of the matter is that the founders of library
economy looked upon it as a "new science"--a new method of
advancing librarianship, which was to search the best thought
and experience of the period and codify those norms, rules
or standards which control, or ought to control, professional
work. In the same article, Nelson summarizes the content
of Library Journal, the pace-setter of the movement, and the
same idea predominates. The 827 pages of the first 11 volumes, he writes, "constitute a body of bibliothecal literature
unsurpassed in value and extent and 'accepted as the highest
authority in this country as well as in England and on the
Continent. ' Here may be found practical and suggestive discussions on the construction of buildings, on the classification of books, on cataloguing with condensed rules for the
same, reports on library aids, on reading for the young, on
libraries and schools, on fiction in libraries, on library legislation, on methods of co-operation ... and all the details of
the internal administration of a library. "

Acceptance of the Mastercraftsman as
the Model of Library Scholarship

        Library economy in time came into bad odor for over-

emphasizing tedium and minutiae, and grounds for the criticism are plentiful. Frank W. Gunsaulus, devoted bookman
and founder of Armour Institute of Technology, lectured to
Katherine Sharp's library-school students, and early Illinois
alumni liked to describe, with appropriate body English, his
demonstrations of how to sweep a floor without letting the
broom stir up the dust. Melvil Dewey went into minute details on how to do janitorial work. He damned feather dust-
ers for merely redistributing dust, advocated cleaning books
"by slapping them sharply together over a shallow pan of
water which catches the dust," and further advocated scat-
tering moist sawdust over the floor before sweeping. It
caused the dust to collect in little balls, and this the Gunsaulus method laid no sure claim to doing!

        All this is good fun, but to stop there is to caricature
the subject, not to get a balanced view of it. We can reject
the idea of training professionals in minutiae and manual routines without rejecting the idea of searching study by professionals of all library methods, whether manual or intellectual.
The point we are leading up to is an elemental way of thinking which the profession was to be slow to catch hold of well
enough to see how weighty it was. Library economy was
more than practical expertise: it was new knowledge--the
heart and nature of serious professional learning. Dewey
liked to think it all began with him. According to Poole, it
was rather C. C. Jewett who first aroused this new "spirit
of inquiry and search after better methods."

        Be that as it may, the new search as well as the
learning it led to deserves high praise, not scorn. For back
of the great innovators beginning with Panizzi, Jewett and
Dewey, to name but a few, stands a long line of librarians,
of whom the most gifted had left operational details in dis-
dain to functionaries who were not qualified for searching
scholarship. It was left to these later nineteenth century librarians to discover that libraries are no better than their
methods. In the language of the football field, the leaders
of the modern movement reversed the strategy of their ivory-
tower predecessors and ran the play straight through the
"thousand and one details" of library management which before had been so loftily avoided. Library economy stands
for the timeless insight that the path of library progress lies
through, and not around, problems of method and supporting
technology; and stands, too, for the down-to-earth practical
learning that accumulates through the ceaseless quest for better methods.

The importance of the "new science" was heightened
because it was developed at a time when the fostering of high
standards and wide diffusion of knowledge of them were both
paramount.   "I wish here to acknowledge the debt I owe the
[Library] Journal," a Baltimore librarian wrote in 1879 (p.
377). "I have read every number which has appeared and
have derived much benefit from so doing.   I have learned
things before unknown, and have gained a clear conception of
many other things which before I saw but dimly. " The search
for better methods was attuned perfectly to the felt needs of
a whole generation of librarians who, like this Baltimorean,
worked alone and in the dark.

But we have to end on another note.   The greatest
dangers along a path are the ones that take us unawares.
The learning exemplified by the ivory tower librarians was
too sterile to appeal to the new breed that set librarianship
on its modern course.   The latter, unawares, therefore
stumbled into accepting the only other model in sight by confusing the ABC's of good craftsmanship with science.   What
was it that separated the men from the boys--separated the
Deweys, Pooles and Cutters from backwoods tyros as well as
from the tested theoretical knowledge developed and acquired
by academic study?   It was their mastery of a new art--the
demonstrated capacity to organize and run a library in conformance with the highest standards set and maintained by
one's peers.   Call this sort of learning library economy or
expert know-how or what we please, it exemplifies the model
that had been the mastercraftsman's from time immemorial.
Here we come upon one of the weightiest and one of the least
noticed ways of thinking of the period, so it needs further
attention.

Resultant Characteristics of Professional Learning

Nelson's early summary of professional thought contains but "four grand divisions": the principles to observe
in constructing library buildings, in book selection, classification, and preparing library catalogues.   Librarianship
continued to stride ahead and branched out as it did so.
The best general summary as of the turn of the century appears in the New International Encyclopedia of 1903, with
Daniel Coit Gilman as chief editor.   The article on "Libraries"
by Melvil Dewey (v. 12, pp. 193-206) pays superficial attention to library history, then concisely expounds accepted
methods of housing, equipping and furnishing libraries, meth-

ods to use in administering each of the standard departments
of library work (executive, accession, reference, loan, binding, shelf, janitorial); methods of library training; the work
of library associations and clubs; and emerging practices of
state aid. The treatment of classification is noticeably more
full-bodied than Nelson's.

For the period as a whole, the ALA publishing program provides as faithful a reflection of the character and
structure of prewar library thought as we have. The National Union Catalog: Pre-1956 Imprints lists 82 book titles
(some in several editions) published up to 1920, and these
break down as follows:

Bibliographic aids	28	Library methods	44
Bibliography	2	Library promotion and	
Reference works	5	development	6
Indexes and catalogs	8	Exhibits of library	
Reading lists	12	methods	4
Government documents	1	Standards for library	
		legislation	1
ALA and related activities	6	Library buildings	1
Library training	2	State and county li-	
Library history	2	braries	3
		Internal organization	
		and management	5
		Book selection	2
		Accession work	1
		Cataloguing and clas-	
		sification	11
		Filing	1
		Service activities in-	
		cluding service to	
		children and schools	9

The same catalog lists 25 books by Dewey, not count-
ing separate editions and translations. Five are on non-li-
brary subjects; two are reports; and five deal with librarianship in general. The remaining 13 consist of: (1) recommended methods for use in administering libraries (e. g., his
Simplified Library School Rules: Card Catalog, Accession,
Book Numbers, Shelf List, Capitals, Punctuation, Abbreviations, Library Handwriting); and (2) tools to use for the purpose (e. g., the Decimal Classification and Relative Index).

In these and other prewar writings, three character-

istics stand out. First, the content is practical, didactic.
The object was to aid and indoctrinate librarians, readers
and the public at large at local and higher levels. Areas
of study like bibliography, history or sociology which were
not directly relevant to organizing and running libraries were
either brushed aside as impractical or slanted so as to be
immediately useful. Bibliography is an example. The blurb
for Kroeger's Guide to Reference Books reads, "Designed to
help library assistants, library school students, college and
normal students, teachers, etc. , in gaining a knowledge of
reference books quickly"; the one for the ALA Catalog, "Designed as a guide in buying books for public and private libraries; as a guide to readers in choosing the best books on
a given subject, etc. "

It is a characteristic whose roots sank deep. In 1886,
the ALA Publishing Section was organized to further cooperation in producing useful bibliographical tools along lines suggested by Poole's index. Its successor, the ALA Publishing
Board, obtained a Carnegie grant of $100,000 in 1902 and
used the income to produce "desirable library aids. " Again
and again, the same motif finds expression. Typical is a
popular series of Library tracts[4] on how to campaign for,
start, house, organize, and run a library. Some of these
tracts are notable not only as illustrations of where the best
energies of the profession were being invested, but also for
achieving their helpful aim so well. Examples are C. C.
Soule, Library Rooms and Buildings, 1902; L. E. Stearns,
Essentials of Library Administration, 1905; and Theresa
Hitchler, Cataloguing for Small Libraries, 1905.

Second, it is normative. The main thrust of library
economy was toward better-run libraries, toward excellence,
toward what ought to be. It was an aspiration that shaped
the goals of professional organization and activities, discussions at professional meetings, and the proliferating bibles
of library procedure.

Nothing better illustrates this characteristic than the
persistent effort to produce a manual which could be accepted
as a definitive guide to good library practice. We have already spoken of the first attempt--the non-statistical part of
the Centennial report. The second attempt produced the
Papers Prepared for the World's Library Congress, Held at
the Columbian Exposition, ed. by Melvil Dewey (Washington:
Govt. Print. Off. , 1896).[5] Dewey explains the background in
the opening chapter. During his 15 years as Secretary of the

American Library Association, he explains, "the need of a
manual of library economy was constantly felt." The Centennial report was out of print and no longer adequate. He
had hoped to produce an authoritative manual by himself, but
the World's Fair meeting made it fitting to produce one in
cooperation with other ranking librarians, among whom were
A. R. Spofford, Hannah P. James, and Samuel Swett Green.
All these contributors were each charged to prepare a two-
part paper which would (1) consolidate the conclusions that
informed librarians were agreed upon, and (2) state problems
on which further consensus was needed. The plan was to
distribute these papers in advance, to focus discussion at
the Congress itself on unresolved problems, and thereby
achieve further consensus. By revising the papers to include
these additional conclusions, the published volume was to be
"a compact and judicial summing up of the principles of library economy. "

    The Columbian Papers succeeded in collating nine-
teenth century professional thought and experience better than
any other single source. The robust volume brings together
how-it-ought-to-be-done particulars across the whole face of
library organization and management, from how libraries
should be governed to whether they should maintain scrap-
books of newspaper clippings. But the procedure broke down.
Library work was already becoming too complex for consensus based on group experience to have much validity, so the
dream of a code of good practice which once and for all
would tell practitioners how libraries ought to be run failed
to materialize.

    But the dream persisted, and the search went on to
its finest hour with the publication of the American Library
Association's Manual of Library Economy. Preprints (1911-
1918?). This time the ALA recognized that specialists would
have to have freer rein, but the procedure in other respects
resembled that of the Columbian Papers. The chapter of
each authority was to be preprinted as a pamphlet and its
acceptability assessed, the object again being a published
version as definitive as pooled judgment could make it. The
carefully worked out list of chapters follows. Dates are
given for those that are known to have been published:

Types of libraries

    American library history   1911
    Library of Congress   1911

The state library   1911
The college and university library   1911
Proprietary and mercantile libraries   1917
The free public library   1914
The high-school library   1915
Special libraries   1915

Organization and administration

Library legislation   1915
Library architecture   1912
Fixtures, furniture, fittings   1916
Administration of a public library   1911
Training for librarianship   1913
Library service   1914
Branch libraries and other distributing
    agencies   1911
Book selection   1915
Order and accession department   1916
Classification   1916
The catalog   ----
Shelf department   1918
Loan work   1914
Reference department   1911
Government documents (state and city)   1915
Bibliography   1915
Pamphlets, clippings, maps, music, prints   1917
Bookbinding   1911

Special forms of work

Commissions, state aid and state agencies   1913
The public library and the public schools   ----
Library work with children   1914
Library work with the blind   1915
Museums, lectures, art galleries, and
    libraries   ----
Library printing   1913

The new manual, better organized and more instructive
than the Columbian Papers, is the most comprehensive summary we have of prewar library learning. Its least satisfactory feature is illustrated by Linda E. Eastman's Branch
Libraries and Other Distributing Agencies. This capable librarian found herself trying to compress a rich fund of experience into too few pages. A meaty outline for the specialist, it leaves out too much grist to be widely informative.

Topics like the state library, the order and accessions department, and bookbinding were easier to capsule.   They are
superb contemporary treatments.   Wyer's The State Library
is an early classic.   But once again definitiveness proved
elusive.   The project died where the preprints left it.

We have noted the virtues of the "new science."   It
is now time to make the sterner observation that library
economy was not science at all.   If not, one is entitled to
ask, what is to be said of all the learning that was so energetically developed between the 1880s and 1920?

It was the workable result of empirical effort in problem-solving, and this is the third characteristic.   According
to the dictionary, "empirical," a term of plural meanings,
refers in its less technical sense, to thought and action that
is "guided by practical experience and not theory."   Theory
was suspect.   The term seldom appears in the literature and
when it does, it usually means the opposite of "practical,"
and in this sense of course is no good.   Librarianship was
in the position of technology in the days of Edison and Ford,
when problem-solving hinged less on developing and applying
a supporting body of tested theory than on inventive genius
devoted to trying and doggedly trying again until a workable
solution was hit upon.   The difference is effectively brought
out by refining the dictionary definition of "empirical" as John
Dewey does in his perceptive little volume, How We Think:
a Restatement of the Relation of Reflective Thinking to the
Educative Process (Boston: Heath, 1933).   "Empirical
thought," he says, "is the process and product of making
judgments based on experience but not regulated or controlled
by scientific method."[6]   Science in this stricter sense is a
sophisticated process of learning which, as we know, was
long in the making and is mastered only by special training.
The empirical process is as old as the most ancient mastercraftsman, and it was his patient method of trial and success
on which the prewar generation relied for what it learned.

Alienation from Academic Scholarship

The alienation is best seen as the cumulative effect of:
(1) abdicating responsibility for relating the profession in
more than a superficial way to the rest of society; (2) failure
to close the gap between empirical and theoretical learning;
and (3) consequent treatment of librarianship as a branch of
library administration, not as a branch of theoretical learning.

Social orientation of library training. The library
school's abdication of responsibility for relating the profession in more than a superficial way to the rest of society
followed naturally from alliance with a form of education
which, as Chapter 2 brings out, originated in the Old World
when class lines were more sharply drawn than they are today.   The business of the upper class was to steer the nation's course, to rule; while that of the working people was
to do the nation's work, in particular all work not based on
learning.   Learning beyond the minimum necessary to qualify
the worker to earn a livelihood was considered a waste and,
by some, a danger.   Who can say, an anonymous pamphle-
teer asked in opposing early moves to improve the education
of the working people of England--who can say they would not
then "take the helm into their own hands" and plunge the
country into "irretrievable ruin and despair"? [7]

Failure to relate librarianship to theoretical learning.
The function of theory in science is to put things known, believed or conjectured (hypothesized) into an orderly system
to give them sense, comprehensive intelligibility.   One of our
most lucid writers on the nature of knowledge and how we
develop it looks upon theory formation as perhaps the most
important and distinctive activity of the intellectual enterprise
and, in any case, the most important and distinctive human
activity. [8]   He brings out this significance by observing that
other animals learn from experience, the same as man does;
but other animals stop short of abstract theory construction,
the process by which we derive the coherent network of ideas
which is the fabric of tested knowledge.   Put another way,
an animal has the capacity to learn that the port and shore
recede, or seem to recede, from the departing vessel, but
invariably stops short of using the observation, as Copernicus
did, to help him construct and defend a heliocentric theory
of the universe.

Science in the stricter sense is the name we give a
body of theory which is developed: (1) with controls designed
to insure the validity or objectivity of human judgments, and
(2) with the further expertise required to reconstruct the
whole system of judgments as findings derived in this manner
may prescribe.   In a looser sense, science refers to any
species of scholarship that is designed to lower the degree
of dependence that is placed on the empirical process in solving problems.   In either case, the normal modern method of
problem-solving is to develop and apply a reliable body of
theoretical learning, whereas the empirical method is that of

trial and success which man excels in but other animals use
too.

Librarianship remained undeveloped as a field of serious scholarship by glorying in the empirical process and
showing little interest in and less capacity for lowering dependence on it. Other nineteenth century professions nurtured in an academic environment went on to discover, one
by one, that the best long-range attack on problem-solving
is to back up practitioners in the field by developing a supporting fund of tested theoretical knowledge; but there was no
place in prewar librarianship for testing judgments by objective inquiry. The basic test of an idea was to try it out to
see if it worked. Another was to test it against group judgment, the highest tribunal being one's professional associates.
It was a method that cut a wide swath at the outset, and it
still has its place. By the time it reached a point of dimin-
ishing returns as problems became more intricate, the established way weighed so heavily on professional thought and
practice that the advancement of librarianship was left ex-
cessively dependent on local trial and success, on observing
what worked elsewhere, and on the pooling of judgments
through committees, conferences, etc. It had the further effect of leaving ingrained beliefs to gain veneration and to be
handed on unexamined.

Deepening alienation. William F. Poole based his opposition to formal training on the contention, first, that the
librarian's competence must be developed through practical
experience and, second, that "The work can be learned nowhere else than a large library." He conceived librarianship
as less a branch of study than as plain work--as an art that
"cannot be imparted by lectures." The success of library
schools swept aside his opposition to organized study, but
his conception of librarianship as a practical art which is
learned by doing it and therefore has no fruitful interconnection with, or foundation in, theoretical learning was never
challenged during the prewar period.

Harold Taylor refers to Woodrow Wilson's plea to
Princetonians to make of their University "a home for the
spirit of learning," then goes on to observe that "the spirit
of learning is a delicate plant that grows only in the most
favorable environments."[9] The School of Library Economy
as of 1887 was committed to technical education no more and
no less than Columbia's School of Mining or the College of Physicians and Surgeons, both of which were to go on and become

major centers of professional instruction and scientific research.   We shall never know what difference it would have
made had the first library school remained in the same environment.   What we do know is that a Columbia crisis over
admissions policy was resolved by the transfer to Albany.
It was a trauma that affected the lives of individuals, of the
School and the profession; but any heaviness of heart was
mitigated by a magnificent adjustment.   An ALA Committee
made its proud appraisal in 1890.   It was full of loyalty to
an idea and to the man who had turned defeat into triumph.
The line taken was that the change from academic sponsorship to library sponsorship was beneficial.   It provided a
strictly professional (meaning a strictly library) environment
where students could better give undivided attention to their
work, free of the distractions of stimulating outside interests.
The struggle for survival at a crucial moment had succeeded
in polarizing sentiment in favor of the new type of sponsorship, and it remained that way. [10]

     Acceptance of the well-managed library as a suitable
environment for nurturing professional education was accompanied by a chain of side effects, some beneficial, some not.

     It made training a separate department of library work
but an integral part of the establishment.   Ordinarily the local library director directed the library school.   There were
exceptions.   For awhile the Secretary of the Wisconsin Library Commission continued to direct its school after it was
affiliated with the University, and we noticed earlier that the
Public Librarian continued to direct the Cleveland school
many years after the transfer to Western Reserve.   Such
variations, however, fit into the general pattern, which was
to treat library education and training as a part-time responsibility subordinate to library management and to put someone in direct charge of the program who reported to the chief
along with other heads of departments.   It had the effect of
isolating professional study from other studies to a degree
that was to become increasingly less common among professions.

     There were other effects.   Library schools enjoyed
the interest and support often of directors whose services
might otherwise have been denied them.   They benefited also
from part-time teachers who, immersed in the work of great
libraries, were well placed to make the realities of library
work vivid and alive.   On the other hand, training programs
often suffered from lack of independent budgets as well as

from lack of full-time personnel--complaints which led steadily to greater independence after the organization of the Association of American Library Schools.   And there were less
tangible effects.

First, the subordinate position of library study and
teaching denied library scholarship a status that ranked with
library management.   This affected the selection, training,
recognition and career incentives of library school teachers;
helped to establish and perpetuate a followership role on the
part of the schools; and stifled the maturing of the new
branch of study as a field of serious inquiry.

Second, the arrangement slowed encouragement of professional growth as a responsibility of administration.   It
tended to be left instead to a separate training department.
Closely related is the fact that the arrangement led both to
condoning weaknesses and to abnormal uses of library schools.
Edwin Hatfield Anderson, a college man, tells us that on
going to library school he found himself in a program which
placed a premium, not on his educational preparation, but on
sheer patience to master tedious details, some of them manual.   "When I tried to write catalog cards in 'library hand',"
he was to write later, "I felt like an elephant trying to do
fancy needlework."[11]   Failure to relate the educational experience in library school to what the student was ready for
in terms of intellectual maturity proved to be a continuing
problem.   Within a decade after Anderson's experience, Albany became a graduate library school.   Admission was
limited to "collegebred candidates," not because the work of
the curriculum made it necessary, but because these were
the pick of the nation's young people; they had a liberal education, and had learned how to work with their minds.   The
action amounted to saying that, although these assets were
not required for library school work, they were required to
raise manpower standards, and the use of admission requirements was the best means within reach.

The Profession's Working Philosophy Not a Subject of Study

An undistinguished biography entitled Melvil Dewey:
Seer, Inspirer, Doer, 1851-1931 has already been cited.   It
traces the modernization of librarianship to Dewey's intervention with Destiny to bring it about.   It is hardly at vari-
ance with Dewey's own account.   "I am profoundly grateful
about these matters," he said in 1916, alluding to early pro-

fessional breakthroughs, "that the Lord let me be the particular Moses to lead those particular children of Israel into the
promised land... " (p. 191). The present study treats Dewey's
work as singularly important but finds the parallel with the
Moses epic misleading. It is more accurate to say that the
origin of the librarian's profession fits into a pattern common
to professions generally and that interconnected forces of social change, not sudden intervention, generated the need for
a new division of labor which librarians developed the competence to supply.

But the title and text of the biography put well a point
sometimes overlooked, that back of the achievements of the
great doers of the era was a great philosophy that inspired
and guided them. Not that the term itself was used. In the
lexicon of early librarianship, "philosophy" could not be said
to be a dirty word, just something scorned--as the deer in
the fable scorned his feet before the hunters came. The ill
repute was not the fault of librarians but the result of having
allowed one of the great tools of thought to degenerate so far
into speculative metaphysics. It was this descent into intellectual irrelevance that led Henry Adams to denounce philosophy as a source of unintelligible answers to insoluble problems. Philosophy, however, is an instrument which is normally used wherever there is a search for depth of understanding, and is present in the life of a major professional
movement whether it is spelled out coherently or left confused and inchoate. Will Durant related this elemental search
for coherent meaning to more rigorous inquiry by saying that
"Philosophy accepts the hard and hazardous task of dealing
with problems not yet open to the methods of science ... so
soon as a field of inquiry yields knowledge susceptible of
exact formulation, it is called science. "

As early librarians confronted the hard and hazardous
task of figuring out how to solve their problems, a rationale
of their role gradually took form. What was it like? What
elemental ideas did they fervently seize, or get seized by,
and pour their lives into achieving? For, as Whitehead says
in his Adventures, great ideas won't keep free of personal
commitment. They matter too much: something has to be
done about them.

We know that one such idea was library economy. It
was embraced so fervently that at times it eclipsed the rest
of what the grand adventure was all about. We have seen
Dewey--as much of a prototype of the new librarian as we

have--characterized by one of his students as first of all a
great mechanician, uncommonly concerned to make the library machine a good one.   And yet the bright vision of well-
designed and properly functioning library machinery--absorb-
ing as that subject was and is--was but a means of accom-
plishing a larger mission.   How is that mission to be described in rational terms?

Browning's Fra Lippo complained at the assignment
to paint spirit without body, and the library historian has a
similar complaint.   For the philosophy of the library movement was less a rational body of codified theory than a body
of sentiment which, transcending searching inquiry, belonged
or seemed to belong in the mystical realm of the seer and
inspirer.   Here and there the "library spirit," as it was
called, surfaces in the literature, but it does so quickly and
is gone.   As illuminating as any is a brief reference in a
review of the year's work for 1908[12] which ascribes the
greatness of the modern library era to "that indefinable something we called the 'library spirit' of the A. L. A. "   The as-
cription of the vitality of the movement to the new library
spirit was common--as well as discerning.   But the passage
is also useful in another way.   For the context indicates that
the library spirit was that something which gave librarians
their "common, noble end": their professional ideals and de-
light in working together, their cohesion and ennobling influence.

Dana once described the library spirit as range of
vision coupled with zeal--the latter a rough equivalent of professional commitment.   But for aid in spelling out the rational components of the library spirit, perhaps no passage
surpasses the one that is fittingly included in a 55-page appendix to the International Yearbook: a Compendium of the
World's Progress, 1900 (N. Y. : Dodd, 1901) entitled, "Progress of the century. "   Assessing the century's progress in
library development, George F. Bowerman devotes about a
third of his article on "Libraries" to "The new spirit. "   The
argument is that the nineteenth century transformed the li-
brary--its aims, character, atmosphere and place in society.
It is no longer a repository serving a select few, a place of
formality, frigidity and cumbersomeness; it is instead a cordial, attractive service center for all the people.   The transformation had been accompanied and effected by a new type
of librarian.   "Trustees are now likely to seek vigorous men
and women, endowed with special aptitude for the work and
equipped with a collegiate education, supplemented by a tech-

nical course in one of the training schools for librarians.
The head librarian of a great modern library is more of an
executive officer than a scholar. He thinks first of the educational work his library is doing and inspires his staff with
the same spirit. " While the whole undertaking is thus professionally staffed and directed, its roots reach deep into the
modern life that envelops the library's walls. The larger
society that is served considers the mission essential and in
consequence the library enjoys full community support.

    The picture suggests how rich the unverbalized body
of thought was that mattered most to early librarians--and,
because it mattered, it gave form, cohesion and vitality to
the new movement they devoted their lives to. It also suggests how intimately these sentiments were bound up with
what our German colleagues would call the Zeitgeist of the
nineteenth century--the deeper current of thought and feeling
which shaped the institution-building that was going on. Ben-
jamin Franklin had launched the idea that learning is a process of self-development in which good books were necessary
but formal schooling is not. In a prose poem on republican
government, Edward Everett had expressed the idea, with the
aged Lafayette sitting in the audience, that the genius of a
people, knowing no class lines, appears in the humblest
homes and that the young republic was forging institutions to
visit it there and nurture it to full flower. Horace Mann
had pictured the library and the school as two arms of popular enlightenment to cradle the capabilities of the populace
from birth to death. Carlyle and Emerson were saying that
higher learning should be book-centered, not lectern-centered.
And if all this ferment made a new role for public, school
and research libraries opportune, the industrial revolution
was convincing thinkers as hard-headed as Bismarck that the
might of nations was no longer to reside in arms so much
as in the cultivation and use of intelligence. Knowledge
would have to come down from medieval towers and be taken
by special librarians to the marketplace, to parliaments and
chancellories.

    Pursuit of the task of correlating these germinal ideas
has two advantages. It enlarges understanding by placing the
advent of the library movement in historical and social context. Second, the pursuit of the rationale of the movement
serves to bring the profession's role in the cultural process
down from the elusive realm of the spirit and the seer to
where it becomes a rewarding field of objective inquiry.

II.   UNWRITTEN EDUCATIONAL NORMS

We are now ready to outline specific norms of educational thought that gained acceptance during the period.   They stand alone as presented, but together formed a single, well integrated system.

The Purpose of Professional Education

1.   The object is to train students to do effectively the work which the calling requires.

The seven-year span of time (more or less) which old style apprenticeship entailed had a dual function.   It was the period used to help a boy get ready for all of the responsibilities of mature life.   With this in mind, New Englanders of the seventeenth century began to require masters to give their apprentices general education.   The innovation was one of the stepping stones toward creating public schools and public libraries which New England came to consider essential to the type of society that her people wished to create.

More commonly and especially in Europe, apprenticeship meant using the seven-year period to get the young workman ready to go to work on his own--just that and no more. The first two chapters bring out the point that technical education fell heir to the office of apprenticeship in this narrower sense of the term, and library training took over the same aim upon aligning itself with the technical education movement.   In Dewey's neat, often-quoted phrase, the norm for professional education was to confine itself to "its peculiar work," leaving any additional preparation for mature life to be acquired in some other manner.

Nature of Professional Learning

2.   Professional learning is practical, not theoretical, and as such is separate and distinct from the aims, methods and results of academic scholarship.

Conflicting conceptions of professional learning were making a bid for acceptance when library schooling was born. One took learning to mean the competence which reputable practitioners perfect and consider essential to success.   For

purposes of describing the characteristics of early library
learning, we have borrowed the nomenclature of apprenticeship and likened it to the learning of the mastercraftsman.
It may help free the meaning from time and circumstance to
observe that the nineteenth century saw self-made men succeed the vanishing race of mastercraftsmen and apprentices;
and they rose to fame and fortune by relying on the same
model.   Their learning also was divorced from academic
scholarship and consisted of conclusions and skills relevant
to job performance which are the result of first-hand experience.

    The other type of professional learning aimed, in Hux-
ley's phrase, at making the mind a useful instrument for independent work, and associated searching theoretical learning
with the development of higher professional competencies.
The most influential adherent of this conception who is known
to have been close to library education was John Burgess.
As one of the architects of the American university, where
professional education was to become a focal area of creative
effort, Burgess urged all learned professions (meaning those
special divisions of labor which rest or deserve to rest on a
foundation of special learning) to get away from the type of
education which connects itself directly with practice and to
engage in studies designed to lift their callings "out of the
condition of a mere technique into the position of a true science. "

    The first circular presented the School of Library
Economy as accepting responsibility for "laying a deep and
broad foundation and for acquiring the inspiration and mo-
mentum essential to the most successful start in one's chosen
life work. "13   To paraphrase Mark Twain, the words were
those of learned professions, but the music was that of library economy.

        3.   The creative work of advancing librarianship is
             the responsibility of practicing librarians and li-
             brary associations.   The responsibility of the
             scholar in the profession is the subordinate one of
             indoctrinating students in the best methods that
             such advances originate.

    This division of responsibility follows from the empir-
ical and normative character of professional learning.   It
was those masters who manned the front line of library pro-
gress--the doers and seers, not the teachers--that the young

profession relied upon for innovations as well as for judging which ones should be put into general use. Scholarship is a term rarely encountered in early library literature but in practice it was equated with transmitting the best results of front-line experience.

For the performance of his assigned role what sort or sorts of competence did the library scholar find necessary? The AALS supplied one of the fullest replies on record at a discussion December 30, 1916, on "What qualifications should be considered essential in choosing members of a library school staff?"[14]

One qualification is "the ability to teach--to really make the subject alive, and to put it in such a way that the student warms up to it and grapples with it. " This is a personal gift, but one which "can be emphasized by proper training. " The consensus was that library-school faculties needed help here and that summer roundtables and workshops for teachers under appointment would probably offer the best means of improvement. A second essential is "vital touch with the work [of libraries]. " "The great danger of the library school today, " the Albany representative observed, "is that there is too much theoretical teaching; too few people have had practical experience. " Others stressed the troublesome problem of continuing contact with front-line experience, pointing out that even teachers who commenced with adequate practical experience were, by enforced isolation, cut off from front-line advances in the field. Thus severed from the stalk that nourishes their strength, their vitality as teachers tends "to dry up. " June Donnelly, the President, sharpened the point by saying that "If every two or three years we could stop and take a year off, " it would enable teachers to keep abreast of progress, but "if you have been teaching five or six years without any intermission the library work gets beyond you. " It was an excellent formulation of a problem which probably every teacher in a professional school has at one time or another felt.

In sum, two qualifications were expected of those who dedicated their powers to professional learning: sound practical experience, updated as much as possible, plus the personal gifts necessary to teach effectively. Common criticisms of the scholarship of the period focussed on lack of up-to-date knowledge of libraries, on dullness, lack of depth and bogging down into minutiae. No profession can downgrade thorough knowledge of what is going on within it, but contem-

porary critics overlooked the fact that all the enumerated
shortcomings back up into an indictment of the system: it
narrowed the assigned task to indoctrination, stifled free, creative inquiry, and militated against the use of the scholar's
powers as a resource for the advancement of librarianship.

Methods and Results of Professional Education

4.   Professional education should produce the same or
     similar results as learning by doing, and is at its
     best when it condenses experience, thereby pro-
     ducing these results in less time and more sys-
     tematically.

Library schooling took over the bias of early technical
education against theory and sought the same practical results that it sought.   There was considerable experimentation
to determine how best to produce the results desired.   Was it
best to mix classroom indoctrination with practice work or to
figure out the ABC's of library operations and cover generally
applicable methods in class, thereby cutting down on actual
library work?

Throughout the search for the best answer, the profession remained intent on the use of schooling as a more or
less systematic apprenticeship which condenses into less time
the mastery of the lessons of hard-won experience.   In 1891,
for example, Dewey reconciled the competing claims of classwork and practical work as follows:

> However excellent may be the results from lectures,
> instruction, seminars, problems and visits, the
> main reliance must be on experience. As time is
> so important, the school aims to condense into its
> limited course as much experience as is possible
> without confusing the minds of the learners with too
> great variety. [15]

Ten years later, in 1901, Richardson reported for the ALA
Committee on Library Schools, and complained that the emphasis on technical aspects of library work was overdone.
He rated library schools "above the average of that of technical schools," but held that technical instruction was not
enough--that students ought in addition to have access, at a
few centers, to "post-graduate courses in highly scientific
bibliographical lines leading to a Ph. D. "[16] His proposed

improvements were too vague to be constructive, but the report forms part of the boldest wave of criticism that the
schools had to stem.   It was Dewey who made the defense
and turned the tide.   He saw no justification in terms of existing conditions and demands in the field, for modifying the
technical focus, and aggressively reiterated the claims of
practical training, repeating the very words of his well-known
policy statements of 1886 and 1891.   Speaking specifically for
the Albany School, he thus says again as of 1901: it "offers
only a technical course," employs methods which "have less
of the usual textbook and recitation and more of apprenticeship," concentrates on "practical subjects ... the thousand
and one details which make up efficient and economical administration," and has little time "for subjects not so urgent"
in terms of what is "directly valuable" in getting the assistant ready to start work in a library. [17]

   In a contribution to the slender volume entitled The
First Quarter Century of the New York State Library School,
1887-1912, a dozen years later, Edwin Hatfield Anderson
agrees with Dewey.   Anderson was one of the first graduates
to move into an administrative position of major importance.
He was at the time Librarian of the New York Public Library,
where he was in charge of his third library school.

>   In general [he says], I believe the advantage of li-
>   brary school training over mere experience in a li-
>   brary without the special training, is due to the
>   fact that at the schools there is a concentration of
>   experience. [18]

   The amount of practical work done at different schools
steadily declined especially during the 1890s.   As the two
quotations suggest, however, it would be a mistake to inter-
pret this as altering the importance of experience.   The decline reflects rather the growing success of classwork as a
condenser of experience.   Organized instruction was proving
flexible enough to serve as a practical method of getting the
same or similar results in less time.

>   5.   The best tactic for implementing a program of
>   systematic apprenticeship is to school recruits in
>   how to do efficient work on the lower rungs of
>   the ladder.

   The special thing about special education for librarianship as of the first period was the adoption of the aims and

methods of technical education.   As a result, it excelled in
inculcating the practical know-how required in jobs at the
operating level.   Considerable emphasis fell on clerical and
semiprofessional training at the expense of professional education and on equipping the student for early job effectiveness
more than on career-length effectiveness.   To keep our balance, however, in saying this we must bear in mind that
great teachers and librarians are never complete captives of
a system.   Mark Hopkins needed only a log to fire a student's
imagination and awaken other dormant powers.   What student
could work with Dewey, an imaginative innovator in the organization and management of libraries, with a man of Dana's
insight into the library's service potential, with Frances
Jenkins Olcott as a founder of children's library work, and
gain no more than a technician's grasp of what the library
movement is all about?

        That much came through to perceptive students be-
sides indoctrination in methods is well documented.   While
Dana scored library schools for overemphasizing technical
work, he warmly praised the "breadth of vision and zeal"
that students caught between the lines and took with them as
graduates into the field.   Arne Kildal (Albany '07) once came
close to saying that the best of American librarianship before World War I was thus caught, not taught.   Stressing the
importance to European libraries of American methods, he
goes on to say, in assessing the American contribution:

        More important still to the Old World has been the
        influence of what may be called the 'library spirit'
        of America, that is to say, the idealism, the en-
        thusiasm and the unshakeable belief in the far-reach-
        ing mission of libraries which run as an undercur-
        rent to the work of daily routine. [19]

The Curriculum: Organization of the Learning Experience

        6.   The professional curriculum should provide the
             practical instruction that is needed to acquaint
             the student with library work and how to do it.

        Being interested in their students and the success of
their careers, library schools tried out various modifications
of the original program of library economy.   Pratt, under
Mary Wright Plummer, departed from the conventional second year of advanced work in subjects studied the first year

and, with the cooperation of Wilberforce Eames and other NYC scholars and librarians, tested the usefulness of certain historical and bibliographical courses. Included were: subject bibliography, Latin paleography, history of learning, history of classical studies, cataloging of incunabula. Wisconsin tried out a course on "Current sociological material." Pratt, Drexel, Wisconsin, Syracuse, Pittsburgh, the New York Public Library and Los Angeles did considerable experimentation, mainly with bibliography. Syracuse offered for many years up to 1927-28 one of the most successful of these courses. Los Angeles, the New York Public Library, Pratt and St. Louis all offered survey courses on fiction, the first two offering further work on belletristic literature besides these. Drexel and Armour share responsibility for original work on the History of books. The teachers, James Mac-Alister and Frank W. Gunsaulus, were friends and were library-minded Presidents of their institutions. Other courses tried out were Children's literature, first developed at Pittsburgh, and The library and the community, which went by various names--The library and public affairs at Los Angeles, The public library and community welfare at Western Reserve.

The general course of curricular evolution, however, is marked first by a search for what was practical enough for "getting the assistant ready to start work" to be worth spending time on. Some of the courses just mentioned were too specialized to be practical for the rank and file. Some failed from being feeble make-up work for educational deficiencies. Others were of questionable depth. But the ones that were directly valuable in terms of the accepted purpose of the curriculum caught on. [20]

A second line of evolution was an unobtrusive shift from training in actual library work to training in the ABC's of library work--that is, to training in methods that had more than local applicability. Armour's 1894-95 course of study below was "based on the experience" of older training centers (Albany, Pratt, Drexel and Los Angeles) and may be taken as representative of that time. Underlines identify fields studied longer than one quarter:

Fall	Winter	Spring
Cataloging	Shelf Department	Loan System
Library Handwriting	Dictionary Cata-loging	Binding
Order Department	Classification	Reference Work

Accession Depart- ment	Loan System	Bibliography
Reference Work	Reference Work	History of Books and Printing
Bibliography	Bibliography	Visits to Other Li- braries

"The course in Library Science," the 1894-95 announcement
goes on to say, "at present consists of one year of technical
training in the elements of each department of library
work...."[21]and the course structure is seen on examination
to follow closely the departmental lines of library work.
This was changed after the transfer to Illinois (1897): the
announcement for 1908-09, likewise prepared by Katherine
Sharp, shows a different structure as follows. Underlines identify required courses, while arabic numerals indicate the
numbers of semesters the work was taught:

For 4th-year Students		For 5th-year Students	
Elementary Library Econ- omy	2	Advanced Library Economy	2
Elementary Reference	2	Bibliography	2
Selection of Books	2	Advanced Reference	1
History of Libraries	1	Public Documents	1
Library Extension	2	Advanced Laboratory	
Elementary Laboratory		Course	2
Course	2	Bookmaking	1
		Seminary	2

Here, the close parallel between the organization of
the curriculum and the departmental organization of libraries
had disappeared--except for the Laboratory courses, in which
the student was familiarized with the activities and the records of the several departments, one by one. The change
in course structure reflects a growth in thinking that had
come with experience. It was observed that if a student is
taught the duties of a given administrative department, the
substance of instruction is indefinite, for the duties vary in
detail from one library to another. The basic aim in 1908-
09, however, was the same as before: it was to teach "the
elements of each department of library work." It was the
tactics that had changed. In career terms, it was more
"practical" to teach the elements of method that had general
applicability, the ABC's of library work, than to spend the
time on the actual doing of the work. "Library economy"
in the later program was given a narrow meaning: the course
took in ordering, accessioning, shelf work and cataloging,
considered as standard operating procedure for all libraries.

We saw in Chapter 4 how the curriculum of the Albany School became stable well before 1920. We are now in a better position to see that the profession had had time to sift accepted methods for organizing and running libraries down to their essentials. There was substantial but by no means complete agreement on what the essentials were. As of the early 1920s, Illinois, Pittsburgh, St. Louis, Syracuse and Washington were in the habit of indicating which among the several courses they offered were required. By examining these, we can get a better idea of what courses gained top priority. These five schools required no less than twenty courses. The total number offered was still greater. Within this broad spread, however, nine courses stand out as the seed-core of the curriculum:

Selection of books   Classification and subject head-
Order and accession work   ing work
Bibliography   Loan Department work
Reference   Library administration
Cataloging   History of books and libraries

These were required by all five of the schools. Only two other courses were required by as many as three of them: (a) Bookbinding and printing, and (b) Practice work. The subjects indicate that the course of study continued to be organized around practical library work, but the conception of what is most "practical" to spend time on had changed.

> 7. The way to keep library training practical is to add new courses on new specialties in library work as they arise.

This is a curriculum-building corollary of the one just discussed. It worked well during the nineteenth century, then became a source of perplexity. For the new century, continuing to make America a land of libraries began early to make librarianship more specialized, and by 1909 the pressure to add courses to cover new types of work was on. The outstanding early picture of the emerging dilemma was presented as follows at the Bretton Woods Conference in 1909:[22]

> The task of library schools is to keep themselves well informed on the work of libraries and to teach approved methods. A one-year course must of necessity limit itself to basic technical operations, to book selection and related subjects having a

practical emphasis. The course of study has been
fashioned largely by the demands of college and
public libraries, the latter especially. Limitations
of time as well as the greatest good of the greatest number of students leave little room for any
change in the existing program. Under these circumstances, what are library schools to do about
rapid changes that are taking place in the library
world? Library work is getting more complex:
there has been a phenomenal increase, not merely
in number of libraries, but in variety of types and
variety of positions in each type. On one hand,
library schools are by virtue of the task they exist
to handle enjoined to provide a chance to learn the
essentials of method used in any and all libraries;
while on the other, the rapid diversification of library work makes such provision increasingly prob-
lematical. Some idea of the seriousness of the
problem can be gained from the fact that the activities in libraries of only one class, the public
library, have since the opening of the first school
increased enough that it would take a year's study
just to become proficient in all of them.

Library schools struggled to follow the logic of the
accepted norm. Resultant additions included courses on Library Extension, County libraries, Small libraries, Large
libraries, Branch and department administration, Business
methods, Bibliographical cataloging, and others. But as we
have seen,[23] Wyer followed a year later with his warning
that fragmentation of the curriculum could not go on endless-
ly. His speaking out against the "minute subdivision of
courses" was not a solution, but the Rathbone paper cited in
the same context[24] struck a suggestive note, for she was obviously groping for a restatement of the mission of the library school in terms which would preclude the necessity of
endless fragmentation.

In view of how the library profession was expanding
and maturing, was it possible that the elements of library
work and the elements of librarianship were no longer synony-
mous? To keep instruction student-centered, had the time
come to consider how to modify the structure of the learning experience? The problem made itself felt, but the prewar generation found no answer.

8. Basic preparation for a career as librarian should

consist of a course of study concentrated into a
single academic year.

Library schools followed the lead of Albany in most
respects, but the tide of opinion swung away from its two-
year program for the BLS.   The younger schools tried out
concentration of the work into a single year.   Not everyone
was happy with the result.   One speaker at the Ottawa Conference in 1912, for example, complained that a year was too
short, that "most library school graduates lack a sufficient
background," and that the problem was complicated by "the
varying courses and requirements of the different schools."
But the approval of the AALS made one year the norm.   By
1920 only Albany and Illinois held to a two-year curriculum.

How the Profession Procures High-Grade Manpower

   9.   Library schools should not be held responsible
        for developing high-grade professional manpower.
        Great librarians are born, not made.

In 1885, Dewey stated that his plans "all contemplate
special facilities and inducements for cataloguers and assistants who do not expect or desire the first place."   His reports continue to speak of the job of the school as that of
producing "trained help" to serve those at the top.   In 1898,
W. I. Fletcher praised library schools for their usefulness
in raising the grade of detailed, routine work of libraries,
especially the smaller ones, but considered their training not
geared to the needs of the upper grades of librarianship. [25]
These grades were the province of "men of genius rather
than men of routine," so Fletcher anticipated that our foremost librarians would never "owe their power to library
school training."

No public event did more to crystallize sentiment on
the subject than the Portland Conference of 1905.   The program sought to resolve a sensitive issue.   Library schools
were multiplying, and bright young graduates were rising to
higher and higher positions of responsibility.   More than one
senior librarian was made to feel "a little sensitive sometimes because we have not had library school training."[26]

Mary Wright Plummer, whose qualifications as spokesman for library schools were unsurpassed, undertook to medi-
ate the issue.   Starting from Fletcher's position and using a

list of distinguished librarians as examples, she conceded
that library statesmen are born, not made. Library-school
training, she reasoned, while certainly of value to any and
all who take it, provides the potentially great with nothing
that can be deemed truly essential. Then came a second
surprising concession: after erecting a clear distinction between the born librarian and the library employee, she states
that it is for the lowlier employee ''that our schools are at
present intended. ''

As we saw in another context, there was no dissent
from Miss Plummer. Three reasons for this deserve to be
briefly restated. Library schools took it as their job to
produce good craftsmanship, and field conditions at the time
froze it in place as the norm. Second, the modern conception of administration as an art which, like others, can be
learned by study as well as by practice, was to come later.
When a special school of library administration was proposed
for discussion in 1919, Library Journal supported the proposal editorially, but it got nowhere because of the view that
''It is perhaps impossible to evolve by training the executive
ability so much needed in the library profession, for the executive like the poet is born, not made. ''

The third reason lay in the followership role which,
as we have seen, technical education assigned the library
school teacher and student. One speaker summed it up in
1909 this way:

> It is a principle underlying all schools of practical
> instruction that they must follow and not lead in
> the development of a profession.... The chief func-
> tions of the library schools should be to keep in-
> formed of developments in the field and to be highly
> specialized bureaus of cooperation in disseminating
> approved library methods. [27]

10. Manning the profession with capabilities beyond
     those of the good craftsman is a recruiting re-
     sponsibility.

The Dana report at Montreal (1900) was referred to
while we were tracing the development of the program of the
library school. There are few official reports which bring
out so clearly the role assigned to recruiting and admissions.
Dana, an individualist, did not subscribe to the common view
that great librarians are born, but as to recruiting he wound

up in the camp of those who did.   Heartily in favor of training, he was a realist who saw a species of craftsmanship
being produced which, though useful in all clerical and professional work, was overrated.   He scorned the "megaloceph-
aly of the diploma," raining his strictures down on training
classes and the schools alike, and counseled both of them
against permitting "the impression to go abroad that their
work is greater than it is."   He then goes on to say that if
the performance of professional personnel is to be high, the
competence for high achievement has to be recruited.   "Thorough preparation for library work," the report of the Conference reads, "may be secured in a library as well as in
a school, and the chief thing needed to raise library work to
a real professional standard is insistence on sound scholastic
training as necessary to admission to library and school
alike."

      Dewey rose to emphasize this part of the report.   Al-
bany was weighing the possibility of making college graduation a condition of admission, a step taken in 1902.   The
profession supported the step, but ten years later, at the Ottawa Conference, Chalmers Hadley led a discussion on whether raising admission requirements alone was enough. [28]   He
called on librarians in the field to join in recruiting a greater number of persons of stature, then called on the schools
to modify the course of study to attract and adequately train
those qualified for more demanding responsibilities, in administration especially.   Higher capabilities such as book
knowledge, initiative, judgment and high purpose, he felt,
were being "smothered in the stress of technical work."
The commonly held view of the course of study differed from
Hadley's and was reiterated by William H. Brett of Cleveland
and Anderson of the New York Public.   Both argued persuasively that the path of professional development should be
through, not around, "a solid technical course"; and as to
the qualities which make the administrator, Brett considered
them "rather the gift of God to their fortunate possessors
than the work of the library schools."   Anderson's position
differed only in the phrasing:

            Is there a science of administration [he asked]
            which can be taught?   The qualities needed for ad-
            ministrative work, library or other, are the gift
            of the gods, not of the school. [29]

Elsewhere Anderson tells us that he too once had his doubts
about all the preoccupation with detail and routine, but years

of experience had convinced him that the library schools were
on the right track: they "can impart a knowledge of library
methods ... but courses in administrative wisdom are, I fear,
an iridescent dream. "

The outcome of the Ottawa Conference, therefore, was
a reaffirmation of inborn genius as the source of qualifications
for the higher orders of professional work, and of the consequent importance of recruiting. No one summed up the position on recruiting better than Anderson who, noting Robert
G. Ingersoll's criticism of colleges as places "where brick
bats were polished and diamonds dimmed," retorted that Ingersoll made the mistake of expecting the colleges to manufacture
diamonds. He then goes on to say:

> They can refine, not transmute, the material with
> which they work. The like is true of the library
> schools; and we have no right to expect that they
> will turn out library geniuses unless they have po-
> tential geniuses upon which to work. Just now, it
> seems to me, the best way to improve the product
> of the schools is to persuade better equipped people
> to attend them. [30]

In Conclusion

Preceding chapters have shown that in terms of aims,
methods and results, a stable national pattern of professional
education and training took form within 20 to 25 years after
the founding of the first library school. A new era was to
follow the first one. This chapter prepares the ground for
discussing that era by describing the educational norms which
the prewar generation handed on to the post-war generation.
Often standards of library education are thought of in terms
of formal guidelines that have been written down and voted
upon. The only organization of the prewar period which originated standards of this kind was the Association of American
Library Schools, and they were few in number as well as
quite general. We have dealt with standards of another kind.
They consist of ways of thinking which gained acceptance firm
enough to serve as unwritten guidelines of behavior.

Prewar library education exhibited many differences
as to details. The curriculum was not everywhere the same.
Programs varied in length and effectiveness. Some faculties
were much stronger than others. Overall effectiveness was

hampered by lack of coordination. Training classes and summer schools did some jobs better than library schools but
weakened them through competition. A college education was
required here, but only a high school education there. Mani-
festly, ways of organizing and administering library education
would have to be changed to reduce all this confusion; but the
more sensitive--and in some respects the more central--task
of reconstruction was to change ways of thinking which, although no longer adequate, were clung to as a venerated in-
heritance.

    We catch hold of the nature of the forest by examining
representative trees. We have sought to specify representative norms which came to serve as educational guidelines of
the prewar generation. In so doing, we have treated them
as components of an integrated way of thinking about professional education.

REFERENCES

1. U.S. Bureau of Education. Public Libraries in the
    United States of America; Their History, Condition
    and Management; Special Report. Pt. I. Washing-
    ton: Government Printing Office, 1876.

2. For a summary of the earliest library school standards,
    see the report on the Association of American Li-
    brary Schools in the papers and proceedings of the
    Louisville Conference, 1917. ALAB 11:160-162,
    July 1917. The standards consist of requirements
    for membership in the AALS. Particulars which
    applications from schools seeking admission should
    cover are detailed, but the main points are as fol-
    lows:

    Membership in the Association is limited generally
    to those library schools requiring for entrance a
    four-year high school course or its equivalent,
    which offer at least one full academic year of tech-
    nical and professional library courses, which pre-
    pare for general work in the profession rather than
    for positions in any specific library, and whose
    faculty has at least two full time instructors, at
    least two of the members having had one year of
    training in such a library school.

3. U. S. Bureau of Education, op. cit.

4. American Library Association. Library Tracts. Boston: Houghton, 1900-1907?

5. This separate is a reprint of the U. S. Bureau of Education. Commissioner of Education. Report for 1892-93, Chap. 9, pt. 2. (Whole no. 224)

6. See his treatment in pp. 190-194.

7. The Consequences of a Scientific Education to the Working Classes of This Country Pointed Out and the Theories of Mr. Brougham on That Subject Confuted in a Letter to the Marquis of Lansdown, by a country Gentleman. London: Cadell, 1826.

8. Kaplan, Abraham. The Conduct of Inquiry; Methodology for Behavioral Science. San Francisco: Chandler Publishing Co. , 1964. See especially sect. 8, pp. 294-326.

9. Taylor, Harold. New York Times, April 12, 1959, VI, p. 23.

10. It was a fateful course the wisdom of which various librarians came to doubt. Dewey himself reached a different conclusion sometime before the following utterance in 1905:

    I feel more and more strongly that a graduate school should be in a university atmosphere, that its students should be mingling with other university graduates and should have all the facilities of a great university just as the professional and technical schools are usually best carried on as departments of a university and not as independent institutions. --Dawe, Grosvenor. Melvil Dewey: Seer, Inspirer, Doer, 1851-1931. Essex Co. , N. Y. : Lake Placid Club, 1932, p. 203.

11. New York State Library School. The First Quarter Century of the New York State Library School, 1887-1912. Albany, N. Y. : State Education Department: N. Y. State Library School, 1912, p. 43.

12. Public Libraries 14:16, Jan. 1909.

13. Columbia College Library. School of Library Economy. Circular of Information, 1886-87, p. 45.

14. AALS. Report of Meeting, Dec. 30, 1916.

15. New York State Library, Albany. Bulletin. Library School no. 1. Handbook, 1891-92. Aug. 1891, p. 26.

16. Richardson's informal report is quoted at length in the annual report of the School for 1901, p. 442-43. For the original report, see LJ 12: Conf. no., Sept. 1901, pp. 685-86. For an earlier report by Richardson, see LJ: Conf. no., Dec. 1890, pp. 93-94.

17. Handbook, 1901, p. 378-79.

18. New York State Library School. The First Quarter Century of the New York State Library School, 1887-1912. Albany, N.Y.: State Education Department: N.Y. State Library School, 1912, p. 44.

19. Kidal, Arne. "American Influence on European Librarianship," Library Quarterly 7:196-210, Apr. 1937.

20. As an informative sidelight on keeping instruction practical, the AALS deferred approval of the application of the Los Angeles Training Class for admission pending action on work that was "too much on the academic side." AALS. Report of Meeting, Dec. 30, 1916.

21. Armour Institute, Chicago. [Course of Study in the] Department of Library Science, 1894-95. The Institute, [1894].

22. Elliott, Julia E. "Library Conditions Which Confront Library Schools," ALAB 3:427-36, Sept. 1909.

23. p. 75.

24. p. 75.

25. Fletcher, W. I., op. cit.

26. LJ 30: Conf. no., Sept. 1905, p. 166.

27. Elliott, Julia E. , op. cit.

28. Hadley, Chalmers. "What Library Schools Can Do for
    the Profession," ALAB 6:147-51, [Discussion, pp.
    151-58], July 1912.

29. Ibid. , p. 154.

30. New York State Library School. The First Quarter
    Century of the New York State Library School, 1887-
    1912. Albany, N. Y. : State Education Department:
    N. Y. Library School, 1912, pp. 45-46.

Chapter 7

THE CARNEGIE IMPULSE

The break with the early form of library training came in two thrusts. The first one is the subject of this chapter and the next. Harriet Howe, in an account of two decades of library education preceding World War II, discusses the rise of the Graduate Library School of the University of Chicago, but dwells mostly on a reorganization that passed its peak before the new school had time to strike its stride. [1] The present study treats the Graduate Library School as one of the main prongs of the second thrust. It is to the earlier movement that we are to attend now. Miss Howe describes it as a reorganization of national scope that centered on raising entrance requirements, on the connection of library schools with academic institutions, the degree structure, the basic and advanced curriculum; and as commencing with Charles C. Williamson's Training in Library Service (The Carnegie Corporation, 1923).

There is a legend that the Williamson report accounts for the new movement. This classic was the product of the most ambitious research project that had been undertaken in the library field up to that time. When Wilhelm Munthe reviewed the American scene in 1939, he observed that the report had struck the library world like a thunderbolt. [2] By that time, standards associated with the report had become so generally accepted that when Louis R. Wilson took stock of the reconstruction that occurred during the decade of 1926 to 1936, he used the Williamson report as a yardstick to measure progress. [3]

The trouble with the legend, however, is that it raises as many questions as it answers. If the Williamson report is the solitary cause of all the changes, how does one explain the fact that, while some of its proposals were adopted, others which it urged with equal or greater force were re-

157

jected?   Further, one notices at once on reading the study
that it employs a sophisticated method of attack, yet Williamson's career shows no other study of comparable stature.
Was the conception his own or was it modeled on previous
work that was known too well to require mention?   Sarah
Vann's research, which throws fresh light on Dr. Williamson's career and contributions, shows that fundamental ideas
commonly traced to the report did not originate with it. [4]
How then explain the report's impact?   Did the assignment
perhaps center more on originating an effective package of
proposals for action than on the originality of items that went
into the package?   Finally, did the thunderbolt catch librarians unawares or were they prepared for it and if so, how?

When Lincoln first met Harriet Beecher Stowe, he is
reported to have said, "So this is the little woman who wrote
the book that made this big war!"   With similar hyperbole,
we may say that the Williamson report made the new movement, but when closely examined, the movement turns out to
be more complex--the result of a set of several interconnected factors of which the Williamson study was but one.
These factors include the ideas and creative energies of
American librarians working as a body through the American Library Association, but Carnegie interest and experience
shows up conspicuously as a sort of bonding element to give
direction, cohesion and effect to their efforts.

Examination of the literature of the period shows that
knowledgeable librarians explained the new movement in terms
similar to these.   A good example is Carl B. Roden's presi-
dential address to the West Baden Conference of the American Library Association in 1928. [5]   It is a stirring review of
an action-filled decade following the Armistice of 1918 which
pictures Carnegie interest as a powerful new force in American library development.   He treats as common knowledge
the fact that the young Carnegie Corporation had in wartime
first announced the reduction and finally the cessation of the
prewar building program; that it had set about finding new
ways to further library development; that the Williamson study
was a part, but only a part, of the search for a new policy;
and--a point the legend overlooks--that the Williamson study
had been conducted "in line with other investigations of the
educational apparatus of the several professions. "   The stereo-
type of foundation aid that we carry around with us commonly
limits it to financial aid.   The significance of Carnegie aid
as pictured by Roden comes through as partly financial, but
primarily as a forceful impulse to fresh vision, imaginative
planning and concerted action.

Carnegie experience in the reorganization of professional education. We need to begin by reminding ourselves
that the various Carnegie endeavors (Carnegie Institution of
Washington, 1902; Carnegie Foundation for the Advancement
of Teaching, 1905; Carnegie Endowment for International
Peace, 1910; the Carnegie Corporation of New York, 1911;
etc.) were operated less formally up to and immediately following Carnegie's death in 1919 than they are today. There
was an inner circle of control, a closely knit group among
whom the two ablest and most far-sighted, according to
Abraham Flexner, Henry S. Pritchett's biographer, were
Pritchett and Senator Elihu Root. 6 Pritchett helped persuade
Carnegie to create the Carnegie Foundation for the Advancement of Teaching and when, to the surprise of many, he gave
up the presidency of M. I. T. to become President of the new
Foundation, he became a full-time member of the establishment. Because of peer respect, he was soon accorded a
role in Carnegie affairs that reached well beyond the Foundation that he served as President. Flexner quotes the President of the Carnegie Institution of Washington on the scope of
this influence, adding that his backstage contributions "seldom came to the surface. "7 Some did. It is known for example that he was instrumental in creating the Carnegie Corporation in the first place. Mrs. Carnegie's correspondence
also makes it plain that his associates leaned heavily on him
to crystallize policies, interrelations, and programs of the
several Carnegie entities when Carnegie's personal control
ended. 8 Peer dependence surfaced in 1921 when James R.
Angell, after a short term as President of the Carnegie Corporation, 1919-21, went to Yale. Pritchett added the post of
Acting President of the Corporation to his duties as President
of the Carnegie Foundation, serving in this dual role till
Frederick P. Keppel began his 19-year term as President of
the Carnegie Corporation in 1923. To assist him as Acting
President, Pritchett turned to a right-hand member of his
Carnegie Foundation staff, William S. Learned, and assigned
him special responsibility for library problems. Against this
background, it is hardly surprising to find Pritchett involved
with the library training project before and after becoming
Acting President. He shared in all planning by the trustees;
the preface to the published Williamson report of 1923 bears
his signature and approval, although it appears to have been
written by Learned, as were significant portions of various
Carnegie Foundation reports.

The Carnegie investigations to which Roden undoubtedly
refers belong to a remarkable series for which Pritchett's

presidency of the Carnegie Foundation for the Advancement of
Teaching, 1907-1930, is noted. The four following--all
launched well in advance of the library training project--are
perhaps the most relevant to our purpose: Abraham Flexner,
Medical Education in the United States and Canada; a Report
to the Carnegie Foundation for the Advancement of Teaching,
New York: The Foundation, 1910 (Bulletin no. 4), two years
in preparation; Charles R. Mann, A Study of Engineering Education, Prepared for the Joint Committee on Engineering Education of the National Engineering Societies, New York: Carnegie Foundation for the Advancement of Teaching, 1918 (Bulletin no. 11), four years in preparation; William S. Learned
and others, The Professional Preparation of Teachers for
American Public Schools; a Study Based upon an Examination
of Tax-Supported Normal Schools in the State of Missouri,
New York: Carnegie Foundation for the Advancement of
Teaching, 1920 (Bulletin no. 14), six years in preparation;
and Alfred Z. Reed, Training for the Public Profession of
the Law; Historical Development and Principal Contemporary
Problems of Legal Education in the United States, With Some
Account of Conditions in England and Canada, New York:
Carnegie Foundation for the Advancement of Teaching, 1921
(Bulletin no. 15), eight years in preparation.

These studies differ from one another, in some ways
significantly. Professional Preparation of Teachers differs
from the others because the number of professionals was
much greater, the problems were more local in character,
and the raising of professional performance required more
attention to social controls at the state level. The studies
of medicine and law rely on historical analysis more than
the other two. Data for three have a national base: the
fourth is a case study based on one state. Engineering gives
closest attention to curriculum development. Professional
Preparation of Teachers depends the most on a team of experts. The reports are all addressed to the public as well
as to the profession concerned, with some of them treating
professionals as the primary audience. All of them bore
prefaces or introductions by Pritchett acclaiming the educational and social importance of a "unitary and comprehensive
treatment" of their subject; and while not all of them struck
like thunderbolts, their impact consistently made national
headlines. What else did they have in common that the Williamson study was supposed to be "in line with?"

To make the answer concrete, we shall take a quick
look at the medical education project and add some general

remarks on the Carnegie Foundation's program and procedure.
The Flexner report is singled out because it is as representative as any in the series.   The first of the Foundation's major investigations, it was a sort of trial run of the new Foundation's method of attack.   The project was well known to
Dr. Williamson and Alvin S. Johnson, of whom more is to be
said later.   Perhaps none of the other investigations is so
well documented.   And Pritchett came to regard it as the
most successful of them all in fulfilling the mission he envisaged for the Foundation.

     Abraham Flexner joined the research staff of the Car-
negie Foundation to conduct the study in 1908.   There were
155 medical schools in the United States and Canada, and he
visited them all.   They were predominantly substandard.
Entrance requirements were nominal or not enforced.   Faculty standards were low: one school was using a nearby night
school student as laboratory instructor and lecturer in clinical
microscopy.   Laboratory facilities were limited or nonexis-
tent.   The absence of bedside instruction left students over-
dependent on lectures and textbooks.   Methods of government
and financing were at the root of much of the trouble.   The
position of the handful of schools which were seriously interested in furthering medicine was undermined nationally by
schools which, because of the mercenary interests of their
proprietors, sold out the public for student fees.   Teddy
Roosevelt had in 1906 labeled social critics who exposed cor-
ruption and public abuses as "muckrakers" when they resorted
to sensational and irresponsible methods.   Pritchett and Flexner resorted to no such methods, but the muckrakers' discovery of the power of effectively presented revelations to
arouse public action was not lost on them.   Flexner fearless-
ly named names of schools, ticked off inadequacies, and
drove home the point that, by European standards, most of
them should be closed.

     The report was first of all an exposure of conditions
too far out of line with the obligations that organized society
entrusts to the medical profession to withstand the light of
day; but it went on to propose remedies.   It calls throughout
for higher standards of entrance, equipment and staff; for
higher standards of government and financing; and for ruth-
less weeding out of substandard schools; but the reader who
is accustomed to seeing recommended programs of action
spelled out in detail may find this part of the report surprising.   Flexner, himself not trained in medicine, skirts the
problems of medical education as seen from inside the educa-

tional program and concentrates with singleness of purpose
on how society, including responsible professionals, can so
manage the medical profession as to insure performance at
a level in keeping with its public trust.

The standards of excellence which he advocates reduce
to two principles, the first being what he calls "the university principle. " Looking back years later, he wrote, "The
one bright spot was the Johns Hopkins at Baltimore," whose
work compared favorably with medical education in Europe. [9]
Indeed the advance preparation he made to conduct the investigation consisted of little more than visiting this graduate
school and analyzing the factors that accounted for its eminence. Once in the field, it was the school itself, in its
entirety, that became his beacon and yardstick. He attributed its excellence to Daniel Coit Gilman, the founder and
first President of Hopkins. Deliberately rejecting the technical education model then in vogue among all of the professions, Gilman had followed German precedent and based
medical education on "the university principle. " The defects
of British medical education Flexner traced to the fact that
it had [like library training] "developed outside the universities, not, as in Germany, inside them. "[10] In France as
well as Britain, medical education had originated out of
practice closely associated with the clinic and hospital; in
Germany, by contrast, it had derived from learning, nurtured by Helmholtz' insight into the fruitful interconnection
between teaching and original investigation. [11]

While the call to higher standards was thus expressed
in very broad terms, it was compelling enough to make itself heard. The veteran Independent's overall assessment
of the report was typical when it concluded editorially that
"There is just one ideal that must be striven for in medical
education and that is that every medical school shall have an
organic connection with the university and shall be, in fact,
a post-graduate department of the university. "[12]

The other broad principle was to protect the public
interest by creating the machinery necessary to control access to professional practice. Drawing both on European
precedent and the best American experience, the report
stressed the responsibility of the American Medical Association and of duly empowered, properly administered boards of
certification to exert this control. It could be exerted, Flexner concluded, by certifying individual candidates (1) who pass
a satisfactory examination, (2) who have in addition graduated

from reputable medical schools (3) which enforce high standards of admission.

Flexner's Medical Education in Europe[13] was written
as a sequel to further enlighten and guide the public; and it
forcefully buttresses both principles. The best features of
European medical education are traced to "the high and uniform entrance basis and to the vigor of university ideals,"
backed up by state oversight and "stringent regulations."[14]
Speaking elsewhere of the superiority of German medical
schools, Flexner asks, "to what is this superiority, if such
it be, due?"[15] and he goes on to reply, "It is to be attributed
in the first place to the fact that a wise and powerful government has drawn a sharp line below which no medical school
can live. "

The two reports were widely distributed at Foundation
expense to professional groups, to educational establishments,
government authorities, and the press; they were widely read,
and served as a catalyst for an "epoch-making transformation. " Publication of the first report created a furor. At
one point, Flexner's life was threatened. The Foundation
was sued.[16] But the facts had been gathered with too much
care to be knocked down, and their disclosure was followed
up with "pitiless publicity. " Pritchett publicly denounced conditions as "scandalous," as "a farce"--as a betrayal of a
public trust.[17] The popular press joined in. The Independent denounced the practice of allowing a semiliterate mer-
cenary-school graduate "to practice on his patients until he
learned some medicine."[18] Current Literature (later entitled,
Current Opinion) headed its story on Medical Education in
Europe as "An indictment of medical education as our greatest national scandal" and used "A peep into the medical in-
ferno" as a running title.[19]

In 1910, the American Medical Association commended
the first report for its thoroughness, its objectivity, and its
farsighted conception of medical schools as public-service
corporations having inescapable obligations to serve the general interest.[20] A 1912 editorial on the second report returns to the importance of attacking the problem on this plane,
saying that public disclosure of the facts "will the sooner
bring about a removal of the disgrace and the establishment
of better conditions."[21] By 1920, the battlefield had quieted.
Inferior schools totalling 76 had disappeared. The field was
left to survivors of higher calibre, which continued step by
step to upgrade their standards still further.[22]

We are now ready for a few generalizations.

1.   The series of investigations of professional training form a unified program of promoting the common welfare.
This was the mission the Foundation had assigned itself.
Deeply committed to the democratic way of life, Pritchett had
seen more clearly than many that critical problems on the
plane of social policy which are the concern of everybody
were not being imaginatively attacked by anybody.   By the
twentieth century, it took little mother wit to perceive the
implications of entrusting ever heavier responsibilities to
professions, old and new, from chemical engineering to children's librarianship.   How does a nation advance--develop--
all these professions?   To Andrew Carnegie, library development meant primarily buildings and books.   And the development of other professions tended to be thought of in similar
logistical terms.   The Carnegie Foundation had struck out on
a new path.   It treated manpower development as the master
key to the process.   Pritchett had perceived that a professional service rises, or tends to rise, to the water level of
qualified personnel but never any higher than that.

2.   If raising professional qualifications is the lever
to use in raising the service capability of a profession, the
process by which the leverage is exerted is education.   Why
had education throughout the civilized world become the universal business of society if not because it had across the
years proved itself to be the most powerful instrument that
a people can use to consciously shape its future and thereby
raise--if it wills to do so--the level of its civilization?
Learned, who served on the staff of the Foundation from
1913 to 1946, helped articulate and propagate this conception
of the power of education. [23]   It is incompatible with the
standards of technical education as summarized in the last
chapter, holding them to be essentially irresponsible.   If the
nation's interests require professional service of a higher
order than it is getting, the profession is obligated to turn
on the power to produce the higher capability: it is not
enough to shrug off low-grade performance as due to lack of
inborn genius.

3.   As to mounting the necessary effort to reconstruct
the jerrybuilt system of professional schooling, the most visible element was the investigation.   In detail, procedure
varied with different investigations, as we have noticed; but
in general the improvement of the student's educational experience and related problems internal to an educational pro-

gram were left to faculties. The Foundation concentrated on
those changes in organization and management which sound
performance of the profession's social obligations require--
on "conditions surrounding" the educational process, as it is
aptly put in one place.

  The yardstick consistently used to take the measure
of a training program was the duty entrusted to it by society.
In the investigation of legal training, for example, the yardstick was how well the student's training qualified him to
perform "that serious and high duty to organized society"
which is the solemn trust of the profession of law;[24] while
the yardstick applied to medical education was how well the
schools enabled organized society to attain its aspirations for
good health, public sanitation, and so on. The investigations
culminated in reports designed to stimulate change, innovation. The goal was a "unitary and comprehensive treatment"
consisting of proposed improvements supported by a sound
factual analysis--a document of the kind that would be useful
at each level of social action. Pritchett once summed up
the overall task of leadership as being "to procure first of
all the facts, secondly to study these facts critically, and
finally to marshall them in such form that they shall be available to those in the teaching profession, to those charged
with its supervision, and to the general public for whose
progress and development the school [in the broadest sense]
exists."[25]

  4. Innovation is something people do, not a report
gathering dust somewhere. "The indispensable steering-gear
of all democratic progress," Learned says in the Preparation of Teachers, is "the effectual organization and thrust of
a resolute public opinion."[26] Factual reporting of shortcomings with constructive proposals for action was a high order
of stewardship, a form of crusading for progress. "The attitude of the Foundation"--Pritchett says in his preface to the
original Flexner report--"is that all colleges and universities,
whether supported by taxation or by private endowment, are
in truth public service corporations.... We believe, therefore, that in seeking to present an accurate and fair statement of the work and the facilities of the medical schools of
this country, we are serving the best possible purpose which
such an agency as the Foundation can serve; and, furthermore, that only by such publicity can the true interests of
education and of the universities themselves be subserved."[27]
The plane on which the Foundation pitched its crusading for
change caught the public imagination. The old Outlook spoke

for many besides itself when it said in 1912: "The Carnegie
Foundation for the Advancement of Teaching would have justified its existence by [these] two remarkable reports if it
never accomplished anything else. "28

5. A final generalization could well be put first. It
has to do with timing and with leadership machinery to strike
while the iron is hot. Pritchett gave close attention to this
subject. For example, the investigation of the preparation
of teachers took form rapidly upon receipt of an official request from the Governor of Missouri in July, 1914, for the
Foundation's cooperation in deciding what improvements should
be made. The study was launched the following November,
but not until President Pritchett had personally conferred at
length with about a hundred Missouri educational leaders and
received their pledge of cooperation. 29

The legal education project has a similar but more
complex history. It began to take form rapidly after receipt
of a letter of February 7, 1913, from the American Bar Association's Committee on Legal Education and Admissions to
the Bar saying that it had been greatly impressed by the medical education study and "is most anxious to have a similar
investigation made by the Carnegie Foundation for the Advancement of Teaching into the conditions under which the
work of legal education is carried on. " The Committee felt
"an imperative need for such an investigation, equally searching and far-reaching with the other, and one equally frank
and fearless in its statement of the facts which the investigation may reveal. "30 It too pledged full cooperation. There
is, however, an earlier chapter to the story. From obscure
minutes of a preparatory meeting of Pritchett and Flexner
with the American Medical Association's Council on Medical
Education in 1907, we learn that medicine was chosen then,
in place of law, as the first profession to investigate: leaders in medicine were prepared to go to bat to improve educational standards whereas the law profession, as of that date,
was not ready to do so. 31 Pritchett had waited for a favorable climate and for leadership machinery to be put in good
working order.

Before we turn to the next topic, it should be added
that, while the Flexner reports and attendant publicity were
the most visible causes of the transformation of medical education, the American Medical Association played a major
backstage role, not only by helping make the 1910 report a
telling one, but with follow-up work which the Foundation

could not do. The Council of Medical Education, one of the
few agencies to be cited in the Williamson report by name,
had been created as early as 1904 to investigate educational
conditions and to act as the Association's agent in seeking
reform. While it was devoid of statutory authority, it filled
a national leadership vacuum--a point which did not escape
Williamson's notice--and quickly gained de facto authority
through the public confidence that its procedures and findings
won. By 1907, the Council was able to make available to the
Carnegie Foundation an enormous amount of useful data on
medical schools. Its Secretary accompanied Flexner to every
school. It helped shape opinion among recognized leaders of
the profession. It worked closely with state legislatures and
boards of licensure, and developed a practical plan of ranking
medical schools, at first by the percentage of their graduates
who failed their Board examinations and, later, by their showing on a rounded ten-point measure of excellence. [32] Through
these unpublicized efforts, the Council played a powerful inside role in escalating educational standards one attainable
step at a time.

    Schools for Training Librarians: an Inquiry. The
library training project employed the same procedure, with
allowance for different circumstances. Unlike the Carnegie
Foundation for the Advancement of Teaching, Carnegie Corporation activities were pointed toward making grants; while
library service, when compared with older professions, was
underdeveloped. As a result, library training problems were
harder to separate from problems of organization and administration.

    Not long after Frederick P. Keppel became President
of the Carnegie Corporation, the Trustees, in 1925, ear-
marked $5,000,000 for a special program of American li-
brary development. This sum, less than Pritchett and
Learned had considered necessary, but liberal, was allocated
as follows: $2,510,000 for support of existing library schools
($1,125,000) and for the establishment of a graduate library
school of a new type at the University of Chicago ($1,385,000);
the remainder, $2,490,000, for endowment and support of the
American Library Association. [33]

    The new program was first of all a fresh assertion of
faith in the importance of library service as a fundamental
branch of public service. It was a corporate commitment
that had to be weighed carefully; for, backed by the power of

the purse, it would inevitably influence city and state govern-
ments, colleges and universities, and the public at large.
In 1911, the Corporation had been chartered to promote the
advancement and diffusion of knowledge; so by way of keeping
its money and policy decisions in glass pockets for all to see,
Acting President Pritchett had assigned William S. Learned
to determine the relevance of the public library--still as of
the 1920s the spearhead of the library movement--to the foundation's stated purpose. The result was Learned's well
known American Public Library and the Diffusion of Knowledge. 34 It too is a classic. In language that requires but
slight change today, he pictures the library as the principal
instrument by which man retains and utilizes the ever-accum-
ulating intelligence of the race, an information or intelligence
service whose potential for diffusing knowledge is limited
mainly by the resourcefulness with which we put it to use.
Constructive aid to this fundamental branch of public service,
the report concludes, would be a sound foundation investment.

        A second characteristic of the new program is the high
priority given to library training. The evidence brought together in the preceding section suggests that Carnegie Foundation experience had a good deal to do with this, but the earliest documented proposal to give more attention to training
as a means of furthering library development which the writer
has seen is the one contained in Alvin S. Johnson's A Report
to Carnegie Corporation on the Policy of Donations to Free
Public Libraries, printed by the Corporation late in 1915 or
in 1916. 35 Johnson at the time was Professor of Economics
at Cornell University. He was given a broad assignment to
examine and report upon "the results of the wise provision
of Public Library Buildings ... with such recommendations
as the study may lead him to propose. " He found that while
the Carnegie building program had exerted great influence on
the library movement, its weakness lay in supplying nothing
but the permanent plant for a public service the effective performance of which depends essentially upon competent personnel. The manpower problem was getting to be doubly urgent:
the country needed a larger number of trained librarians and
needed also a higher order of professional training than existing schools were providing. Johnson nowhere minimized
the importance of good buildings, but emphasized that the
Corporation was up against a stern fact of economic life--
the impossibility of extricating the problem of efficient use
of capital invested in library development from the development of efficient personnel. His conclusion, accordingly,
was that it would benefit the service and would be a sound

philanthropic investment to join in raising the water-level of
professional competence. He cited the rapid progress that
was then being made in medicine--five years after the Flexner report--to reinforce the point that the standing of professional workers, no less than the social worth of their profession, follows--but does not precede--the development of
professional training of high standard.

America entered the war during the gestation period
of the new idea. Sometime before March 11, 1918, the
Trustees of the Corporation agreed in principle to make "an
inquiry into the subject of schools for training librarians."[36]
Dr. Williamson joined the staff of the Corporation shortly
afterwards. Formally he was head of the Department of
Statistics and Information's Study of Methods of Americaniza-
tion (and on half-time leave from the New York Public Library); but James Bertram, Secretary of the Corporation,
quickly involved him in the planning of the inquiry. The
earliest plan was to use a team, much as Learned had done
in conducting the teacher training project. On behalf of the
Corporation, Williamson attended the Conference of the American Library Association at Saratoga Springs, July 1-6, 1918,
to confer with library leaders on the organization of the inquiry, especially on persons best qualified to serve on the
survey team.[37] On March 28, 1919, four months after the
Armistice, the Trustees decided to go ahead, and appointed
Pritchett and Bertram, named in that order, to invite Williamson to make the study. They had decided against the
use of a team in favor of a study by one man supported by
a strong "advisory council."[38] Preliminary research and
consultation, coupled with other professional responsibilities,
deferred the field work until late 1920 and the first part of
1921. The report was completed around the end of 1921,
was approved by the Advisory Committee not later than March,
1922, but was not published till the middle of 1923, just before Pritchett concluded his term as Acting President.

The slender report, Training in Library Service, deserves reading in full, and the more so because it has been
referred to and commented on oftener than it has been read.
Following is a general summary of its contents.

National library development is held back, the central
argument runs, by a shortage of competent manpower more
than by anything else. To put library service on a sound
professional footing calls for higher standards both of managing libraries and managing library training. Library schools

have tried to train for all grades of library work indiscriminately. As now set up, they are capable of producing lower
orders of competence, but are not capable of producing the
competence for community leadership which library service
at its best requires. Attached as they usually are to public
libraries, the schools are at a disadvantage in trying to compete for and train young men and women of first-rate ability.
They should be attached to universities where all other professional education is rapidly going, and they "should be
modified to any extent that may be necessary to make them
gateways to professional work for college men and women. "

        The recommendations propose modification of admis-
sion standards, curriculum, methods of instruction, and financial support. One of the two main proposals is to locate
library schools at universities and to require college graduation for admission, leaving to training classes at libraries
the responsibility for training of a lower order. The schools
so placed should offer a one-year curriculum devoted to the
essentials of library work that are common to libraries of
all types. A second year of advanced study should be set
up for superior, experienced graduates of the first-year program, and should be devoted to specialized forms of library
work not common to libraries of all types--including but not
limited to school library work, cataloging and classification,
library administration, children's work, county and rural library work. Instruction should be improved by reducing dependence on the lecture method, by producing essential textbooks, and by extension of access to organized instruction,
such access to be facilitated by additional scholarships and
by correspondence study when resident instruction is out of
reach. Better financing is needed for all these improvements,
but particularly for scholarships and to promote staff development.

        There is another side of the coin, the report continues.
The planning of library training has to be tied in closely with
the organization of library service. To attract as well as to
provide career incentives for high-grade professionals, a
graded service needs to be developed. Library work falls
into two basic grades, each of which is further divisible:
they consist respectively of clerical work and professional
work. Library management must differentiate between the
two and observe the difference in organizing library work
into jobs; but so far this has not been done. Training at
both professional and subprofessional levels is needed but can
best be conducted by separate agencies--library schools for

professionals, training classes for subprofessionals. The
multiplicity of small public libraries creates a problem but
they can be fitted into a graded national service by mounting
a three-pronged attack on the problem--i. e. , by absorption
of small libraries into larger units, by appointing whenever
possible a professional librarian and, when this is not possible, by giving the librarian while in service the training
necessary to qualify for a subprofessional certificate. The
training can be provided through short courses nearby or by
correspondence study conducted farther away.

The whole program of raising standards calls for the
establishment of a National Certification Board, and here is
the second main proposal. This Board should be empowered
to exert leadership in, and control over, the standardization
of library training and personnel administration. To this
end, the Board would be responsible for investigating all
training agencies, for evaluating their work for purposes of
accreditation, and gradually correlating into an organized
system the disparate array of training programs at different
levels. Second, it would head up and operate a national system for the certification of individual librarians, much as a
state department of education certifies the individual teacher
for the grade for which he has qualified himself by training
and experience. Third, the Board would be a central agency
for promoting professional training in such additional ways as
it finds possible. The NCB, in short, is conceived as playing a role "analogous to that of the Council on Medical Education of the American Medical Association. "

The report thus presented an integrated set of proposals for remedial action, but like the Flexner report it did
more than that. It was a forthright disclosure of conditions
too untenable to withstand public gaze. The study was hard-
hitting in this respect. It dug out for example and published
the fact that about half (48 per cent) of library school teachers were not college graduates, some having gone little beyond high school. Williamson drove the point home, observing that in no part of this country could a well-organized high
school be found with standards so low. Forty-two per cent
of the teachers taught in the schools which trained them.
Caught in a vicious circle of habitual training practices coupled with habitually neglected grading of library positions, library schools were still trying to do the impossible by training workers for all grades of positions--clerical and profes-
sional--in the same classes and in the same way.

There were side effects of all this. The practice of
trying to give the student a cursory acquaintance with every
grade and kind of library work and with every problem he is
likely to meet is well calculated to reduce instruction to superficial routine, deadening to students and teachers alike.
Sterile overdependence on the lecture method could be reduced
with suitable teaching aids, but nobody had the time to write
them, workloads being what they were. All schools required
contact with some phase of actual library work, but conditions
were in intolerable disarray, with the amount of work varying from four weeks to a third of the school-year and with
comparable confusion as to purpose, method and location in
the program. Meanwhile, standards of fitness were sorely
at odds with professional pretensions. Librarians sought public recognition as intellectual and educational leaders, yet a
survey of a representative state, Minnesota, revealed that,
outside of the Twin Cities and Duluth, only nine librarians of
public libraries had a college education although there were
in all 104 public libraries and 237 high schools. Finally the
schools were heroically trying to make bricks without straw.
Only four of them spent more than $10,000 a year and fewer
still had independent budgets. Surely here was a branch of
public service that could be better managed: reform was
overdue.

No one knows why the ink dried on the report more
than a year before it was published. The inquiry was to
serve two purposes--to aid in reshaping Corporation library
development policy and to aid in reshaping library education.
Professor Vann's valuable work on unpublished papers in the
Williamson and the Corporation files brings out the fact that
confidential material on individual library schools was deleted
from the original report and that other changes were made to
enhance its usefulness to the public. Does this mean that the
delay is to be explained by the Foundation's preoccupation
with grants and with information needed to make them?

Possibly, but one would not suppose so. The two
purposes are distinct though not in conflict. A report which
served no public purpose would hardly serve the grant-making
needs of an organization chartered specifically to serve philanthropic purposes. The overriding interest of the foundation
was the general welfare--a "unitary and comprehensive treatment" of the training problem which would help raise standards of library service. This being true, it is more plausi-
ble to attribute the delay to the pace of the times, to check-
ing findings with selected consultants, and especially to wait-

ing on the American Library Association to develop the leadership machinery to strike energetically for reform once the
report was released.

Machinery for determining and enforcing standards of
admission to library work. Active cooperation with American librarians began with Williamson's contacts at the Saratoga conference of July, 1918, and awareness on all sides of
his position as the emissary of the Carnegie Corporation cat-
apulted him into a succession of speaking and committee activities. First came his plea on "The need of a plan for library development" in September of the same year. [39] Air-
ing problems as seen from the Foundation's side, he called
on the ALA to fall in with a trend of the times toward large-
scale planning. The point is stressed that public officials
and philanthropists cannot be expected to thrust upon an in-
different or hostile profession forward-looking development
plans and funds to boot: the responsibility for taking the
lead in these matters rests squarely on the profession. He
considered it all the more incumbent on the profession to
bestir itself because much of the development work that
needed doing called rather more for vision than for money.
Then, singling out for special attention the problem of small
libraries, in which the Carnegie Corporation had a large
stake, Williamson develops at some length the possibility of
using extension and correspondence courses to give small
public library and business office personnel better access to
instruction in technical processes. The two problems--high-
level planning and the small library--are loosely tied together by the suggestion that professional training should occupy
a central place in imaginative planning of library development. He thus supports Pritchett and Johnson on where the
entering wedge for raising standards of library service should
be driven, but fails to supply an equally cogent rationale for
his position.

Roden refers to the "responsive enthusiasm" with
which the Carnegie Corporation's overtures were greeted and
to the fact that Williamson's early suggestions as its emissary fell on fertile ground. [40] The record bears him out.
Service men from all sections of the population had shown
keen interest in the good library service they had received
in wartime, and their response had electrified the American
Library Association, the sponsor of the program. The man
who had led it (under the direction of the Librarian of Congress) was Carl H. Milam. On January 1, 1919, Milam be-

gan his 28-year career as Executive Secretary of the ALA,
which, with Foundation aid, he was to elevate to responsibilities of national leadership unsurpassed by any other library
association or ministry of education. Even before he took
office, librarians were busy trying to blueprint an Enlarged
Program of American Library Service to give effect to the re-
vitalized dream of equal library opportunity for all of the people. Therefore, the September admonition to the profession
to further bestir itself did not fall on deaf ears. On January
11 following, the ALA Executive Board authorized the creation of a Committee of five to survey the whole field of library
service as an aid to planning future lines of development. "In
short," President William Warner Bishop's letter of appointment read, "we should do consciously and objectively the sort
of thing the Carnegie Foundation has done for legal and medical education...."41 Williamson was appointed to serve as
one of the five, and was given special responsibility for library personnel.

      Two months later came his appointment to conduct the
library training study, at which time the Trustees broadened
their contact with the public by setting up an advisory council (commonly referred to as an Advisory Committee) to aid
in seeing that "no well-founded criticism should be directed
against the findings in the report on the score of partiality,
either by librarians, state library commissions, library trustees or the general public. "42 James H. Kirkland (Chan-
cellor of Vanderbilt University), Wilson Farrand (Principal of
Newark Academy), and Carl H. Milam (listed as Librarian,
Public Library, Birmingham; and as assistant to Herbert
Putnam, Director of the Library War Service, American Library Association) were invited to accept appointment. Milam's new post as Executive Secretary of the ALA gave him
a relation to the project too close to accept: Dr. Putnam
took his place on the committee.

      Carl Milam had a penchant for following up fresh
leads, so it is hardly surprising to find Charles Williamson
appearing on the program of the ALA conference at Asbury
Park in 1919, not once but twice. "A look ahead for the
small library" was read before the League of Library Commissions. While the small public library as of that date--
Williamson argued persuasively--served as the only doorway
toward the goal of equal library opportunity for two-thirds of
the people, it was an anachronism. The best experience of
the nation suggests, he goes on, that its future lies in extending the movement to organize county systems of cooper-

ating libraries, with each system heading up in a strong state
library commission. This would do away with independent
units that were too small and too weak to be viable.

The second paper, on "Some present-day aspects of
library training," a highlight of the conference, was read before a general session. 43 It was a dramatic moment in the
life of the new project and of its director. Williamson used
the occasion to propose new national machinery to control
access to library work. Adequate control would require organization of all training activities into a single, orderly system under the general direction of an ALA Training Board.
Manned by a permanent staff, the Board would be empowered
to work out and adopt a scheme of standards of fitness for
all grades of library service and to grant appropriate certificates to properly qualified persons. Holding that this was
a task that would test the metal of librarians as an organized
body, he asked searchingly, "Shall this Association sit back
and expect others to plan a system of training and certification? Nothing ever happens that way. Progress in library
service, as in everything, has always been and will always
be the direct result of vision and purposeful planning on the
part of those engaged in the work. ... The Association must
become more than a debating society or a social club. "44

It was a bold proposal which bears the main thrust of
his thinking. He had swung in behind the trend to vest in
universities responsibility for developing professional education, but the acumen and weight of scholarship summoned to
justify that part of his move proved to be pallid and disappointing. That part of the report does its best work in showing that public libraries are not set up to serve as seats of
formal education. But he addresses himself to setting up an
ALA Training Board with livelier interest and greater personal authority. 45 He gives the conception the breadth necessary to encompass all of the main streams of thought that
find expression in the final report: (1) the inseparability of
standards of organizing and administering library service from
standards of training; (2) effective professional control over
the admission of recruits to the profession; (3) a unified career service encompassing professional and subprofessional
grades of work; (4) a unified training system encompassing
accredited library schools and accredited training classes;
(5) the use of correspondence study to facilitate upward mo-
bility in the service; and (6) improvement of the value of the
professional curriculum by requiring more general education.
It was an imaginative proposal which neatly packaged contribu-

tions from several sources. It drew inspiration from medicine's double-edged control over professional manpower development by certifying individual practitioners and accrediting all training agencies. Further, as Librarian of the Municipal Reference Library of New York City, 1914-18, he had
watched a surging national movement--civil service reform--
which had been transforming personnel management, especially in government, with the idea of a graded career service. 46

His plea to develop a national library service along
similar lines voices a convert's enthusiasm to share with his
profession all that he had learned about the importance of
this new tool. And from the field of business and industry,
he drew inspiration from the example of the American Bankers Association. In 1901, it had launched a centralized national program of training and certification of bank employees,
and it was still relying heavily on correspondence courses
when the young Carnegie investigator looked into what it was
doing. 47 Brilliantly led, the ABA program had become a
success story at once. Nathaniel Peffer said of it 31 years
later, in 1932, that "there is no branch of industry [using
the word in the broadest sense] in which the problem of educating employees has been approached with greater thoroughness. There is none in which a higher degree of success
has been attained. "48 This precedent of continuing success
must surely have given the speaker reassurance as he presented a related proposal to the Asbury Park audience of
1919.

The address was given a bandwagon reception that
soon spent itself. It was referred to the powerful committee
on an Enlarged Program, which invited Williamson to present
at greater length, in person, "the merits of a system of
standardization of library service and national certification of
librarians. "49 The Committee acted promptly, recommending
the creation of a National Library Examining Board to determine grades of service, conduct suitable examinations,
and award certificates to successful candidates.

Reverses followed, but official ALA support of Williamson's efforts to get the proposal off the ground remained
as steady throughout as membership support permitted. The
year 1920 brought a divided house and growing reserve.
The establishment of an Examining Board was shunted aside
because of criticism, originating with the ALA Committee on
Training, that the proposal failed to come to grips with the
problem of uncorrelated kinds and levels of training. 50 There-

upon a special Committee of five, including Williamson, was
appointed "to consider the subjects of standardization, certification and library training. "51

This committee's report turned out to be the high
water mark of the movement sparked by the Asbury Park
proposal. It recommended a National Board of Certification
for Librarians. Consciously modeled after boards of accreditation and licensure in medicine and law, the plan went a
step farther and proposed that it establish grades of library
service including but not limited to professional grades. To
discharge its responsibilities, the Board would be empowered
to certify individual workers, to correlate training agencies
into an organized system and to evaluate their work for purposes of certification. 52

The report was hailed by Library Journal as "a mas-
terly piece of forethought" which would "lift the whole
scheme of certification and standardization to a higher plane
than it has hitherto reached. "53   But there were roadblocks
--financing, need of an amended ALA constitution, a wave of
state legislation extending the jurisdiction of civil service,
and mounting membership resistance. The ALA Council and
Executive Board adroitly hedged: the report was formally
"accepted" but handed on for further study to a new Committee of nine on Certification headed by Williamson.

The movement folded in 1921. The Committee of
nine's efforts crested with a resolution proposed for adoption
at the Midwinter conference in December. The object was
to commit the Association in principle to a graded service
and--this time--to voluntary certification. The program would
be headed up by an independently financed national board, a
majority of whose members would be ALA appointees. Means
of financing would be the responsibility of a special committee.
The Chairman, who was absent, was quoted as holding that
"the national scheme would make it easier to find support for
a certification board. " There was some support from the
floor and from the President, who was in the chair, but it
was not enough. The Council killed the proposal by recom-
mitting it to the committee and directing the committee to
confine its attention to formulating measures to facilitate ALA
cooperation with the growing movement to enact certification
legislation in individual states. Thus the prospect of control
by certification shifted from the national to the state level. 54

Williamson resigned from the committee shortly thereafter.

178 Library Education

Action from another quarter followed swiftly. The
ALA Committee on Training had remained unconvinced that
standardization and accreditation of training agencies, if
approached from the side of certification as Williamson was
doing, would receive the attention that it deserved. In 1922,
Malcolm Wyer, Chairman of this Committee, repeated its
plea for "the development of a more uniform system of library training by bringing the various agencies into a closer
cooperation and correlation of work," adding that he was
loath to make further demands on his committee in view of
the scant notice that had been taken of their past efforts. [55]
But events were to prove that these efforts had not gone un-
noticed. Secretary Milam had, the preceding year, 1921,
been directed by the Council to communicate in person to the
Carnegie Corporation, ALA's interest in seeing it resume a
program in behalf of libraries. [56] Promoters with his finesse rarely require such injunctions; but with a sense of
timing that was characteristic, he brought forward early in
1923 a list of 19 things that ought to be done to accelerate
manpower development and arouse grass-roots support for a
constantly improving grade of library service. [57]

Five items dealt specifically with training, and the
first among them was: "Some scheme should be devised for
accrediting library training agencies--perhaps a library training board." Concurrently, Wyer and his committee came to
life with a report that was to become historic. It opened
with a cogent analysis of the record, showing that American
librarians had, since the Williamson paper of 1919, consistently favored the use of the national professional association to correlate and accredit training agencies on the basis
of their fitness to qualify manpower for library service of a
high order. Second, the success of professional control over
training standards in medicine and law had established the
principle of accreditation well enough that the American Library Association should not shrink from following suit.
The Committee accordingly recommended the appointment of
an ALA training board "to survey and investigate the field
of library training agencies for the purpose of defining stand-
ards--devising a plan for evaluating or accrediting, [for] organizing all training activities into a general system, [for]
suggesting improvements, [for] recommending the establishment of new agencies and promoting education for librarianship in every way."[58]

The Council authorized a temporary Library Training
Board with these general powers on April 24, 1923. [59] The

preface of the Carnegie report, Training in Library Service,
was signed June 1; the report was released in the summer;
and a Carnegie grant to support the Board followed in the
fall, not long after the Executive Board set it up.

In Conclusion

This chapter relates the Williamson report as well as
the opening of a new era in library education to the seminal
influence on American professional education of the Carnegie
Foundation for the Advancement of Teaching and the Carnegie
Corporation.   That influence stemmed from recognizing the
importance to civilized life of professional services of high
standard and from recognizing that raising professional qualifications is the main leverage to use to improve a profession's service capabilities.   Carnegie experience with raising
the service capabilities of professions began with the modernization of medical education.   The most visible aspect of the
project was the Flexner investigation, which became the pace-
maker and supplied a model for a series of investigations of
other professions.   Conducted by a scholar of stature who was
untrained in medicine, the investigation gave but perfunctory
attention to problems internal to the educational process and
concentrated on changes of organization and management required to produce a service capability commensurate with the
profession's obligations to society.   The report's disclosure
of shortcomings and proposals for remedial action fitted into
a more inclusive effort.   It was not enough to show the way
to needed change and let a report on the subject gather dust:
the Foundation considered it a part of its duty to cooperate
in bringing change about.

As the trustee of Andrew Carnegie's library program,
the Carnegie Corporation decided to shift its policy and to
use similar leverage to help raise the service capability of
the library profession.   But there was a problem.   The
young profession's leadership structure was underdeveloped.
Machinery to set and enforce standards was lacking: the
Association of American Library Schools was not doing the
job effectively, and practicing librarians were not yet agreed
that professional control was needed.   Concurrent, therefore,
with plans for an inquiry into schools of library training
went planning for more effective professional control over
educational standards.

Charles C. Williamson, who took charge of the project,

worked on it part time from 1918 through 1921, completing
the written report around the close of that year.   Conclusions
about the project can be brought together under three captions,
the first being the active part played by Williamson in establishing professional control over the formulation and enforcement of educational standards.   He may have stumbled at
times in doing this, but whoever has ventured along a creative path himself knows how poorly it is lit.   The Pritchett
preface suggests two other captions.   By investing four of
the best years of his life, Williamson produced for the first
time a "unitary and comprehensive treatment" of the training
problem, from recruiting and financing to organizing library
work for proper manpower utilization.   Separate findings were
important, but it was their cumulative weight that led librarians, in Roden's words, to receive the contribution "with
frank recognition of [its] significance."[60]

     The report was first of all a disclosure of conditions
which could not be condoned if the full potential of this branch
of public service was to be realized; but it went on to present
an integrated package of proposals for remedial action, ranging
from improving textbooks to improving field work--the longest
chapter.   The proposals were of uneven weight, but of the
two most basic, one was the proposal to transfer sponsorship
of library schools to universities, to adopt in so doing the
majority practice among library schools of limiting the basic
professional curriculum to one year and to adopt the practice
of the schools of best reputation of admitting college graduates only.   This reorganization would fit in with the modern
trend in professional education and would materially raise the
level of general education of librarians.   Training for subprofessional grades would remain the responsibility of training classes operated by libraries accredited for the purpose.

     The second main proposal was to establish a National
Certification Board to standardize grades of library service,
certify acceptable recruits for each grade, accredit training
agencies on the basis of their fitness to qualify recruits for
effective service, and promote library manpower development
in other ways found to be desirable.   This was the boldest
and most original of the Williamson proposals.   First presented to American librarians in 1918, it was debated and
finally rejected in favor of an ALA Training Board.   The
worth of a man's work tends to be measured by public acceptance.   It is not always a kind or reliable measure.   In
this case, however, Williamson in losing could take heart;
for despite the differences between the two conceptions, the

type of board approved, the same as the one rejected, could
be used to protect high standards of public service by assert-
ing control by the profession over the qualifications of recruits admitted to professional standing. This was the objective, and it was the address at Asbury Park of 1918 that
had led to the innovation.

The report also gained acceptability and strength--
some would say its greatest strength--from the fact that "the
most expert opinions on the problem [of library training]
were analyzed and compared" in preparing it. We have referred to outside sources of ideas that went into its prepara-
tion--Carnegie experience with professional training and the
great burst of contemporary effort that was producing invalu-
able new tools of personnel management. There were other
sources, not least of which was the now-forgotten vogue of
correspondence study which was then near an all-time peak
of popularity. But the library profession itself was the most
prolific source of ideas, and the nature of the inquiry made
it fitting to utilize them. If anything was to come of the inquiry, its findings would have to command a following from
within the ranks. An added incentive to draw liberally on
the best expertise in the field lay perhaps in Williamson's
prior contact with library schools, which had been limited.
In any case, the bulk of findings might be described as
consolidating, or attempting to consolidate, the best professional judgment of the time, the end in view being a higher
common ground which thoughtful librarians in the country
over could accept as tenable.

A couple of examples will make this clear. As of
1918, Williamson was considering whether a graduate school
which admitted only graduates of other schools would not be
a good thing. 61 The report settles on a different solution--
specialization by type of library work during a second year
of study. The more conservative solution was found to be in
an incipient stage of development already, and was more consistent with prevailing opinion. The chapter on the curriculum, the second longest, is another example. Devoid of
searching analysis, it accepts the existing curriculum as
satisfactorily adapted to the profession's demands. The treatment gains historic significance from using a composite statement of assorted library school subjects to suggest improvements in the organization of the curriculum. First, this
composite of experience unveiled priorities in actual use,
showing that four subjects absorbed about half of the student's
time: cataloging, book selection, reference work, and clas-

sification.   They were in practice the mainstays of the basic
curriculum.   Second, it was obviously difficult to do justice
to a total of twenty-five or more distinct subjects in one
year's time, and hence a need for two degree programs,
each of a year's duration.   Third, the technical nature of
the subjects supported the main proposition that such a program "should be based on a broad general education. "

REFERENCES

1.   Howe, Harriet E.   "Two Decades in Education for Li-
        brarianship," Library Quarterly 12, 1942, 557-70.

2.   Munthe, Wilhelm.   American Librarianship from a Euro-
        pean Angle; an Attempt at an Evaluation of Policies
        and Activities.   Chicago: American Library Asso-
        ciation, 1939, p. 132.

3.   Wilson, Louis R.   "The American Library School To-
        day," Library Quarterly 7, 1937, 211-45.

4.   Vann, Sarah K.   Training for Librarianship before 1923;
        Education for Librarianship Prior to the Publica-
        tion of Williamson's Report on "Training for library
        service. "   Chicago: American Library Association,
        1961; and her The Williamson Reports: a Study.
        Metuchen, N. J. :   Scarecrow Press, 1971.

5.   Roden, Carl B.   "President's Address: Ten Years,"
        ALAB 22, 1928, 311-18.

6.   Flexner, Abraham.   Henry S. Pritchett, a Biography.
        New York: Columbia University Press, 1943.
        Hereafter referred to as Flexner's Pritchett.

7.   Ibid. , p. 158.   Pritchett's capacity to deal with prob-
        lems of policy and management did not go unnoticed
        outside the Carnegie circle.   Flexner describes his
        being sought as director or trustee by organiza-
        tions as diverse as the Atchison, Topeka and Santa
        Fe Railway and the New York Metropolitan Museum
        of Art.

8.   My source on Mrs. Carnegie's correspondence is Flex-
        ner's Pritchett.   She follows up correspondence on
        the subjects noted in the text with a letter to Prit-

chett when he concluded his tenure as Acting President of the Carnegie Corporation in which she expresses heartfelt gratitude for the fact that "Great
things were done," then adds that "I feel this was
due almost entirely to the splendid work of the Acting President."

9.   Flexner, Abraham.   Abraham Flexner: an Autobiography.
     Introduction by Allan Nevins.   New York: Simon
     and Schuster, 1960, p. 85.

10. Ibid., p. 93.

11. Flexner, Abraham.   Medical Education, a Comparative
     Study.   New York: Macmillan, 1925.

12. Independent 68, 1910, 1407-08.

13. Flexner, Abraham.   Medical Education in Europe; a
     Report to the Carnegie Foundation for the Advance-
     ment of Teaching.   Introduction by Henry S. Prit-
     chett.   New York, 1912.   (Carnegie Foundation for
     the Advancement of Teaching.   Bulletin, no. 6)

14. The phrasing is from Flexner's Pritchett, but the points
     were first made in the original Flexner reports.

15. Flexner, Abraham.   "The German Side of Medical Edu-
     cation," Atlantic Monthly 112, 1913, 665.

16. Burrow, James G.   AMA: Voice of American Medicine.
     Baltimore: Johns Hopkins University Press, 1963,
     p. 35 and 35n.

17. See his introduction to Bulletin 6, Flexner's Medical
     Education in Europe, cited above.

18. Independent 68, 1910, 1407-08.

19. Current Literature 53, 1912, 306-07.

20. American Medical Association.   Journal 54, 1910, pp.
     1948-49.

21. American Medical Association.   Journal 59, 1912, 40-
     41.

22. Fishbein, Morris. A History of the American Medical
    Association, 1847 to 1947. Philadelphia: Saunders,
    1947. Fishbein has a good section on the history
    of the Council on Medical Education whose work in-
    fluenced Williamson.

23. This summary follows closely Bulletin 14, William S.
    Learned and others, The Professional Preparation
    of Teachers, cited in full in the text. The point
    of view pervades Pritchett's writings.

24. See Pritchett's introduction to Bulletin 15, Alfred Z.
    Reed, Training for the Public Profession of the
    Law, cited in full in the text.

25. Ibid.

26. Bulletin 14, supra, p. 15.

27. Bulletin 4, supra, p. ix.

28. Outlook 101, 1912, 465-66.

29. See Pritchett's introduction to Bulletin 14, supra.

30. See Pritchett's introduction to Bulletin 15, supra.

31. Fishbein, op. cit., 897-98. Fishbein quotes minutes
    of the Council on Medical Education on a prelim-
    inary conference with Pritchett and Flexner saying
    that the plan was "to investigate all the profes-
    sions, law, medicine and theology." Pritchett
    "found no efforts being made by law to better the
    conditions in legal education and had met with
    some slight opposition in the efforts he was mak-
    ing." He was on the other hand "agreeably sur-
    prised not only at the efforts being made to cor-
    rect conditions surrounding medical education but
    at the enormous amount of data collected." The
    Foundation would proceed on its own responsibility.
    "The report would therefore be, and have the weight
    of an independent report of a disinterested body,
    which would then be published far and wide. It
    would do much to develop public opinion."

32. Fishbein, op. cit., passim.

33. Carnegie Corporation of New York. "Proposed Program
     in Library Service; Office Memorandum, November
     10, 1925. " New York, 1925.

34. Learned, William S. The American Public Library and
     the Diffusion of Knowledge. New York: Harcourt,
     1924.

35. Through the courtesy of the Carnegie Corporation, I
     was permitted to examine copy no. 7 of this 67-
     page report along with certain other papers which
     were utilized in preparing this chapter. Robert M.
     Lester, in his preface to Joseph L. Wheeler, Pro-
     gress and Problems in Education for Librarianship
     (N. Y. : Carnegie Corporation, 1946), names the
     Johnson study as the first of a series of influential
     reports on libraries and library training prepared
     under the Corporation's sponsorship.

36. Vann, Sarah K. The Williamson Reports; a Study.
     Metuchen, N. J. : Scarecrow Press, 1971, p. 13.
     The context discloses the Corporation's intention to
     review existing library activities and commitments
     in the light of the survey findings.

37. Ibid. , pp. 46-50. Professor Vann provides a detailed
     account of this mission.

38. Based on official proceedings as quoted in a letter of
     January 24, 1922, from Acting President Pritchett
     to Robert A. Franks, Treasurer of the Corporation.

39. LJ 43, 1918, 649-55.

40. Op. cit.

41. ALAB 13, 1919, 32-33.

42. Letter of January 24, 1922, Pritchett to Franks, supra.

43. ALAB 13, 1919, 141-46.

44. ALAB 13, 1919, 120-26.

45. Probably no librarian of his time was better informed
     than Williamson on developments that were modern-
     izing management in government and industry. His

awareness of their implications for librarianship is
shown in other writings besides those cited in the
text, as: "Efficiency in Library Management," LJ
44, 1919, 67-77, and "Personnel Specifications for
Library Work: a Project," Public Libraries 26,
1921, 297-301.

46. The verdict of Williamson's peers was that he exagger-
ated the close relation of personnel development to
the organization of libraries and personnel management; but if one feels his way into the novelty and
excitement of the career service concept at the time,
Williamson's slant is made understandable. Following are a few references which furnish contemporary
background: Jane S. Dahlberg, The New York Bureau of Municipal Research; Pioneer in Government
Administration, with a foreword by Luther Gulick.
New York: New York University Press, 1966; Henry
Moskowitz [President, Municipal Civil Service Commission, New York City], "Old and New Problems
of Civil Service, Annals of the American Academy
of Political and Social Science 64, 1916, 153-67;
Charles A. Beard, "Training for Efficient Public
Service," Annals of the American Academy of Political and Social Science 64, 1916, 215-26; H. D.
Kitson, "Scientific Method in Job Analysis," Journal
of Political Economy 29, 1921, 508-14; and the his-
torical section of Civil Service Assembly of the
United States and Canada. Committee on Position-
Classification and Pay Plans in the Public Service.
Position-Classification in the Public Service. Chi-
cago: The Assembly, 1942.

47. Schneider, Wilbert M. The American Bankers Association; Its Past and Present. Washington: Public
Affairs Press, 1956. For further insight into the
vogue of correspondence study, see James A. Moy-
er, "The 'People's University' of Massachusetts,"
Annals of the American Academy of Social and Political Science 67, 1916, 193-201; and Lee Gallo-
way, "Correspondence School Instruction by Non-
academic Institutions," Annals of the American
Academy of Social and Political Science 67, 1916,
202-09.

48. Quoted by Schneider, op. cit., p. 61.

49. LJ 44, 1919, 651-52.

50. ALAB 14, 1920, 72-73.

51. ALAB 14, 1920, 78.

52. ALAB 14, 1920, 311-13.

53. LJ 45, 1920, 937.

54. ALAB 16, 1922, 12-14.

55. ALAB 16, 1922, 206-09.

56. ALAB 15, 1921, 169.

57. ALAB 17, 1923, 156-57.

58. ALAB 17, 1923, 152, 153, 194-96.

59. ALAB 17, 1923, 153.

60. Roden, op. cit.

61. LJ 43, 1918, 654.

Chapter 8

THE GENERATION OF REORGANIZATION

The period between the two world wars saw confusion
over educational policy give way to extensive reorganization
and end in renewed tranquility. Looking back in 1936, the
ALA Board of Education for Librarianship described as follows the new pattern which had by that time become a reality:

> According to this pattern, a first year of profes-
> sional instruction is given usually in an academic
> institution following four years, or in some cases
> three years of college work; effort is made to se-
> lect students who show aptitude for library work;
> members of the faculty meet qualifications which
> entitle them to faculty status; library and other
> facilities appropriate for professional instruction
> are developed. Advanced study based on the first
> year's work and leading to an advanced degree is
> available in seven library schools. . . . Twenty-six
> of the forty schools have been accredited by the
> board, of which twenty-three are general schools
> and three give courses in school library work
> only. [1]

To the Temporary Library Training Board fell the responsibility of finding a viable plan to bring this change about.
This chapter tells what happened to library schools of the
rank and file. The story of the Graduate Library School of
the University of Chicago belongs in the chapter that is to
follow.

Design for Change. Publication of the Williamson report in the summer of 1923 intensified the national dialogue
on educational policy and organization that had been inaugurated at Asbury Park in 1918. Library Journal published the

reactions of library schools in November, 1923,[2] and followed up with reactions of selected librarians in December.[3] The picture is a whirlpool of divergent views. Library Journal, a supporter of national certification, considered the report "the most important ever presented in the library field." By contrast, Carl B. Roden found in it "little that is new, and even less that is startling, to any one familiar with library affairs." He considered the disclosure of compelling reasons for reorganization timely, but scored the author for continually brandishing "a small hatchet labeled National Certification." One critic complained that library schools and their graduates were being pilloried; another considered criticisms of the schools as "the only vital ones that I have had the pleasure of reading. We have been so sentimentally good to ourselves that we have not dared to criticize ourselves searchingly." Clarence Sherman, of the Providence Public Library, held that the survey would have been a success had it done nothing more than emphasize the importance of distinguishing between library work of clerical and professional grade, while Arthur E. Bostwick, of the St. Louis Public Library, challenged the whole idea and regretted that Williamson had deemed it unnecessary to defend with more care something as basic as this, "his principal thesis." Josephine Rathbone opposed prescribing college graduation for admission to library school on the ground that it would exclude many deserving selfmade applicants who could "acquit themselves quite as well as the collegians." Sydney Mitchell, of California, on the other hand, supported requiring college graduation before technical training even though his university had not at that stage adopted the requirement.

Milton J. Ferguson, of the California State Library, advocated leaving any necessary changes in the curriculum to be "dictated somehow" by experience, and giving priority to "recommendations that schools be placed on a firmer financial basis; that schools become departments of universities thereby putting themselves in touch with a student supply and also ranging library instruction on a plane with other professions; and that instructors be required to be better trained for their job and very much better paid." By contrast, William Warner Bishop favored giving high priority to curriculum development. "I differ," he says, "from Dr. Williamson quite radically" about transferring the existing curriculum bodily to the graduate level, on the ground that students with a bachelor's degree would find the content too elementary. "The study of these elementary subjects," he continues, "and the time necessarily devoted to them, is, I fear, the

very factor which renders library school instruction so jejune
and unsatisfactory. Graduate students should be put at graduate work under teachers trained to handle mature students.
The elements should be gained in the undergraduate years..."
Some points were not contested--e. g. , that the essential elements of the profession can be mastered in one year and
that library schools urgently needed to be strengthened financially.

     The longer reviews throw better light on the report's
acceptability for planning purposes. Examining it first as the
handiwork of an individual inquirer, the New York State Library School Faculty[4] regretted the "pervasive disparage-
ment" of the schools, remained unconvinced that all of the
report's conclusions were sound, believed some of the investigator's ideals were beyond immediate accomplishment and
that others were nearer realization than he had discovered;
but agreed in principle with all of his larger ideals and objectives. Foremost among these was the proposition that librarianship should rank as an equal among the learned professions. The guidelines laid down for achieving this goal,
the Faculty agreed, undoubtedly mark out the great future
lines of advance--emphasis on education of professional grade,
strengthening instruction and the teaching staff, standardizing
entrance requirements, better textbooks, better arrangements
for specialized and advanced study. Other aspirations supported by the Faculty included national certification, graduate
footing for all library schools, a policy of strengthening existing schools in place of establishing new ones, and closer
affiliation with universities.

     The report was deemed significant, second, as "a re-
port to (and of) the Carnegie Corporation. " It was not sponsored by the Carnegie Foundation for the Advancement of
Teaching, "as have [been] the earlier momentous reports on
various departments of professional training, but in content,
method and motive, it forms one of the series. " Previous
Carnegie successes had demonstrated the value of unsparing
criticism as an aid to educational statesmanship:

          An immense advance in professional education is due
          largely to its criticisms, recommendations and fi-
          nancial aid.... It has never been content to rest
          in the first critical stage of its activities, but has
          proceeded thru cooperative efforts with schools and
          education associations to a common agreement on
          programs and reforms. Does not this fact promise

a similar cooperation with the American Library
Association and the Association of American Library
Schools for the reform and advancement of library
training?

Frank K. Walter, in a review of September 1, 1923,[5]
spoke as one who had worked closely with the ALA on training problems throughout the interval since Asbury Park.   He
likewise associated the survey with the Carnegie Foundation
series, observing that all of these reports "have a way of
stirring things up" and that this one was no exception.   "Never in the history of the modern library movement," he says
in praise of the project, "has so careful a study of a specific phase of library activity been made by an investigator
as professionally well qualified. "

But the outcome is viewed in a less favorable light.
The conclusions and recommendations are seen as forming a
unified program centering on the proposal to standardize library positions and certify individual librarians who qualify
for them.   This would provide the schools with standards
for admitting students as well as guidelines for building the
curriculum and developing faculty manpower.   The schools
would require "a reputable representative and authoritative
body to assist them not only in formulating standards, but
particularly in enforcing standards agreed upon. "   Attainabil-
ity of the standards, in turn, would depend on getting more
money both to operate the schools and to operate libraries
at salary levels which their graduates would require.   The
program would permit specialization along really professional
lines and aid in properly differentiating professional and
clerical work and workers.   Turning then to the practical
merits of the program, Walter holds that it would not be acceptable without considerable alteration for three reasons:
the recent rejection by the American Library Association of
national certification, the absence of a system of training
having the coordination necessary to support it, and cost requirements which could not be met with the funds in sight.
The review applauds the forceful disclosure of conditions that
clamored for change but criticizes some interpretations of the
facts as lacking authority--a shortcoming attributed to the investigator's limited first-hand contact with the work of the
schools.   He concludes that "one cannot help but feeling that
the author is more at home with the economic aspects of the
problem than with the pedagogical. "

Edwin H. Anderson, Librarian of the New York Public

Library, praised the Carnegie Corporation for the survey and
the choice of Williamson, a member of his staff, to conduct
it, saying, "I do not see where they could have found a better man to make it."[6] He foresaw the likelihood that the creation of the Temporary Library Training Board would prove
to be the outstanding result of the five-year project, but commended various features of the report itself: the findings on
curriculum and instruction, the need of better textbooks, and
the financial plight of the schools. The whole study, in his
view, was "an attempt to prove the thesis that the schools
cannot do their work as it should be done because of lack of
adequate funds. "

Much of the Anderson review is devoted to criticizing
the report as impractical ("out of touch with realities") and
for overemphasizing "academic mechanics. " With a rare
burst of feeling, he says that "The whole attitude seems to
me too academic to meet the existing conditions. There appears to be a rather unconvincing assumption that we can
raise our standards in schools and library service by pulling
at our own academic bootstraps, as it were. " As an example, he agrees that, within limits, it is possible to demar-
cate professional from clerical work, but contends that Williamson draws the line too sharply to be practical. Likewise
he agrees that, in general, it is better to have library
schools located at academic institutions, but holds it to be
"entirely too sweeping" to rule out sponsorship by a public
library. He agrees that the use of personal interviews is an
imperfect method of selecting library-school applicants, but
holds that the substitution of psychological testing would as of
that stage of the art be ill-advised. Anderson also scores
the tone of presentation, saying that "All through the report,
there is an air of certitude which, as usual, rouses a spirit
of opposition in the reader. A little indication that he was
merely handing down an opinion, and not the tables of the
law, would have made his arguments more ingratiating and
persuasive. "

Given the overall state of opinion, it devolved upon
the newly created Library Training Board to suggest a line
of action that the profession could better unite behind. Five
years of give and take had supplied valuable leads. By 1923,
it was agreed on all sides that professional manpower development was the key to the advancement of library service.
Second, the appointment of the Board signified a common desire to follow the example of established professions and to
experiment with empowering a central agency to exercise, on

behalf of society and the profession, the initiative and authority required to put into effect national standards for attaining
professional status.   Third, Williamson had, by frank disclosure of conditions, aroused determination to improve library schools; and most of his critics, even, would agree
that he had done more.   For he had held aloft, as no one
else had done, the possibility of lifting library education to
a higher plane commensurate with other professions, and this
was acknowledged to be desirable too.   His grand design for
the purpose might require alteration; but it had been worked
out in light of the "most expert opinions" obtainable, so opin-
ion-makers who had thus helped shape the thinking of the report might in the end find themselves coming around to much
of it.   Meanwhile, the new Board treated the Williamson report not as a blueprint to follow but more as a stimulus to
produce one.   In this vein, the Chairman, in his first address to the ALA Council, held that the main job lay ahead
but indicated that it was Dr. Williamson who had "vitalized
the silent thoughts, the deep concerns, the earnest hopes of
a good many of us.... We are aroused."[7]

The Temporary Board was one of high calibre, with
Adam Strohm, Librarian of the Detroit Public Library, as
Chairman; Harrison W. Craver, Director of the Engineering
Societies Library; Andrew Keogh, Librarian of Yale University; Linda A. Eastman, Librarian of the Cleveland Public
Library; and Malcolm G. Wyer, Librarian of the Denver Public Library。 Packed into the single year of its existence
were visits to library schools, voluminous correspondence,
and systematic gathering of hitherto inaccessible data to assist in making decisions.   But none of its activities was
more productive than the working conferences that it conducted across the country.   These open meetings permitted
all shades of opinion to be heard, drew out and enlisted the
best thought in the field, and in the process promoted national solidarity.   The progress of other professions that had
been making the headlines since 1910 was not lost on librarians.   "Librarianship, despite our yearnings," said Milton J.
Ferguson in the symposium of 1923, "has so far failed to
reach professional standing in the sense we consider medicine,
law and even teaching professions. " And this discrepancy
kindled interest in having outsiders participate in the national dialogue。 At a notable meeting in New York, William S.
Learned of the Carnegie Foundation spoke on the personnel
implications of the library's expanding role in the diffusion
of knowledge, and was followed by N. P. Colwell, Secretary
of the Council on Medical Education of the American Medical

Association. The experience of the medical profession, coupled with the advice of Colwell, influenced librarians as nothing else had done to consider the "analogies" between the educational problems of different professions and in particular the importance of organizing a scheme of library education which would be "in harmony with what here in America is coming to be a pretty well recognized system of professional education."[8] It was a turning point--when discord began to give way to resolution to fall in with basic contemporary trends in professional education generally.

The Board presented its report on May 20, 1924.[9]
It found the educational and social significance of libraries in American life to be rapidly expanding and stressed the conviction that in developing adequate service capabilities, "no other essential is so important as carefully chosen, well educated and thoroughly trained librarians." The changing character of library service was placing a higher premium on trained minds of a high order, but the demand was greatest in positions requiring specialized knowledge and leadership. There was already a scarcity of librarians of suitable calibre, and the scarcity was rising. The findings further indicated that the problem of closing the gap between supply and demand was complicated by the condition of training agencies, especially by their financial condition. They were all in need of money and all offered courses having a family resemblance, but they differed in other respects--in entrance requirements, length of curriculum, strength of faculty and equipment. No formal national standards of excellence existed to guide them and, to add to the disarray, there was no orderly process of formulating and approving such standards.

To fill the void of central leadership and professional supervision, the Board recommended that the American Library Association establish a permanent Board of Education for Librarianship and give it a strong mandate to study library service and its changing needs and to promote the further development of education for librarianship; to determine the extent to which existing agencies meet the profession's needs; to formulate for the approval of the ALA Council minimum standards for all types of library education agencies (library schools, summer schools, training classes); to classify them in accordance with approved standards; and to publish annually a list of the ones accredited. It further recommended that this new instrument be empowered to correlate the work of the several types of training agencies, establish close relations with similar educational bodies, advise on

grants for library education, reduce the chaos in educational
terminology (which left basic terms like "library training" and
"library schools" ambiguous), serve in any other matters that
"would fall logically within the functions of the Board," and
report progress annually to the ALA Council.

   Minimum Standards for Library Schools.   The Council
adopted this blueprint for central leadership and supervision
on June 30, 1924. [10]   The resultant Board of Education for
Librarianship (referred to hereafter as the BEL), formally
organized September 4, consisted of the original members except for the withdrawal of Miss Eastman, who was replaced
by Elizabeth M. Smith, Director of the Albany Public Library.
It was thus composed entirely of administrators of stature in
a profession where study and teaching were by tradition subordinate to administration.   It was generously financed during its early years by Carnegie Corporation grants, was cap-
ably assisted by Sarah N. Bogle, Secretary, and Harriet E.
Howe, Executive Assistant, and had a clear mandate for
vigorous action.   It is therefore hardly surprising to find the
BEL emerging in the second half of the 1920s as the most
powerful and the most discussed arm of the American Library
Association and one of the most dynamic agencies of its kind
on the continent.

   One of its services was to establish good working re-
lations with foundations and appropriate educational organiza-
tions--the National Education Association, the Council on
Legal Education and Admission to the Bar of the American
Bar Association, the Dental Council of America, the American Association of Colleges of Pharmacy, the Associations of
Colleges and Secondary Schools of the North Central and
Southern States, and similar organizations.   Of these, the
Association of American Universities played the most strategic role in library educational history.   Following up conversations initiated by the Temporary Board, the BEL developed
for its own guidance a summary of an AAU committee's
recommended specifications for library education standards, [11]
as follows:

1.   Four years of academic work leading to a bachelor's
     degree with a major in any humanities or scientific
     subject, to be prerequisite to admission to a profes-
     sional library curriculum.

2.   Two years of professional study to be required for the

master's degree.

    a.   The first year to consist of professional courses in library science, or equivalent experience, for which a certificate should be granted.

    b.   The second year to be organized and conducted on a strictly graduate basis, for which a master's degree should be granted.

3.   Provisional approval of a library science major for inclusion in a four-year college program leading to a bachelor's degree.

4.   Discouragement of planning work beyond the master's degree except in established fields of scholarship.

5.   Counsel to delay requirement of higher degrees for library-school faculties no longer than necessary.

There are two arresting things about these recommendations. One is the low esteem they reflect for the existing library school curriculum; the other, their ready acceptance by the library profession, which probed some issues of less importance with greater persistence. Acceptance of the recommendations established terms of reference which were to control the degree structure for a quarter of a century. The only important change in the interval came in 1929 when member universities were authorized to confer a second ("fifth-year") bachelor's degree, in place of a certificate, for a year of professional study at the graduate level, if they chose to do so.

Aided by further open meetings, the BEL filled in this general framework with an informal set of policy guidelines which were used to formulate specific standards for use in accreditation. The guidelines represent the best judgment of the profession on next steps required to further the progress of library education and can be summed up briefly as follows: (1) remedy confusion by converting all training agencies (library schools, summer schools and training classes) into an orderly system within which the work of each is coordinated with the others; (2) connect library schools, which should occupy the central place in the training system, with academic institutions; (3) raise entrance requirements and place as high a premium as circumstances permit on college graduation as a prerequisite; (4) use one year of approved professional study as the basis of admission to professional status; (5) uphold the importance of full-time, high-quality staff for conducting

an effective educational program; and (6) insist on provision
by the sponsoring institution of the administrative authority
as well as the operating resources (financing, size of staff
and physical facilities) necessary to do work of creditable
grade.

The Temporary Board had produced a first draft of
standards for use in measuring excellence in accordance with
these goals.   The draft was revised by the new Board and
approved by the ALA Council July 7, 1925.[12]   These, the
first national standards to be formally established by the profession, provided for accrediting two classes of schools.
Each class was in turn subdivided into two groups, making
four in all.   Status within the resultant hierarchy was de-
termined mainly by (1) the amount of preprofessional education required for admission and (2) affiliation or nonaffiliation
with an academic institution.   Following is the BEL's own
outline of the principal differentiae of the four grades of program:

Undergraduate library schools:

1.   Junior undergraduate library school

Connected with an approved library, college or
university
Requires for entrance one year of college work
Grants a certificate

2.   Senior undergraduate library school

Connected with an approved degree-conferring
institution.
Requires for entrance three years of college
work
Grants a bachelor's degree

Graduate library schools:

3.   Graduate library school

Connected with an approved degree-conferring
institution
Requires for entrance a college degree
Grants a certificate

4.   Advanced graduate library school

Integral part of the university
Requires for entrance a college degree
Grants a master's degree

Changes did not await formal adoption of the standards.
The Library School, Carnegie Library of Atlanta, affiliated
with Emory University in November, 1925, and in doing so
foreshadowed a general movement.   The BEL reported for
1925-26 that "One of the most important changes in the library school world is the consolidation of the New York
State Library School and the Library School of the New York
Public Library with the Columbia University School of Library Service ... opening September, 1926.   Two highly successful schools thus are given university connection and an
environment offering unequalled opportunities for observation
and practical work."   Table I (see pp. 200-201) gives a
graphic picture of some of the major changes made during
the decade following adoption of the new standards.   The
rapid transfer of library education to an academic environment stands out prominently.   Five of the 14 library schools
first accredited (one out of every three) were connected with
libraries at the time of accreditation: the Carnegie Library
of Atlanta, the Los Angeles Public Library, New York Public
Library, New York State Library, and the St. Louis Public
Library.   By 1933, none of the five, which included some of
the foremost schools of the time, was still in operation.
Meanwhile, the number of accredited schools rose from 14
to 26, and all of the latter were connected with degree-granting institutions.

Another striking change occurred in admission requirements.   California and Drexel began to limit admission to
college graduates in the fall of 1925.   The same year Simmons, which already had a program for graduates, further
tightened admission by concentrating its undergraduate program in the senior year.   St. Louis, where entering students
in 1925 normally had about one year of college, announced
that educational requirements would be progressively raised
in the future.   The table shows that other schools used the
same method of gradual escalation--Greensboro, Hampton,
McGill, Western Reserve.   Ten of the 26 schools had graduate-level programs by 1932, and the number rose to 16 by
1935.

The escalation of preprofessional education standards
can be stated in another interesting way.   As of 1925-26,
65 per cent of a total enrollment of 553 in 14 accredited

schools were college graduates, 13 per cent had three years
of college, but 11 per cent had gone no farther than high
school.   Three years later, in 1928-29, 68 per cent of an
enrollment of 1,019 in 18 accredited schools were college or
teachers college graduates, an additional four per cent held
a master's degree, 19 per cent had three years of college,
while only three per cent had gone no farther than high
school.

There were other advances.   Enrollment rose from
553 in 1926 to 1,121 in 1933, and was even higher before the
depression struck.   Recruiting benefited from placing the
schools in the main stream of higher education.   Quiet progress was made in developing a more orderly course structure and better coordinating educational programs nationally.
The schools fared better financially; they gained ground in
full-time staff and gained from being governed by the same
institutional code as other professional schools.   But if one
were singling out the respects in which the 1925 standards
were most successful, it would be their contribution toward
the transfer of library education to established seats of learning, enforcement of higher standards of preprofessional education, and better relating the degree structure to approved
academic practice.

Triumph and Failure.   In a way the breadth of its
mandate put it up to the BEL to find out for itself how far
the uses of centralized initiative and authority should be carried.   Upon assessing the situation, it had decided at the outset to concentrate on converting the disarray of training establishments into a more orderly system of higher standard,
and this in turn spurred management activity in other directions.   The need to bring the output of qualified librarians
in line with growing demands in the field led the Board to
bolster recruiting and it was so successful in interpreting
opportunities for useful careers in library service that the
ALA, in acknowledgment, later added recruiting to its formal
responsibilities.   When output lagged behind anyway, the
Board went to work on the establishment of new library
schools in strategic centers, and provided helpful guidance
in shaping plans to insure their healthy development.   The
part it played in distributing foundation grants to library
schools drew it farther into a national role of professional
and educational management.   It nurtured respect for librarianship as an emerging profession, and in the process opened
new doors to students to apply for scholarships and fellow-
(cont. on p. 202)

TABLE 1: ACCREDITED LIBRARY SCHOOLS, 1926-1935

Name of School	1925-1926	1926-1927
Albany--N. Y. State College for Teachers (1926)		
Atlanta--Library School, Carnegie Library (1905)	4	2
California--U of Calif School of Librarianship (1919)	2	2
Chicago--U of Chicago Graduate Library School (1926)		
Columbia--Columbia U School of Library Serv. (1887)		2
Denver--U of Denver Sch of Librarianship (1931)		
Drexel--Drexel I. School of Lib Science (1892)	2	2
Emory--Emory U. Library School (1905)		
Emporia--Kansas State TC Library School (1928)		
Greensboro--Women's Coll UNC Dept of L S (1928)		
Hampton--Hampton I Library School (1925)		Pro
Illinois--U of I Library School (1893)	2	2
Los Angeles--LA Public Library, Lib Sch (1914)	4	4
Louisiana--LSU School of Lib Science (1931)		
McGill--McGill U Library School (1927)		
Michigan--U of M Dept of Library Science (1926)		Pro
New Jersey--NJ Col for Women Lib School (1927)		
NYPL--NY Public Library, Library School (1911)	4	
NYS--NY State Library, Library School (1887)	2	
North Carolina--UNC School of Lib Science (1931)		
Oklahoma--OU School of Library Science (1929)		
Peabody--Geo Peabody College Library School (1928)		
Pittsburgh--Carnegie Inst of Tech. Lib School (1901)	4	4
Pratt--Pratt Inst School of Lib Science (1890)	4	4
St. Catherine--Col of St. Catherine Lib School (1929)		
St. Louis--St. Louis Public Library, Lib School (1917)	4	4
Simmons--Simmons College School of Lib Science (1902)	2&3	2&3
Syracuse--Syracuse U School of Lib Science (1908)		
Tennessee--Univ of Tenn Dept of Lib Science (1928)		
Washington--Univ of Wash Library School (1911)	3	3
Western Reserve--WRU School of Lib Science (1904)	4	4
Wisconsin--Univ of Wis Library School (1906)	4	4

Symbol	Meaning
1	Advanced graduate library school--1925 standards
2	Graduate library school--1925 standards
3	Senior undergraduate library school--1925 standards
4	Junior undergraduate library school--1925 standards
I	Type I library school--1933 standards
II	Type II library school--1933 standards
III	Type III library school--1933 standards
Pro	Provisional or tentative accreditation
Acc	Accredited but not classified
Sch	Accredited for school library work only
Sch 16	Accredited for 16 hour curriculum for school librarians

1927-1928	1928-1929	1929-1930	1930-1931	1931-1932	1932-1933	1933-1934	1934-1935
			4 Sch	4 Sch	4 Sch	III Sch	III Sch
2	2	2					
2	2	2	2	2	2	I	I
						I	I
2	2	2	2	2	2	I	I
				Pro 3	3	Pro III	III
2	2	2	2	2	2	II	II
			2	2	2	II	II
			3 Sch	3 Sch	3 Sch	III Sch	III Sch
			4 Sch	3 Sch	3 Sch	Discd June, 1933	
4	4	4	3	3	3	Pro III	II
2	2	2	2	2	2	I	I
4	4	4	4	4	Discd June, 1932		
				2	2	II	II
Pro	4	4	2	2	2	II	II
2&3	2&3	2&3	2	2	2	I	I
	Pro	3	3	3	3	III	III
Merged with NYS to form the Columbia School of Lib Service, 1926							
Merged with NYPL to form the Columbia School of Lib Service, 1926							
				2	2	Pro II & III	II & III
				3	3	III	III
				3 Sch	3 Sch	Pro III	Pro III
4	4	4	3	3	3	Pro III	II
4	4	Acc	Acc	Acc	Acc	III	III
			3	3	3	III	III
4	4	4	4	Suspended operation June, 1932			
2&3	2&3	2&3	2&3	2&3	2&3	II &III	II & III
	Pro	3	3	3	3	Pro III	II
			Sch 16	Sch 16	Sch 16	Sch 16	Sch 16
3	3	3	3	3	3	Pro III	II
4	4	4	3	3	3	Pro III	II
4	4	4	4	4	4	III	III

ships for advanced study. It did yeoman's service for a more
exact professional vocabulary, producing in 1927 a thirteen-
page glossary entitled Standard Terminology in Education
With Special Reference to Librarianship. 13 This all but forgotten predecessor of the ALA Glossary of Terms14 defined
terms which were the source of most confusion and changed
usage for the better several years before the ambitious project that it initiated came to fruition.

If the Board's main achievements lay in helping American librarians manage the reorganization of manpower development and in creating a better climate for library schools
to thrive in, its main failures lay in taking over, or trying
to take over, responsibilities for research and curriculum
development. The short-lived trend toward centering library
research in the BEL dates from around 1928. The 1924 mandate directed the Board, as we have seen, to study the changing needs of library service, and in 1928 that clause began
to be referred to as "the Board's major duty."15 Carl Roden,
while serving as President in 1928, said that the coordination
of training programs and the improvement of the curriculum
were but necessary first steps which cultivate only "a small
corner" of the BEL's field of responsibility. He foresaw
great unspecified advances in the next ten years as the rest
of the field was cultivated and the profession began to reap
the benefits of its research. 16

The Board's report for 1930-3117 goes on to designate
thorough-going study of the conditions and needs of the profession as "first and always the project of paramount importance,"
and the report the following year is more specific. There,
questions as to what the main functions of the Board should be
and whether the original charter should be amended to define
them better are answered by saying that it is probably "a
primary duty" of each major ALA board and committee, "and
particularly of the Board of Education for Librarianship, to
be continually interested in the advancement of professional
knowledge through original research and through service
studies. " In 1932 a special committee was assigned to propose a form of organization through which the ALA could effectively operate as a promoter of the advancement of knowledge. 18 Shortly afterwards, an audit of progress and problems of library education, prepared by Ralph Munn at the request of the Carnegie Corporation, recommended that the
Board be considered the most appropriate agency to initiate
and supervise studies in education for librarianship. 19

The move to assign an agency of the American Library
Association a major role in library research seems to have
gained its plausibility from a combination of circumstances,
but particularly from the need for service studies to promote
enlightened management of the development of librarianship.
When the burgeoning Graduate Library School found this conception of the research function too restricted, the ALA tried
to take over the job itself.   Two other considerations argued
in favor of doing so.   One was the part that reliable information had played in hammering out the national consensus
which made five years of harmonious progress realizable.
We have already observed how the BEL dug out facts that
nobody knew and everybody needed.   Reliable data on shortages, enrollment, characteristics and regional origins of students, their scholastic preparation, the colleges that educated
them, the library schools that consistently attracted college
graduates, and where young librarians went on leaving library
school--all this information, hitherto unavailable, proved
crucial to formulating policy and bringing about a meeting of
minds.   As of October, 1924, for example, only two of the
existing 18 library schools required college graduation for
admission.   The Board was able to disarm objections to
raising admission standards when it was able to show that,
in spite of formal requirements, 48 per cent of all the students enrolled were in reality college graduates.   Similarly,
the profession had supported the Williamson proposal to
strengthen existing library schools in place of establishing
new ones until BEL research revealed that the Williamson
data were dated and that additional schools were required to
meet rising postwar demands.

The second consideration follows from the first.   Looking back over the first five years, the Board could see by
1928 that the creative phase of reorganization was ending.
What was the next big job?   In all of its proud efforts to
generate change, the Board had been preoccupied with the
educational requirements of library work as currently prac-
ticed.   Was existing service adequate or should the sights be
raised?   Since this fundamental question had been skirted,
was it not time to tackle it?   The problem was to determine
the course that fundamental development of library service
ought to take, to measure modern society's library needs
against those cherished ideals of which "we speak in glitter-
ing sentences, " and to relate manpower development closely
to the results of the inquiry.   This meant long-range research not only to ascertain whether a more powerful instrument of service was needed but to develop a branch of learn-

ing on how to relate library service to people's actual needs.
It was a job, the report suggested, that might take up to 25
years. 20

The surprise in all this is that the Board showed no
interest in nor inclination toward developing library schools
as centers of research, and the reason is puzzling in spite
of the logic of the situation just analyzed. Whatever the
answer, neither the Executive Board nor the Carnegie Corporation supported the idea of BEL as a central research
bureau. The 1928 proposal to appraise library service as
one of the fundamental branches of public service was a lineal
predecessor of the one-shot Public Library Inquiry conducted
20 years later, but the closest the BEL came to its dream
was to conduct a few service studies in the 1930s which the
Corporation financed shortly after receiving the Munn report.

The BEL looked upon curriculum development to start
with as one of its most important tasks. 21 It delegated responsibility for determining the nature and content of the curriculum, then dropped the project when it proved to be a misguided move.

Here, in bare outline, is the disappointing story that
opens with an announcement in the first annual report that,
"At every turn, the Board is confronted with divergent views
concerning curricula content and is convinced that a scientific analysis of library work is a requisite preliminary to a
correlated system of education for librarianship. The fundamental facts on which to build curricula can be obtained only
from a thorough study of duties incident to the various positions in libraries. As soon as money is available such a
study will be undertaken under the direction of Dr. W. W.
Charters, who has made studies of other professions for similar purposes. "22

The tradition of technical education still weighed "like
an Alp" on thinking about the curriculum, and this reinforced
the profession's confidence in the Charters approach. He had
had successful experience with trades and related vocations
where good training consists in finding out which operations
are most basic--or standard--and in learning the best methods of performing them. One of his successes involved developing a training program for 125 secretaries by using the
type of job analysis that the Russians had used to devise
their training in the ABC's of shopwork, the breakthrough
which created a sensation at Philadelphia in 1876 (see Chapter

2). Charters found that the job performances of the secretaries could be broken down into 871 elements or skills, and
further found, through frequency tabulations, that some of
these ABC's of the work formed the core of daily duties
while other elements of the job stood at the periphery. On
the basis of this information, a training program was planned
which sought to develop specific skills known to be involved
in secretarial work and which gave top priority to those
skills known to be most essential to effective job performance.

The Curriculum Study undertook to use the same procedure to identify a core of standard library skills. The
first step was to take a single library and compile an ex-
haustive list of the work elements or duties in acquisitions,
cataloging, circulation and other departments of library activity; second, to ask experts in each activity in other libraries to expand the original list until the inventory within that
area was found to be complete. Third, these experts would
then be asked to pool judgments as to the most skillful method to use in performing each duty. When tabulated, the results would then be turned over to authors commissioned to
prepare definitive treatises on the best methods to use in the
several departments of work. Each treatise would be referred
to other experts while in draft and would be published when
revised in the light of their criticisms.

The higher skills of a profession cannot be encapsu-
lated so easily, so the project ran into trouble. A storm
broke and it was halted; the specialists who were already at
work on treatises were encouraged to give up the elaborate
reduction of library procedures into their ABC's and to complete the books in their own way. This was done. The following were all published by the ALA, and were widely used.
Figures to the right show dates of publication and copies sold as
of March, 1931. 23 A final report on the project was promised but failed to materialize.

Flexner, Jennie M.	Circulation work in public libraries	Oct. , 1927	2,536
Wyer, James I.	Reference work	Dec. , 1929	2,032
Mann, Margaret	Introduction to cata- loging and the classi- fication of books	Mar. , 1930	2,956
Fargo, Lucile F.	Library in the school	Mar. , 1930	2,664
Drury, F. K. W.	Book selection	June, 1930	1,860
Drury, F. K. W.	Order work for libraries	June, 1930	1,348
Power, Effie L.	Library service	Nov. , 1930	1,169

The storm that broke the calm was loosed by John
Cotton Dana, December 20, 1927, when he criticized the
American Library Association for overcentralization of power,
wasting money and ineptitude. [24] He attacked various specially financed projects including (1) a recently completed three-
year survey of administrative and service practices of American libraries;[25] the activities of (2) the Adult Education and
(3) Library Extension committees; but (4) BEL activities were
the main target.   Dana considered the BEL well-intentioned,
but objected to their work as an intrusion of outsiders who
were expert neither in education nor in library-school management.   That was not the worst of it in his view.   Backed
by the ALA and the power of the purse, the Bel move toward
"standardization" was seen as fostering the goosestep and
creating timidity in schools whose past strength had sprung
from their unstifled freedom.

He considered the Curriculum Study exorbitantly expensive and the most inept of all.   He could not understand
how librarians had been led to believe that this elaborate exercise of job analysis "could furnish material for treatises
of the first quality...   But I do understand," he adds, "how
an expert in the curriculum study of hand-work in factories,
and certain trades, could be self-deceived into thinking that
this same curriculum study formula would produce valuable
results" by mistaking operating routines for the sum and substance of professional competence.   He had read the Flexner
and Wyer books, had found them helpful, but felt sure that
the two authors had produced "almost precisely the books
that their several native talents and forms of experience and
education would have impelled ... them to write had they
never heard of $30,000 worth of questions and answers ac-
quired via a curriculum study. "

A special committee appointed to consider the Dana
letter found it too harsh but symptomatic of unrest that was
entitled to examination, and proposed, in a landmark recommendation, that an overall evaluation of ALA activities be
made periodically. [26]   Approval of the recommendation led,
across the years, to a series of major policy and organization reports, the first of which was in 1930. [27]   In it, the
BEL found itself once again at the center of attention.   "The
task of our committee in reaching a just conclusion regarding
the Board," the Activities Committee states, "is the most difficult it has before it.   The letters regarding the Board, considering the number of agencies affected, have been more
critical, more numerous, more voluminous than regards any

other activity. " Several pages of letters, mostly excerpts,
are quoted to document the full range of membership opinion,
pro and con, but the Activities Committee itself narrowed attention to the power vested in the Board and to the two major areas into which it found the actual work of the BEL to
classify itself namely (1) the study of training and related
problems and (2) accreditation of training agencies.

The Committee agreed with critics that the broad
powers of the Board posed a bureaucratic danger but held
that these powers were being used too wisely to be curbed.
It had nothing but praise for the fund of fresh information
that the Board had gathered and disseminated. But it supported membership complaints that the program of accreditation was not satisfactory, suggested clarification of BEL
policy on foundation grants, and concluded with two drastic
recommendations. One proposed reconstitution of the Board
so as to include (1) a representative of the Association of
American Library Schools as well as (2) a representative
chosen from those members of ALA who were engaged in library training outside of accredited library schools. The
second recommendation was not to scrap accreditation, as
some were ready to do, but to place all schools, once accredited by the Board, on the approved list without being
classified.

It was a recoil from the high resolves of 1924. The
force of inertia described in the chapter, "The Sway of Unwritten Standards, " had found powerful expression and threatened the reorganization. In a brilliant, conciliatory reply, [28]
Louis R. Wilson, Chairman of BEL, agreed that the classification "has not provided exact places into which all schools
could be fitted in a manner altogether satisfactory to themselves, " but observed that the profession in approving an accreditation program in 1924 had in mind a new and better
pattern of library education, and that while the resultant
duties had at times been unpleasant, the Board had "performed them frankly, openly and impartially to the best of
its ability. " He opposed turning the clock back either by
block representation on the Board or by abandoning classification of library schools. Defensible weaknesses of the
standards, including weaknesses of classification, could be
remedied by revision. It was not necessary to kill a fly
with a hatchet.

The response was decisive and statesmanly. The
Executive Board, acting on behalf of the profession, turned

down the recommendations.   The principle of broad professional control over educational standards had weathered the
storm, and the BEL, already at work on revision, moved
rapidly ahead to complete the job.

        The 1933 Standards.   The revised standards were sub-
mitted to the ALA Council and approved October 21, 1933. [29]
They mark an advance over the 1925 standards in four ways.
First, they brought library education in line with a general
trend in accreditation to seek educational improvements by
placing a higher premium on local interest and initiative.
The 1925 standards relied heavily on specific requirements,
imposed from outside, and were often quantitative in nature.
Examples selected at random from standards for graduate library schools include: a suggested curriculum of up to 36
hours, complete with proposed credit for each course; the
requirement of not fewer than four full-time teachers for an
enrollment of 50 students; and restriction of admission to bona
fide graduates of approved colleges and universities with at
least two months of experience in an approved library.   Given
the conditions which the original standards were designed to
correct, requirements of this degree of specificity had their
place, but the 1933 standards shifted away from such specifics
and focused on what a school was trying to do, on how intel-
ligently the program was related to the manpower needs of
the profession, on administrative requirements of the program, and how well those requirements were being met.
The course structure was left to the local faculty.   Faculty
strength was to be measured in terms of program demands,
and more leeway was left to select students on the basis of
their aptitude and their fitness to benefit from the program.

        Second, the revision corrected inequities.   Built into
the 1925 standards were tests of acceptability which served
the cause of reorganization better than the cause of educational excellence.   Take the case of two schools accredited as
of junior grade, one at a university, the other at a public library.   All the university library school had to do to move
up to senior grade was to raise admission requirements, but
this opportunity was denied the public library school regard-
less of the quality of its educational program.   Quantitative
measures caused trouble in other ways.   For example, the
ratio of admissions from leading Eastern women's colleges
began to decline in the late 1920s as the ratio of admissions
from teachers colleges rose.   By dwelling on the superiority
of four years of undergraduate preparation, it was complained,

the standards minimized the significance of a trend of this
kind and discouraged the use of qualitative criteria in the selection of students.

Third, the basis of classification was changed. Graduate library schools were to find that the change had the defect of its virtues in that it amounted to being discriminatory,
but the object was to soften the rigidity of the standards in
the face of criticism by the Activities Committee. One cor-
rective was to reclassify accredited schools in terms of the
overall character of their program. The lowest of the new
classes, Type III, comprised those library schools which gave
only the first full academic year of library science without
requiring four years of college work for admission. Type II
comprised library schools which also gave only the first full
academic year of library science but required four years of
appropriate college work for admission. Type I comprised
the schools where the most advanced work was done--schools
which required at least a bachelor's degree for admission to
the first academic year of library science and/or gave advanced training beyond this first year.

A second change was to employ a single standard for
rating purposes. The object was to base accreditation on
one decision and one only: is the work which this school is
ready to do of a standard that deserves accreditation or not?
And to confirm this, the annual list of accredited schools beginning in 1936 stated that "Classification as Type I, Type
II, or Type III neither includes nor implies a comparative
rating or grading of the schools." It was this second cor-
rective that graduate library schools found discriminatory.

Type I and Type II library schools had to be an integral part of a degree-conferring institution, but for Type
III schools this requirement was optional.

A fourth advance was to consolidate the gains of reorganization. Perhaps no gain was more significant than the
triumph of a full year of professional study as the criterion
of professional standing. As of 1923, the profession was
being served, as we have seen, by an ill-coordinated array
of training agencies, often referred to indiscriminately as
"library schools"; and, while the duration of their programs
ranged from a few weeks up to two years, each agency laid
some claim to qualifying recruits for professional standing.
While all of this was confusing, the mandate of the BEL assumed that all components of the training system in existence

at the time (training classes, summer schools as well as library schools) were to have a permanent place: the job was
simply one of better coordination--some orderly division of
labor among the competing agencies.

The outcome of the Board's work was different--and
unforeseen. Its first step had been to formulate and obtain
ALA approval, not of one set of standards but five. The
other four besides those for bona fide library schools were
for: (1) short-term summer schools in library science, approved January 1, 1926;[30] (2) short-term training classes,
March 7, 1926;[31] (3) short-term apprentice classes, also
March 7;[32] and (4) curricula for school library work, approved the following October. [33] The important thing to observe, however, in comparing the five sets is that they were
all given a common polarity--the use of a full year of basic
study as the standard for obtaining recognition as a professional librarian.

This cornerstone of the whole accreditation program
was cemented into the standards in different ways. For example, minimum standards for summer schools divided these
so-called "schools" into four categories, Types I to IV. The
two of top rank, Types I and II, were the ones that met minimum standards of accredited library schools, the sole difference between the two being that Type I had in fact to be
conducted by such a school. Types III and IV provided room
for "schools" of lower rank.

Training in school library work had to be handled dif-
ferently. Minimum standards encouraged the slanting of instruction in the fundamentals of general library work so as
to acquaint students with problems peculiar to school library
service, and they also encouraged opening the instruction to
college seniors. For teachers who were to handle the library as a part-time responsibility, the standards made room
for a short-term, 16-semester hour program narrowed to instruction as practical for the purpose as possible. But all
this was done as a concession to emergency conditions: the
premise of the whole school library training program was
that all full-time school librarians should receive their library
education in an accredited library school.

Training classes were oriented to the basic first year
in yet another way. Their function was looked upon as being
essentially auxiliary--to relieve accredited library schools of
responsibility for training in elementary library operations and

by so doing to supply the local library, but not the profession at large, with subprofessional assistants with at least a high school education. In these several ways, the entire structure of standards and accreditation was built on the principle that no one was to be regarded as suitably prepared for a professional career who had not covered the ground represented by the first-year curriculum.

The experiment in this regard was doubly successful. Manpower standards for library service were rising. A full year of professional study was an attainable minimum standard for professionals, and library-school graduates, by their performance, confirmed the wisdom of using a full year's training as a norm. But the success did not end there. The profession needed an acceptable method of telling whether a person was a qualified librarian or not. Experience with national standards demonstrated the practicability of using graduation from an accredited library school for this purpose. The effect was for library-school training to gain acceptance as a de facto substitute for national certification.

What was the effect of the ascendancy of the library school on the permanence of other components of the training system?

The fact that the BEL produced but one set of minimum standards in 1933, not five sets as in 1925, hints at the answer. The other components disappeared or underwent changes to fit into a more unified system. Training classes were the first to lose out. Public interest and support for them waned as university-supported library schools gained strength, and financial difficulties of the depression sounded their death knell. Their final bid for survival as a formal component of the training system may be said to have been made in 1932 in a spirited debate, "Resolved, that the training class is passing."[34] The affirmative treated training classes and library schools as rivals and contended that the classes lacked the institutional base as well as the financial and professional resources required to compete with the schools any longer. In fact, the higher order of preparation increasingly being demanded by twentieth-century libraries was rendering training classes as formal centers of professional education obsolete. They tended to produce "a spurious class of workers halfway between clerical and professional grades, too good for one and not good enough for the other." The negative contended, on the other hand, that training classes and library schools each had a necessary

contribution to make, that the training class gave better training for a specific set of known tasks, and hence that the quality of work done by its graduates was actually better than
that of the imported library school graduate during the first
year or two while the latter was catching on to what to do.
While points were thus scored on both sides, an audience
vote upheld the position that the training class was passing
into history.   Individual classes survived and the gap in subprofessional training left by discontinuance of others was felt
for years; but no case was made for them better than the one
in 1932, and it was not enough.

        Summer schools survived a bit longer.   These
"schools" were short, their programs were adjustable, and
they were comparatively easy to staff.   Across the years,
they had proved their capacity to serve small libraries, and
the school library movement that got underway in the 1920s
enhanced their usefulness in this regard.   The number of
known schools climbed to 80 by 1930 and to more than a hundred by 1932.   This was their banner year, and enrollment
soared to well over 4,000.   Their gradual disappearance
thereafter is attributable to various influences of which the
most decisive were three which the BEL had a part in gen-
erating: (1) the success of summer sessions conducted as an
integral part of the programs of accredited library schools;
(2) growing awareness of the drawbacks of throwing on the
market "a lot of poor, cheap competition for those who are
better prepared;" and (3) better cooperation between educators
and librarians in upholding high standards of professional
training.

        It took several years to resolve a couple of abrasive
problems that interfered with the cooperation of these two
professions, educators and librarians, in matters of library
training.   One problem was whether the local public library
or the local board of education was to be responsible for library service to public schools.   The last sharp debate on
the subject, in 1934,[35] signals in a general way the beginning of undisputed acceptance of school libraries, manned by
personnel employed by the schools themselves, as the standard form of service.

        The second issue is often said to have arisen in 1926
when the ALA took the stand, in support of the BEL, that
full-time school librarians should all have a basic year of
library education the same as other librarians.   The criticism that educators dragged their feet on this is true of some,

but fails to go to the root of the difficulty. A more typical
attitude was expressed by President William F. Russell, of
Teachers College, whom the BEL retained as a consultant on
educational standards. Russell found the superintendents of
large city school systems to be agreed that "the properly
trained librarian must have all that the good teacher has and,
in addition, library training."[36] In the bright dawn of the
school library movement, these educators looked forward to
the possibility of rewards that would make the longer training
justifiable. When this possibility proved elusive, the only
recourse to many on both sides seemed to be to sacrifice
professional training standards either of teachers or of librarians; and it was this dilemma, created by the economics
of the situation, that strained relations between the two professions. Neither one was ready to make that kind of sacrifice.

        A trial middle-of-the-road solution was worked out by
a joint committee of the American Association of Teachers
Colleges and the American Library Association and was published in 1936 in a report entitled How Shall We Educate
Teachers and Librarians for Library Service in the School?[37]
It is based on a comprehensive analysis of experience with
curricula of different types, differentiates library training
needs for careers in teaching from those in librarianship,
formulates practical guidelines for organizing library instruction for teachers and teacher-librarians, and concludes with
suggested courses for the purpose for inclusion in programs
of teacher education. The report was warmly received on
all sides. It took account of the realities of the school library situation, but safeguarded basic standards both of library education and of teacher education and, in the process,
strengthened the role of the library as an educational instrument. The latter result was achieved by bringing out the
fact that teachers and school administrators were not being
adequately acquainted with the educational uses of the library,
and by showing how this defect in their training could and
should be remedied.

        The Curriculum. When Carl B. Roden criticized the
Williamson report for offering so little that was new,[38] it
was the meagre contribution toward improving the student's
library-school experience that was uppermost in his mind.
When one considers the period as a whole, progress in curriculum development was substantial although outdistanced by
progress made in other areas that have been discussed. It

was a period when the curriculum felt the effects of numerous outside influences--the rising level of student preparation,
changes in the scope and character of library service, and
not least the vogue of electives in American education generally.   As one thumbs contemporary library school catalogs,
nothing stands out more than the use of electives on proliferating specialties to accommodate these changes and enrich
instruction.   But there were other improvements besides
this.

Williamson's call for separate orders or levels of
training, professional and subprofessional, was met halfway
by limiting library-school instruction as much as possible to
library work of professional grade.   Whole sections of instruction in duties considered primarily subprofessional gradually
disappeared from the curriculum as a result--detailed methods
of ordering books, accessioning, shelving, taking inventory,
and circulation desk routines.   The BEL visits revealed inept organization of subjects and stimulated overdue improvements: one program, for example, gave "Women presidents
of the American Library Association" and "Great figures of
the American library world" (with overlap unspecified) co-
ordinate rank with "Cataloging" and "Children's library work."
Tighter organization of course work, shorn of responsibility
for subprofessional duties, facilitated compression of the essentials of general library work into one year.   Joseph
Wheeler was later to single this out as one of the outstanding
educational achievements between the two world wars. [39]

The Williamson report helped catalyze two other developments.   Accepting the curriculum "as it stands" as satisfactorily representing the demands of the profession,[40] Williamson found, on combing through library-school programs,
that, of twenty-five or more subjects in all, four absorbed
about half of the student's time.   These high priority subjects
were cataloging, classification, book selection, and reference
work.   They were further reinforced as the core of basic
professional instruction when the BEL selected them as the
only subjects in the suggested curriculum of accredited library
schools to be studied in both semesters.

A further advance dates from the Williamson proposal
that led to the establishment at California, Columbia, Illinois,
and Michigan of programs of advanced study leading to the
master's degree.   This second year was originally conceived
as the place for instruction dealing with types of work not
common to libraries of all types, but that idea had to be

changed.   School library work, for example, was soon being
taught at all three levels--before and during as well as after
the basic one-year curriculum.   The new master's program
came into its own as an opportunity for more searching study
of any aspect of librarianship, free of stifling restrictions.
It attracted mature librarians of demonstrated ability and
trained some of the foremost leaders of the rising generation.
Wilhelm Munthe, scanning the scene as an outsider, found
these programs well conducted and deplored the fact that
more students were not being drawn into them. 41

Finally, this is the period when library schools of the
rank and file began to come to terms with research.   Given
the long-standing orientation of library education, it was not
an accommodation to be made overnight.   The misgivings with
which the subject was initially approached is illustrated by
Williamson's paper of 1930 on "The place of research in library service. "42   As we have seen, library schools devoted
themselves to empirical learning--the sort that is advanced
by experience, not by research; but Williamson saw that conditions were changing this, and stated the problem well, saying that there was a dearth of library research and that the
reason was not a dearth of problems requiring scientific study
but lack of training.   In consequence, practically no librarians
were qualified to do research.   Having stated the problem,
the paper flounders from then on: it is inconclusive on where
research training fits into the program as well as on how it
is to be conducted.   The discussion ends up in uncertainty as
to what sort of priority research training is really entitled
to.   Research products of students in training were written
off as unlikely to amount to much and, besides, only a small
percentage of students "will ever go on to the doctorate or
engage in scientific research for its own sake. "   The most
to be said, we are told, is that some attention to research
would yield better--more scientific--habits of thinking; and
these would accrue to all, not merely to the few whose special aptitude for research led them to go on and make a career of it.

The historian cannot rest on his oars with a chronicle
of concrete developments such as these and nothing more.
The claims of intelligibility obligate him to look beneath them
for some thread of interconnection with one another and with
the past.   Between the two world wars, new curricula emerged
which were both unlike and akin to their predecessors.   The
best way to express the relationship is to say that the new
curricula offered the student a technical education of higher

grade than before. The point can be given context and perspective by referring briefly to Ernest J. Reece's Curriculum
in Library Schools. 43 Professor Reece's students remember
him as a well-informed expositor of ideas that, as he once
expressed it, were "in the air" around him. This book, the
fruit of his best years, is an illustration. It could hardly
be called a germinal work; but it perceptively sifts out the
most progressive developments of the time, relates them to
the profession's educational patrimony and presents a synthesis of contemporary theory and practice that stands head
and shoulders above anything else we have on the subject for
this period.

    The heart of the Curriculum in Library Schools con-
cerns the genesis, function and structure of the curriculum.
Reece was brought up in the technical education tradition,
and the treatment shows the deep hold that it had upon his
imagination as of the 1930s. The type of learning to be cultivated by library schools remains library economy shorn of
subprofessional activities. The norms of accepted library
practice serve as the fountainhead of the curriculum: the
courses to be mastered are derived and updated by following
the advancement of librarianship as measured by professional
progress out in the field--progress in which the schools are
seen as being at best not more than junior partners. The
function of the curriculum is to condense the best of the practitioner's thought and practice, the test of the good curriculum being how faithfully it represents library work as students have to "face" it on becoming practitioners themselves.
For purposes of shaping the structure of the curriculum,
Reece adopts, with one significant change, the procedure followed by Dewey and his generation. He found these pioneers
to be groping, as indeed they were, for an inventory of practical methods or skills that fall to the staffs of libraries to
perform. The difference is that Reece's analysis is considerably more elaborate and complete: the result is perhaps
the most incisive spelling out of library operations into their
ABC's to be found anywhere in the literature. All of Dewey's
thousand and one duties comprised in library work are broken
down into 13 categories which are brought together under four
main headings: (1) fashioning a library collection, (2) organizing and caring for the collection, (3) using a library collection, and (4) directing a library enterprise. Using accepted
practices in these four areas as raw materials, Reece pro-
ceeds to derive a basic list of close to a hundred topics to
be covered, which are then arranged under ten curriculum
divisions as follows:

Selection and evaluation of stock
Trade and national bibliography
Acquisition methods
Cataloging
Care and preservation of the collection
Reference books and reference work
Guidance of readers
Teaching the use of books and libraries
Administration of libraries
History and production of books

But while traditional curriculum theory remains unchanged, the book shows that the technical education of students was, as of the 1930s, being conducted on a higher
plane. It was higher because, as brought out above, the
newer curricula concentrated on training in the professional
aspects of library work, in the expectation that training
classes would provide such training as was needed in subprofessional duties. It was higher, secondly, because of the
enlarged scope of the new curricula. Library economy tended for
years to dwell on duties within the four walls of a library; but by
the time of Learned's American Public Library and the Diffusion
of Knowledge, [44] this constricted frame of reference was being
pushed aside as library-school courses reached out to encompass all of the responsibilities involved in handling library
service viewed as a major branch of the public service. It
was higher, thirdly, because research was in the air and a
place began to be made for it. It was a somewhat anomalous
place to be sure, but research was no longer left out entirely.
Reece was convinced that field conditions justified "something"
along this line, but the barometer of justifiability used was
the nature of inquiries received by placement officers. It
was a sort of box-office standard of measure which led to
his taking the cautious stand that research training could be
considered an acceptable "extension" of the curriculum but
not an indigenous component of it.

In Conclusion

The cross-currents of thought on educational policy
and organization that date from the Asbury Park meeting
eddied to a crest in the months following publication of the
Williamson report in 1923. It fell to the Temporary Library
Training Board, appointed the same year, to lead the way to
a consensus on what to do. It found the Williamson report
more of a compelling call for reconstruction than a blueprint

to follow, and developed a blueprint of its own. Finding the
demand for librarians of high capability to be expanding, the
Board decided on a strategy that would call on the American
Library Association to accept responsibility for filling a long-
standing void of central leadership and professional control.
To this end, it proposed that the Association establish a permanent Board of Education for Librarianship and empower it
to study library manpower requirements, assess the adequacy
of existing training agencies to meet these requirements, foster educational performance of high standard, and promote in
other ways as needed the interests of library education.

        The ALA approved the proposal and the BEL went to
work in 1924. Composed of librarians of stature, the Board
gathered hitherto inaccessible information, quickly established
a place for itself as a national clearinghouse for information
and counsel, advised on grants to library schools, worked
closely with cognate organizations, and opened new doors
leading to scholarships and fellowships. But its best work
was done in formulating standards for training agencies of
all types and in accrediting library schools. The minimum
standards which were approved in 1925 stimulated rapid progress along a broad front. They benefited recruiting and the
organization of instruction. They upheld the importance of
full-time, high-quality staff, stressed the importance of providing library schools the administrative control, the staff
and the other resources required for work of creditable grade;
but they had their greatest impact in fostering the transfer of
library education to established centers of learning, in raising
the level of preprofessional education and establishing a basic
year of professional study as the minimal requirement for
recognition as a trained librarian.

        In 1933, these original standards for library schools
were revised, and this time no other standards were produced. The BEL had in 1925 and 1926 formulated standards
for the entire array of training agencies (library schools,
summer schools, training and apprentice classes, and special
curricula for school library work), but in so doing had used
the minimum requirement for professional status just mentioned
as the pole toward which all five sets of standards were oriented. The result was the ascendancy of the library school,
the only agency empowered to offer a full year; and the success of the experiment reduced the need of standards for any
of its competitors. The 1933 revision accomplished other results. The new standards removed inequities that had given
rise to complaints, and switched away from specific require-

ments imposed from outside the schools toward greater emphasis on local initiative and responsibility for producing educational results of high quality.   This was in line with a general trend within the accreditation movement.

The BEL was an experiment in centralizing responsibility for initiative in and control over professional education --territory into which the ALA had not ventured before.   It was an experiment that yielded much success and a few failures.   Success in producing information useful for decision-making purposes led the Board to project for itself a continuing role in more basic research which failed to materialize. The principal failure, however, grew out of attempting to take over responsibility for planning the library-school curriculum.

Looking at the period as a whole, the greatest achievements lay in managing the reorganization of library education and in creating a better climate for it to thrive in.   The achievements are at once a tribute to, and consistent with, the competence of a Board of Education for Librarianship composed predominantly--and for years completely--of selected laymen on whom responsibility for much of the creative work of the period fell.   Ernest J. Reece's comprehensive Curriculum in Library Schools shows that the main line of educational progress was toward developing a higher form of technical education.   It was a trend that embraced various specific improvements.   Accelerated progress of the library movement was producing new specialties and library schools accommodated them by adding numerous elective courses as required.   The professional character of the instruction program was improved by leaving responsibility for training in subprofessional duties to local training classes.   Other noteworthy lines of progress included: improved organization of courses and instruction, compression of the essentials of general library work into one year of study, development of a reasonably uniform core of basic instruction, a separate year of advanced study leading to the master's degree, and an awakening of interest in giving professional study and scholarly research a meaningful relation to one another.

REFERENCES

1.   ALA Board of Education for Librarianship.   "12th Annual Report," ALAB 30, 1936, 316-27.

2. The Williamson Report: Comment from the Library
    Schools, " LJ 48, 1923, 899-910.

3. "The Williamson Report II: Comment from Librarians, "
    LJ 48, 1923, 999-1006.

4. LJ 48, 1923, 899-900.

5. Walter, Frank K. "A Dynamic Report, " LJ 48, 1923,
    709-11.

6. Anderson, Edwin H. "Training for Library Service, "
    LJ 49, 1924, 462-66.

7. Strohm, Adam. "Self-measurement, " Public Libraries
    29, 1924, 61-63.

8. "What the Temporary Library Training Board Is Doing, "
    ALAB 18, 1924, 5-9.

9. ALA Temporary Library Training Board. "Report, "
    ALAB 18, 1924, 257-88.

10. ALAB 18, 1924, 197-98.

11. ALA Board of Education for Librarianship. 1st Annual
    Report. Chicago: American Library Association,
    1925, p. 5.

12. Ibid. , pp. 13-14.

13. ALA Board of Education for Librarianship. Committee
    on Terminology. Standard Terminology in Educa-
    tion, with Special Reference to Librarianship. Pro-
    visional ed. Chicago: American Library Associa-
    tion, 1927. Mimeographed.

14. ALA Editorial Committee. Sub-committee on Library
    Terminology. ALA Glossary of Terms, with a
    Selection of Terms in Related Fields, prepared by
    Elizabeth H. Thompson. Chicago: American Li-
    brary Association, 1943.

15. Wilson, Louis R. "Informal Report of the Board of
    Education for Librarianship, " ALAB 22, 1928, 368-
    72.

Generation of Reorganization   221

16. Roden, Carl B. "President's Address: Ten Years,"
    ALAB 22, 1928, 311-18.

17. ALA Board of Education for Librarianship. "7th Annual
    Report," ALAB 25, 1931, 190-217.

18. "ALA Secretary's report," ALAB 26, 1932, 195-96.

19. Munn, Ralph. Conditions and Trends in Education for
    Librarianship; a Report on the Program in Training
    for Library Service Adopted by the Board of Trus-
    tees of Carnegie Corporation of New York, March
    19, 1926, Together with the Report of Committee
    on Library Training, November, 1934--and Other
    Documents. New York: Carnegie Corporation of
    New York, 1936. This was one of three recom-
    mendations. The other two were: (1) to treat the
    one-year course as the area of primary importance
    in the development of library service and (2) to re-
    lieve the BEL, in accordance with its request, of
    responsibility for recommending Corporation grants
    to library schools for purposes of regular main-
    tenance.

20. ALA Board of Education for Librarianship. 4th Annual
    Report. Chicago: American Library Association,
    1928, pp. 14-17.

21. Wilson, Louis R., op. cit.

22. ALA Board of Education for Librarianship. 1st Annual
    Report. Chicago: American Library Association,
    1925, p. 26.

23. ALA Board of Education for Librarianship. "7th Annual
    Report," ALAB 25, 1931, p. 196.

24. "Letter from Mr. Dana to the ALA read at the meeting
    of the Council held at Chicago, December 30, 1927,"
    LJ 53, 1928, 93-95.

25. ALA. A Survey of Libraries in the United States, Con-
    ducted by the American Library Association. Chi-
    cago: American Library Association, 1926-27.
    4v.

26. "Report of Special Committee to Consider Communica-

tion of Mr. John Cotton Dana," ALAB 22, 1928, 384-86.

27. "ALA Activities Committee Report," ALAB 24, 1930, 607-80.

28. Wilson, Louis R. "The Board of Education for Librarianship," ALAB 25, 1931, 5-11.

29. ALA Board of Education for Librarianship. [Report on minimum requirements for library schools], ALAB 27, 1933, 610-13.

30. ALA Board of Education for Librarianship. 2nd Annual Report. Chicago: American Library Association, 1926, pp. 59-64.

31. Ibid., pp. 66-67.

32. Ibid., pp. 68-69.

33. Ibid., pp. 71-74.

34. [Report of the joint meeting of the ALA Professional Training Class Section], ALAB 26, 1932, 603-04. Margie M. Helm, Western Kentucky State Teachers College Library and Harold F. Brigham, Louisville Free Public Library, upheld the affirmative; Rena Reese, Cincinnati Public Library and Clarence E. Sherman, Providence Public Library, the negative.

35. Clark, Charlotte H. and Louis P. Latimer. "The Taxpayer and Reading for Young People: Would a 'Library in Every School' Justify the Cost?" LJ 59, 1934, 9-15. The case for continuing to entrust responsibility for library service to children and young people to public libraries, presented by the Supervisor of Work with Schools and the Directory of Work with Children, of the Washington, D.C., Public Library. They are answered by Lucile F. Fargo and Helen S. Carpenter, " Economy or Efficiency? Let the Taxpayer Decide," LJ 59, 1934, 100-05. Miss Fargo, author of the pioneer work, The Library in the School, Chicago: American Library Association, 1928, was at the time Research Associate in the Columbia University School of Library Service; Miss Carpenter, Assist-

ant to Superintendent of Libraries, N. Y. City Board
of Education.

36. ALA Board of Education for Librarianship. 2nd Annual
Report. Chicago: American Library Association,
1926, pp. 38-39. See also School and Society 24,
1926, 113-18.

37. Joint Committee of the American Association of Teach-
ers Colleges and the American Library Association.
How Shall We Educate Teachers and Librarians for
Library Service in the Schools: Findings and
Recommendations, with a Library Science Curricu-
lum for Teachers and Teacher-librarians. N. Y.:
Columbia University Press, 1936。

38. Op. cit.

39. Wheeler, Joseph L. Progress and Problems in Education for Librarianship. New York: Carnegie Corporation of New York, 1946, p. 59.

40. Op. cit., p. 24.

41. Munthe, Wilhelm. American Librarianship from a
European Angle; an Attempt at an Evaluation of
Policies and Activities. Chicago: American Li-
brary Association, 1939, p. 141.

42. Williamson, Charles C. "The Place of Research in
Library Service," Library Quarterly 1, 1931, 1-17.

43. Reece, Ernest J. The Curriculum in Library Schools.
New York: Columbia University Press, 1936.

44. Op. cit.

Chapter 9

TRANSITION TO UNIVERSITY STANDARDS

The main advances made during the first half of the twentieth century, we said earlier, came in two steps, the first of which has been treated in the preceding chapters. We turn now to the second, which is the climax of the story.

The Standards of 1951 and Their Setting

New standards for accrediting library schools were approved by the American Library Association July 13, 1951.[1] The best way to catch hold of their significance is to call attention to two incompatible conceptions of education that we have encountered. In Chapter 6, we saw how a characteristic pattern of thinking about the nature and function of professional education grew up around the commitment of library schools to library economy--not only grew up but, reinforced by success and overlaid by sentiment, came to serve as the accepted mold for shaping library school training. According to this conception, library economy constitutes the body of knowledge and skills that is the distinctive province of the professional librarian, and it consists of those norms of thought and procedure that govern or ought to govern library practice. This type of learning is of a practical nature in relation to which the modes of thought and procedure employed in the advancement of theoretical learning were deemed to be, if not alien, at least irrelevant; for advances in library economy were understood to be made, not by critical inquiry and research, but by trial and success in the field of practice. Librarianship, we must remember, was still considered not a branch of learning so much as a branch of library administration. Chapter 6 brings out not only how this standard pattern of thinking affected the spirit, content and structure of professional training, but how it downgraded the importance of education in the making of librarians. High-grade pro-

fessional capabilities, as we noticed, had to be recruited, because the qualities required for professional work of distinction were supposed to be inborn. Dewey expressed this point
with his familiar half-truth that you can polish agate, but not
a pumpkin. The often quoted maxim, "Great librarians are
born, not made," put it more bluntly.

Chapter 7 conceives education to be a force capable of
playing a more vital role in the making of the professional.
The Carnegie Foundation for the Advancement of Teaching was
established at the beginning of the twentieth century when the
nation found itself entrusting more and more responsibility
for social leadership to professions--some young, some old
--and addressed itself to the neglected problem of how society
goes about effectively developing a profession. The answer
it hit upon can be expressed in three propositions. First, a
profession's usefulness can be enhanced by well-designed
buildings, suitable equipment, sound legislation and strong
financial support; but the master key is manpower development. A profession's service, the President of the Foundation eloquently emphasized, rises or tends to rise to the water-level set by the qualified personnel available, but never
rises any higher than that. Second, education has become
throughout the civilized world the universal business of society because, when skillfully handled, it has proved to be by
far the most powerful instrument that a people can use consciously to shape its future. If professional education fails
to produce manpower qualified to do this job, it has to try
harder. Third, the most effective strategy for developing
adequate manpower is to adopt the "university principle" in
conducting the professional's education.

The "university principle" introduces a standard that
eludes precise definition. If one asks when does professional
education meet the standard, a pat answer is not possible,
but certain considerations are important to keep in mind. A
university base provides an opportunity to enrich and round
out professional education by drawing freely on supporting
disciplines. A university standard is one that places a high
premium on original and incisive thinking. It fosters critical inquiry and research, which are considered essential to
problem-solving and the advancement of learning in the field.
These considerations are prominent not only in the writings
of Dr. Pritchett and Learned but clearly were in Flexner's
mind when he traced the defects of British and French medical schools to the fact that, in both countries, medical education arose out of medical practice. For a model to use in

establishing the Johns Hopkins University Medical School,
Gilman turned to Germany, where the medical school had
been university-based from the outset.   The close coupling
of university learning and medical practice had been spurred
by Helmholtz's insight into the intimate relation between illuminating teaching and original investigation, around which
insight the modern university took shape.   Hopkins--and the
Carnegie reports--rode the wave of the future.

The rubrics used to outline the 1951 accreditation
standards correspond closely to those of the 1933 standards,
and the trend from centralized to local leadership and control in library education continues; but there are two major
changes.   First, the educational structure is rebuilt around
the master's as the basic professional degree.   The fifth-
year bachelor's vanishes from the scene.   The classification
of schools into Type I, Type II, and Type III is discontinued.
And graduate-level professional education becomes the un-
equivocal aim and standard.

Second, the 1951 document expresses fresh interest in
and compliance with accepted university standards.   This
shows up in various ways, but is nowhere more noticeable
than in ending the academic isolation of the library-school
program.   The entire five years of higher education are
treated as an integral whole and the university is called on
to support efforts to draw on its full resources to produce
imaginatively planned student programs.   This move was foreshadowed by John Dale Russell in connection with the Illinois
survey which is to be discussed farther on. [2]   He observed
that librarians in real life find themselves playing roles (in
administration, community service and leadership, human relations, and scholarship in different areas) that draw on several disciplines, but that contemporary library education was
addressing itself narrowly to roles of within-the-walls technicians.   The five-year program is flexible and is a blend of
fundamental academic and practical purposes. [3]   These purposes stress the value of a sound general education, thorough
comprehension of the theoretical foundations and interdisciplinary aspects of librarianship, and familiarity with the functions and methods of research.   They stress also the importance of general bibliography and reference, of knowledge of
the literature of the broad subject fields, and of the ability
to evaluate library resources in these fields.   Finally, the
list of purposes stresses the importance of an incisive assessment of the state of the art and of being adequately
equipped on graduation to serve in one or more specialized
areas of library work.

The best way to put the matter in historical perspective is to say that the 1951 standards signalled the adoption of a new model of professional education--a shift to a more fruitful conception of the educational process than the outworn model of apprenticeship schooling could be patched up to offer. Spelled out more concretely, the standards obligate the library school, in cooperation with its parent institution, to transmit the cumulated knowledge and intellectual skills required to maximize the social usefulness of librarianship. This fund of knowledge and skill embraces but is considerably broader than library economy. The transmission of existing knowledge, while it continues to be the largest and most obvious element in the educational process, is no longer regarded as the only element. In terms of the university model, the higher levels of the process impose on the school the responsibility to increase knowledge by research, to criticize existing professional practice in the light of advancing knowledge, and to develop manpower with the theoretical insight, critical acumen and research capability to perform at these higher levels.

The object of this concluding chapter is to trace the origins of the trend toward the use of this new model. Chief among the factors that account for the shift were: (1) the gradual acceptance of library education as a university responsibility; (2) the triumph of a bold experiment, the establishment of the Graduate Library School of the University of Chicago; and (3) the fresh thought given in the 1940s to reconstruction of the first-year program. The term "trend" is used to avoid oversimplification of a prolonged transition. Universities have individuality; they do not observe in detail the same standards; and the ALA action of 1951, while it was a milestone in the advance, marks neither its beginning nor end. The Charters curriculum study described in the preceding chapter was the last thoroughgoing attempt to organize library education in accordance with the traditional model. It centered attention on the norms of operating methods and considered the function of the library school to be that of preparing practitioners to perform the round of jobs that are involved in different kinds of library work. It was an approach that was to remain unchallenged at the first-year level until the 1940s; but the collapse of the Charters study in the late 1920s and the deepening tone of criticism of the 1930s make it clear in retrospect that this once-adequate conception of training was breaking down before a better approach was defined, worked out and accepted.

Acceptance of Library Education as a University Responsibility

Until inflation struck American higher education after World War II, the major private universities remained the pacesetters in standards of excellence, or at least considered themselves as being so. As of the time of the Williamson report, a few library schools were located at great state universities but most of them were located, as we have seen, at strong libraries or at degree-granting institutions whose charters emphasized technical education. Not until the library schools of the New York State Library and the New York Public Library merged to form Columbia's School of Library Service in 1926 and until the Graduate Library School was established at the University of Chicago in 1928 was a library school to be found at a ranking private university. The action of these two universities forwarded the movement to transfer library schools to academic surroundings and they were in turn to help library education accommodate itself to university standards.

We need to bear in mind that the policy to be taken as to the place of library education in American universities was but a piece of a larger problem: what to do in the face of the rising demand for training in other newer callings that were also seeking professional recognition. The years following World War I witnessed rapid expansion of courses in social welfare, business, public administration, public health, nursing, teacher education and other fields where trained personnel was in growing demand--expansion which in the aggregate was spectacular. The reasons for the expansion were compelling: the growing fund of knowledge that lent itself to social uses, attendant development of specialized fields, the desire for higher education having relevance to one's life's work, and the popularity of the land-grant colleges in fusing general and vocational education. Universities could hardly be expected to accept responsibility for all kinds of vocations, but where was the line to be drawn?

Nobody bothered to answer at first. Academia had led an encloistered life so long that it was a heady experience to find its usefulness suddenly expanding at such a rate. The generous impulse to be of public service led to excesses that were caustically exposed by Abraham Flexner in his Oxford lectures, Universities: American, English, German, first published in 1930 and reprinted with an introduction by Clark Kerr in 1968. Flexner drew the line at the other ex-

treme. Modern universities, he contended, are not service
stations. They have special functions to perform and weaken
the performance of their big job when they meddle with functions that are properly not theirs. Their proper function is
to address themselves to the advancement of knowledge, to
the study of problems from whatever source they come, and
to the training of men and women--all at the highest level.
This should be done wholeheartedly and unreservedly: the
unique responsibility of the university professor is his responsibility for and commitment to learning. Flexner believed
that a few professional schools belong in the university--
though very few besides medicine and law--and emphasized
that schools or departments of "a vocational character" do
not belong there. Library science is among the fields cited
as belonging "elsewhere than on the university campus."[4]
It was a forceful criticism uttered at a strategic moment
when the depression was stimulating re-examination of university commitments and priorities.

        The case for university responsibility was presented
by William Warner Bishop in October, 1933, to the Association of American Universities.[5] The argument of his paper
on "The status of library schools in universities" is, first,
that training in librarianship must chiefly be the training of
college graduates. No amount of training in library methods,
he contends, will supply an adequate educational foundation
for a profession made up of persons who spend their lives
with books and must perforce be acquainted with ideas and
the content of many books. It is this necessity that has
pushed training in librarianship out of the undergraduate curriculum where part of it at least may be said to belong.
Second, formal instruction is the best and cheapest way to
provide the training. Third, library activities stratify themselves into three fairly distinct grades, and library schools
have pointed their training toward the middle grade. In so
doing, the schools are responsible for features of American
librarianship which are a source of pride even in academic
communities. This training is based on a one-year curriculum which is indispensable for further instruction and professional progress. Universities are well-equipped to conduct a unified program which includes training beyond the
first year. There is a need for such a program, and no
other agency but the university has the resources necessary
to do the job.

        In attaining "true university status," Bishop conceded,
library schools still had a piece to go, especially in faculty

development; but he urged universities to look beyond the depression and beyond current criticism and to take a sympathetic part in furthering their development. Much of the ad-
verse criticism, he believed, came from persons who "have
never studied the curricula of these schools, nor for that
matter, considered carefully the structure and organization
of modern libraries" with their huge numbers of books in
many languages, their intricate services, their direct aid to
scholarship, and their service to the public at large. "Analysis of the modern library's work would reveal to such persons, I am confident, a need for training at the graduate
level and under university control.... It would be a great
pity if the existing financial crisis and the existing confusion
in library training agencies ... should lead to any precipitate
action against library schools in universities. "

     He asked the Association to face the alternative square-
ly. "If the universities decline to continue their responsibility for training librarians; if they decide that this is vocational and not professional training and hence unworthy of a place
in the body politic of the university, what will be the result?"
The training would have to go on somewhere: it would simply
fall to agencies that were not as well-equipped to do it. The
result would be disastrous for libraries, including university
libraries. "In self-protection it would seem that the universities should strengthen their few library schools by every
means within their power. "

     Two other pertinent addresses to the Association of
American Universities were delivered by Dean Guy Stanton
Ford of the University of Minnesota in 1930 and Dean Charles
B. Lipman of the University of California in 1943. These
leading representatives of higher learning, while sharply critical of contemporary library education, both took a broader
view of the university's responsibility than Flexner. The
gist of Dean Ford's position is that graduate study is the distinguishing feature of a university and that the test of what
belongs at the graduate level is not the subject, but the method of study. "Whatever the field, the method and spirit, if
it is to be graduate in the true sense, will be the method of
inquiry and research...."[6] The dilemma to be faced in organizing professional study at the graduate level, he explains,
is that the spirit of inquiry is "alien to most professional
training and tradition, at least in America. " The reason is
that professional study must produce skilled practitioners by
imparting necessary techniques, and American professional
education has set a high standard in this. Without slighting

the responsibility to produce well-trained practitioners, however, various professions have demonstrated that benefits
can be derived from research which eminently reward all efforts to support and inspire it, and "If graduate work is undertaken and the spirit of inquiry moves on the waters of any
profession, change will come not on the surface alone but in
the depths." Medicine and agriculture are cited as convincing examples. Other professions described as having reached
varying stages of research development include education,
business, dentistry, and librarianship. Ford had high expec-
tations of librarianship but found it as of 1930 "one of those
most concerned with expedients and routines.... We now
have a graduate library school [at the University of Chicago]
and so far as I can make out the institution that is blessed
with it would give half the endowment for a program that
would justly be called graduate work."7

Dean Lipman likewise acknowledges a responsibility
for professional education but opposes allowing programs of
inferior quality to drag down academic standards. He had in
mind newer professions, with which he associates librarianship, where "the process of training consists to a large degree ... of pouring information into the minds of the students," a large part of it essentially ephemeral. He questions the justification for a graduate professional curriculum
anywhere that (1) lacks a well organized body of knowledge
of a high order intellectually and (2) consists of courses
"which are entirely (or nearly so) informational in character
and the information such as to be subject to change every
year with the vicissitudes and exigencies through which that
subject passes as time goes on."8

Here are two searching questions brought forward on
behalf of concerned representatives of the American university. One is whether the methods of inquiry and research
that characterize "graduate work in the true sense" can be
fruitfully applied in the study and development of librarianship. The other concerns the intellectual quality of the basic
curriculum as conventionally organized. The rest of the chapter is devoted to the resolution of these two problems.

The Graduate Library School--
A Successful Experiment

In 1926, the University of Chicago accepted an unsoli-
cited Carnegie Corporation gift of a million dollars to estab-

lish a library school of a new type, as different from existing library schools as the Johns Hopkins University Medical
School was at its foundation from existing medical schools.
Two years later, in 1928, the resultant Graduate Library
School set out with four professors, a handful of select students and an unstructured program to blaze a new path in
library education. Other universities were to take a hand in
developing advanced study and research, but Chicago played
the central role and this account is limited to it. The resultant picture will be less general but sharper. George A.
Works, the first head, staked out the course, saying that
when the Board of Education for Librarianship accredits a
library school as "graduate," the term means nothing more
than that college graduation is required for admission: these
schools are primarily concerned with passing on to their students a body of principles and practices that have been found
useful in operating libraries. The University of Chicago authorities were not interested in a school of that type. "They
were interested in a library school only if it were to be a
graduate school in the sense that its primary objective was
the extension of the boundaries of knowledge relating to libraries and librarianship. "9

There were no precedents for the new school to follow and the going was rough the first few years. Thunder
came from the left. Flexner scolded Chicago, Columbia,
Western Reserve and state universities--as well as the Carnegie Corporation--for their part in establishing library
schools, believing as he did that library training was too
vocational to be the province of, or responsive to, serious
inquiry. This dismal view, however, was not shared along
the Midway. Other academic departments took a cordial
view of the new school's platform and cooperated from the
start in carrying it into effect.

A storm came from the right and brought two confron-
tations. The first one is not fully documented, but when
Works abruptly accepted the presidency of Connecticut State
College, the editor of the ALA Bulletin invited an explanation
of why his tenure was cut so short, and the reply indicates
that a major factor had been the policy of the School and
who was to control it. Conditions inside the University, he
wrote, argued well for the School's future: the climate was
congenial and experience with enrollment showed that there
was an adequate supply of qualified students to warrant a
school of this type. Outside the University, however, were
some who were impatient for results, and the context makes

it plain that they had pressed their own ideas as to how to
get them. The School, he urged, "should not be dominated
by any particular interest as to the historical, administrative, etc. " Even more important, it should not "come to
be regarded as an adjunct of an association or organization. "
The University of Chicago should be free to develop it in accord with its ideals of research and the needs of the profession. [10]

       The next bolt struck in 1931. In the first issue of
the Library Quarterly, Douglas Waples outlined the School's
policy at greater length than Works had done, saying that it
sought to meet the University's standards of scholarship; con-
fined its attention to research, leaving to other library
schools responsibility for passing on the profession's accumulated experience in running libraries; concentrated on producing each year, with an enrollment limited to about five, a
few students imbued with the spirit of investigation; sought
to integrate their work with related fields of learning; and
published studies significant enough to justify it.   Then, after
discussing problems of long-range research and the nature of
library science, he concluded with an extensive list of investigations that had been made by the School since 1928. [11]
Seymour Thompson, of the University of Pennsylvania, in a
reply entitled, "Do we want a library science?" saw little
good coming to the profession from studies of the kind the
GLS was conducting. He had rejoiced upon learning that the
dream of a graduate library school was to become an actu-
ality, but was disappointed in a program which he found to
be so obtuse to tradition and practical library needs. If we
can have a science only by adopting the psycho-sociological
laboratory methods used by the School, he concluded, the profession does not want a library science. [12]   The two authors
thereupon each produced a rebuttal to the other[13] but failed
to reconcile differences and left the School bogged in contro-
versy.

       The two incidents are related and gain added meaning
when set in context.   At the time the School was getting under
way, few professions if any depended more on central leader--
ship in and control over the education of recruits than the
library profession.   The practice among professional associations of pressing higher institutions to listen to them on matters of professional education was too common to cause surprise at the ALA's attempts to influence the program of the
new school. [14] Universities were of course entitled to auton-
omy in policy; in time, they demanded it; and the GLS was

the first library school to do it.   Winning this procedural
battle, however, did not settle what the cross-fire was all
about.   The crux of the problem was whether and to what
extent the School could or would produce a program having
demonstrable relevance to the profession's leadership responsibilities and requirements.   Librarians had worked for a
new type of school to do a job that needed doing, but they
were not clear how it was to be done.   All they were clear
about was that the GLS was not fulfilling their hopes and ex-
pectations.   Even among its well-wishers were many who
felt that a program as narrow as the one unveiled so far was
not imaginatively geared to the needs of the profession.

        The sharp Waples-Thompson encounter has commonly
been set down as a conflict of personalities.   It is best understood in impersonal terms as the first major collision of
the two educational traditions mentioned at the beginning of
this chapter, which had yet to be reconciled to one another.
Thompson's background had imbued him with the ways and
values of the technical-education tradition, and he had strong
feelings about preserving them.   On the other hand, the GLS
was undertaking in the best academic tradition to employ the
same tools of scholarship that had demonstrated their usefulness in other fields of professional endeavor.   This was
something new and unsettling.   Here was a small faculty concerned more about training in scientific research than in library economy, more about new sociological data than the
cultivation of genteel learning.   They were questioning rather
than accepting and promoting the best-known library standards,
and looked for future development of librarianship to come
not from the inventiveness of enterprising librarians alone,
but from delineating, testing and developing library theory.
The trouble with it all, in Thompson's view, was its obtuse-
ness to what matters most.   He makes it clear that he considered the main purpose of the profession to be "bibliothecal"--that is, to know good books and diffuse knowledge
and appreciation of them.   Higher educational attainments,
he agreed, were essential to carrying out this mission, but
the education should have a humanistic base and outlook, and
emphasize "the body of techniques and opinion" that library
experience has accumulated.   He loyally claimed for these
bibliothecal principles "a humble place among the sciences
for they have demonstrated their soundness and are no more
subject to change than the principles of other sciences. "

        What then should take priority?   The chief need, in
his estimation, was "to revive the bibliothecal spirit, " not
to exalt the search for minute, sometimes trivial, facts.

By the time of Pearl Harbor a decade later, the Graduate Library School was to become, in the apposite phrase of Jesse Shera, "the greatest single force of its generation in American librarianship and American library education."15 Its triumph over doubt and opposition was the achievement of a capable faculty, of an undivided university, and especially of Louis Round Wilson, who left Chapel Hill with a distinguished record as Librarian of the University of North Carolina to become Dean in 1932. Dr. Wilson was a gifted persuader who undertook both to do a good job and to let it be known. Others shared the role of interpreter with him. Pierce Butler fittingly called his Introduction to Library Science16 a tract of the times because it states the case for treating the professional task of the librarian as being broader than bookmanship: it is to conduct a branch of public service generated and conditioned by society's interests and needs. Publication of this slender 118-page book was a first attempt to rationalize the relation of the profession to society, of library science to social science--a propaedeutic to a new philosophy of librarianship.

Carnovsky followed up in 1937 with a strong case for graduate study of university grade.17 After recounting understandable grounds for skepticism about it, he makes the point that it is not enough for library schools to serve as a training ground where library employees are fitted for work in established libraries. Graduate study has a higher function-- to assess the state of the art, identify problems and develop the competence and insight to solve them. In addition to interpreting the role of scholarship in problem-solving, the paper describes the opportunity for significant investigations that await "those who would be pioneers, provided they are willing to cast off too conventional modes of thought and have the courage to break new ground."

It was imperative that the new experiment be interpreted, but performance speaks louder than words, and in the case of the new School, performance spoke on several fronts. The crucial test was whether the advancement of librarianship could in fact be furthered by scholarly inquiry. Criticism of individual studies came early and was not to end soon, but skepticism about the relevance of scholarship to the future of the profession disappeared rapidly after 1935. Carleton B. Joeckel's dissertation, The Government of the American Public Library, an early product of interdisciplinary research, was published that year and won instant acclaim as a professional contribution of first magnitude.

The Library Quarterly tagged it as "authoritative." The review by Clarence B. Lester in the American Political Science Review was less restrained. Lester pointed out that
this was the first thoroughgoing study of the subject to be
made, and went on to say that "Dr. Joeckel's work is definitive in its presentation of governmental structure as it has
actually developed, and stimulating in its contribution to the
literature of the movement toward the large-area regional system for public library service."[18]

Dean Wilson took the position of Ford and Lipman
above, that because university standards treat research as
essential, it does not follow, as Works and Waples were disposed to assume at the outset, that this is all it should do;
so the program was significantly expanded. One conscious
objective was to strengthen professional literature. The National Union Catalog lists not fewer than 35 pre-1956 imprints
under "Chicago. University. Graduate Library School." The
list includes the Library Quarterly but not the University Library,[19] Post-war Standards for Public Libraries,[20] The
Geography of Reading,[21] and other influential contributions
produced wholly or in part by members of the GLS family.
No other library school approached this record of productiv-
ity.

Many of its publications consist of proceedings of institutes and conferences, a third feature of the expanding
program. The first institute, held for two weeks in 1936,
was on Library Trends.[22] It focused on policy-level problems of interest to city, county and extension-agency librarians. An interdisciplinary panel of sociologists, political
scientists, educators, and librarians reported significant
trends in society which had a bearing on library policies,
and reported findings of recent studies and the results of enterprising work being done in the field. Discussion from the
floor and between sessions went on from there. The ALA
Bulletin called it "one of the most significant events in the
library history of the year 1936,"[23] and the Journal of Higher Education found the proceedings "one of the most interesting and ... readable books that have recently appeared in
the field of library science."[24] The idea caught on because
it met a neglected need. A Library Journal review described
Current Issues in Library Administration,[25] the papers presented before the third institute, as a trail-blazing accomplishment.[26] Not all institutes (later conferences) have been
as germinal as this one; but a style was quickly developed
that has had a high yield of fruitfulness--summit meetings of

selected university scholars and practicing librarians designed
to bring together the most incisive thinking and provocative
experience of the time on problems of current interest. It
was an innovation that became a sort of national fixture.
The topics across the years read like a contents page of contemporary library history.

A fourth feature may be said to have been directed
toward giving the profession better intellectual tools to work
with. The whole GLS program was oriented, not toward
pouring accepted information into passive minds--although it
was recognized that students had to be informed--but toward
acquiring a working philosophy to serve as a compass to
guide them, toward developing their potential for critical and
cogent thinking, and learning how to use research as an instrument of problem-solving. All this took place within the
precincts of the university; but one particular instrument, the
survey, was put to brilliant use in the field. This is not the
place to detail the surveys of public, school and academic
libraries made by Carnovsky, Joeckel, Wilson and their students. They are numerous and their influence has been historic. The point to emphasize here is that the library survey, which has become a valued tool of library management,
was perfected by the GLS in the process of demonstrating
the relevance of scholarship of university grade to the leadership requirements of a vigorous, rapidly evolving profession.

In this way, the Johns Hopkins of American librarianship demonstrated the feasibility and worth of study organized
in accordance with rigorous university standards. From the
side of the consumer, one alumnus speaks of "the intellectual ferment and excitement that animated the atmosphere of
the GLS during the decade of the '30s. "[27] Throughout the
better part if not all of that decade, the thinking of most of
the profession, including the first-year library schools, remained dominated by the spirit and standards of technical
education; but the continued growth and deepening social significance of library service, the presence of the library school
in an academic environment, the growing proportion of uni-
versity-educated librarians, and the triumph of the GLS experiment all thrust into the foreground the problem of how
best to combine in the first-year program the merits of both
traditions, the technical and the academic. Creative work
on that problem dates from the 1940s.

Strengthening the Basic Professional Program*

The purpose of this section is "to throw light on the meaning of the turbulence in education for librarianship since the ALA Midwinter conference of December, 1945, and to relate the Columbia program to the general picture."

That conference is remembered for its concern about library personnel and remembered especially for ALA Council action on the Miller proposal on the future of Type III library schools. He emphasized that, according to ALA accreditation procedures, strengthening their role would not lower educational standards; that graduates of Type II and Type III schools normally receive the same beginning salaries; and that, if we relied on the undergraduate Type III school in place of the graduate-level Type II school, it would save a year's time for students and employers as well. Because of war-born shortages, employers were hard-pressed to wait. Favorable discussion followed, and the Council voted to ask the Board of Education for Librarianship to explore the proposal's possibilities. [28]

1946--Year of Decision

The Council's action threw the future of undergraduate professional education into the center of discussion. In her assessment of the situation as of the spring of 1946, Hazel Dean observed that the Type III solution had become the most popular possibility under consideration. [29] The most effective spokesman for the Type III school to emerge was the respected director of one of them--Harriet Howe, of Denver. She was the one, as she reminds us, who seconded the ALA Council motion to strengthen their position; and, when Joseph Wheeler came out against them in his Progress and Problems in Education for Librarianship, [30] asking why they should exist at all, it was Miss Howe who replied. She upheld the conception and the performance of the Type III schools, saying that when their graduates are compared with those of Type II schools, the difference depends less on the type of school than on how well the students were selected in the first place. [31]

---

*Based on a paper, "Ferment and Change in Education for Librarianship in the 1940's," presented to the Graduate School of the U.S. Department of Agriculture, December 9, 1949. All of the notes are recent.

Against this background, Denver's switch in 1947 to a
fifth-year program leading to the Master's degree was a dramatic event. The suddenly popular movement to strengthen
Type III schools collapsed; and overnight, Denver was in the
vanguard of a different movement altogether. Chicago also
inaugurated a one-year master's program in the fall of 1947,
and other schools followed in rapid succession. Seven
schools made the switch in 1948: Columbia, Emory, Illinois,
Michigan, Pittsburgh, Southern California, and Western Reserve. A letter from ALA of November 17, 1949, indicates
that some 20 of the 32 accredited schools had by then
switched over; and seven more reported plans to do so,
which would bring the total to 27.

The four busy years after December, 1945, had thus
brought a stunning reversal. The widely discussed proposal
to expand dependence on undergraduate professional education
was decisively rejected by the end of 1946, and after that
the profession gave support--unequivocal support for the first
time in our history--to graduate professional education as
the standard. A new and stronger pattern was taking form.
It varied as to details but featured rebuilding the basic program around a fifth-year master's degree. I shall refer to
this trend as "the new movement." It was so general that
further accreditation had stopped, pending development of a
new set of standards.

Origins of the New Movement

The heart of my assignment is to explain where the
character and impetus of the new movement came from, and
this is difficult because the story is not fully documented.
The common explanation goes something like this: "Post-
war conditions happened to be just right, and all it took was
someone to break the ice." But this is too general. It
leaves obscure the very things we need light on.

Take some random examples. In 1942, while the
Graduate Library School was discussing with the BEL their
plans to launch a first-year program, the question was raised
about Chicago's possible interest in developing a program
which the University and the profession would consider acceptable for the master's degree. The action would have
been timely, and was considered to be in line with the
School's record for pioneering action. GLS preferred to
launch a conventional BLS program but shifted to a fifth-

year master's program in 1947. Why in 1947 but not at the outset?

Another example. The Foster study on behalf of the BEL polled the 32 accredited library schools in 1943-44 to determine their attitude toward altering the degree structure and found "practically all of the accredited library schools of the country against granting the Master's degree for the basic library curriculum when it represents a fifth collegiate year,"[32] yet 27 of the schools had by 1949 approved, or were in process of approving, this shift. How account for this wholesale change in a period of time so short?

Or take Denver's quick change of position. The Denver faculty's commitment to the Type III school began to waver in time to signal that fact in July, 1946,[33] but no move was made to join in sweeping schools of this type aside until there was an opportunity to confer with library colleagues at the Midwinter conference in December, 1946. The faculty left that conference, we are told, convinced "that a new alignment of education for the library profession was desired by many librarians ... was imminent, and should not be ignored."[34] In a matter of days, the switch to the new master's program was cleared with Denver University authorities, and by February 7, 1947, clearance was being sought with the BEL. The picture that comes through is that of a responsive group of cooperators taking the initiative to put into effect locally a realignment which was too imminent nationally to be ignored. What snowballing influences persuaded the Denver faculty to favor this step over continuing a Type III program which entitled itself to their pride?

I shall treat factors best known to me and encourage other observers to fill in the gaps. Let us begin with things that set the stage for change, then turn to initiatives of the ALA and accredited library schools which together were, by 1946, precipitating a break with the existing pattern. The position of Type I and Type II schools in the library-education framework had hinged change of much significance on them, but it should be emphasized that library schools as a group united their efforts to bring the movement into being and push it along.

A More Acceptable Degree Structure

In 1924, the profession requested the Association of

American Universities to support awarding the master's degree for the completion of a year of professional study when
preceded by four years of acceptable college work.   The
AAU disapproved on the ground that the conventional library
school program was not worth it, but promised approval, according to James I. Wyer, as soon as graduate standards
were met. 35 The precise nature of these "graduate standards"
was not made clear; but librarians considered neither a certificate nor a second bachelor's degree a deserving professional credential.   Smoldering dissatisfaction became vocal
in the 1940s.   Other influences had to initiate the new movement, but once it got under way perhaps no other factor did
more to solidify national support for it than the chance it
offered to come to terms with a twenty-year old complaint.

Ambiguous Position of Type III Schools

      One of the major goals of the 1926 standards for li-
brary schools was to raise admission requirements.   Accordingly, a weighty criterion of acceptability for accreditation
was the amount of preprofessional education that a school
prescribed.   While the 1926 standards bore good fruit, they
were attacked on the ground that such a measure of acceptability was in reality not a measure of the quality of an instruction program at all.   The 1933 revision improved accreditation standards, but the time was not ripe to shift com-
pletely to graduate professional education, so a laissez-faire
compromise was worked out.   Undergraduate library schools
(Type III) were retained; schools were classified by type so
as to signify whether they operated at the graduate or undergraduate level; but to avoid stigmatizing lower-level programs
as inferior, it was stipulated that a school's classification as
Type I, II or III "neither includes nor implies a comparative
rating or grading. "

      The awkwardness of the result is illustrated by Colum-
bia's experience.   For too many years to remember, Columbia had prescribed but three years, 90 hours, of acceptable
undergraduate credit for admission to its graduate divisions.
This meant that graduates of Type III schools were permitted
to go directly into the master's program in library science--
although surprisingly few did so.   By contrast, Columbia's
own students had to take an additional year in compliance
with minimum ALA requirements for admission to a Type II
school.   It amounted to operating on a double standard.   The
movement underway at the end of the 1940s was attempting

to correct the inequity and in so doing open a more direct
route for advanced study for the doctorate.

ALA Initiative

     Of the numerous ALA activities of the 1940s that in-
fluenced library education, surely one of the least expected
was a general session of the Cincinnati conference of 1940
on the social importance that libraries of different types have
in common. President Ralph Munn chose children's libraries
and university libraries to represent the kindred interests of
the library family as a whole. Jean Roos lucidly developed
the theme that library work with children and youth is the
cornerstone of the whole process of bringing books and people together--the common function of all libraries--and is
critically important because the progress of society in general depends so much on the growth and training of the
young. 36

     I agreed to prepare the other paper on "The Place of
the University Library in the Modern World. "37   The heart
of it can be expressed in three propositions. First, libraries along with universities perform certain functions which
are indispensable to the survival and normal functioning of
our type of society. They conserve for continued use the
recorded experience of the race. They promote enlightened
living and understanding, support formal education, foster
the development and use of professional expertise, and make
possible systematic advancement of knowledge. Second, the
university movement and the library movement were generated by similar historic forces. They both owe their origin
to the fact that, in building Western civilization, a high premium was placed on the emancipation of human intelligence
from tradition, ignorance and arbitrary authority, and on establishing the institutions necessary to sustain free intelligence
and diffuse the results thereof. Third, libraries are indispensable also in an authoritarian society advanced enough to
depend on the communication of modern scientific and technological information; but authoritarian societies rest on a
different system of values from that of free societies. It
is a system that turns back the clock toward enslaving the
mind to arbitrary authority, that stifles free access to reliable information, and that converts libraries into instruments
of propaganda and indoctrination.

     One effect of the program was to suggest to some the

desirability of giving more attention in the first-year library
school to the social origins, goals and position of libraries.
President Munn had wanted American librarians to take stock
of their common interests and purposes at a moment of ALA
history when growing specialization threatened to divide them
into independent organizations, and the times gave point to the
exercise.   Eastern Europe had been subjugated.   The British
had been thrown back to Dunkerque.   France was collapsing.
And the Axis powers were getting poised for the crucial battle of Britain.

What did it all mean to the family of librarians?   For
them as for all others a brutal lesson on the meaning of free
institutions was unfolding.   Sumner Welles tells of the shock
--like a body blow--that he received that year, 1940, on seeing
first hand the raw power which a controlled press bestows on
a government.   He goes on to say in his Time for Decision:
"From that moment I have been convinced that when this war
is over, the peoples of the earth must never again permit a
situation to arise where any people shall be deprived of their
inherent right to know the truth. "38   While most thoughtful
people know deep within themselves that libraries are somehow important in all this, M. Llewellyn Raney, of Chicago,
expressed it in these terms--that Cincinnati put their "ulti-
mate purpose" in plainer light.   Adam Strohm, first Chairman of the BEL, felt that the occasion brought to the foreground a neglected area of study which should be a "must"
for librarians.   Don Coney, Ernest Reece and Carl Roden
agreed.

Another war-time development: when the nation began
to mobilize for war, Secretary Carl Milam noticed the exo-
dus of students from colleges and universities, saw or thought
he saw an opportunity for public service, and moved at once
to inaugurate special training for library careers for selected
young scholars whose classrooms were being emptied.   Mo-
bilization began not long after the MacLeish appointment as
Librarian of Congress; the profession was still smarting from
criticism for lack of effective training of leaders and administrators; and ALA international activities held out hopes for
additional high-level positions.   This was back of the Milam
move.   Being located at nearby Champaign-Urbana, I was
asked to take charge of outlining a curriculum, with the understanding that a fresh look should be taken at what additional training a selected group of young scholars of stature
would require.   All of the librarians who were coopted to discuss the problem recognized the challenge in this--and recog-

nized too that our work might to some extent affect library education generally. The training program never became a reality, for college and university professors who could be spared soon also left their campuses for the duration; but in the meantime a working paper on the basic curriculum was produced, was widely discussed, and in due course was condensed for publication. 39

The heart of the matter was that well-educated, well-motivated recruits should have better professional equipment than the conventional curriculum provided. A dominant purpose of library schools had been to inculcate a mastery of accepted methods of operating libraries. To be sure, library service is no better than its methods; no professional service ever is; but the conventional orientation unduly emphasized library economy, and university education of librarians stood for more than that. We could enrich professional preparation, the paper suggested, with a curriculum designed to give the student: (1) a critical overview of the more basic operating methods; (2) the competence in bookmanship (general reference and bibliography, subject bibliography and collection development) that building up and exploiting the resources for library purposes require; and (3) the background study necessary to understand the theoretical foundations of librarianship. As a minimum, such study should equip the student with a grounding in library practices, a working philosophy of librarianship, and should link library science as a branch of study and research fruitfully with related branches of learning.

The working paper was circulated for criticism the latter part of 1941-42, a year which may be said to mark the beginning of the new movement. For this was the year when the University of Illinois Library School launched its fiftieth-anniversary appraisal of library education, of which more later, and also the year when the BEL first took official notice of "dissatisfaction with a system which grants a bachelor's instead of a master's degree for completion of a program requiring five years of study at the college level."40 Following up a meeting at ALA headquarters in 1942-43 where these matters were discussed, Donald Coney, Chairman of the BEL, was to predict that "Changes in the pattern of education for librarianship are inevitable."41

While some members of the BEL favored specific changes, the Board officially took a neutral position, limiting itself to sponsoring relevant studies, special papers, and public discussions "to stimulate more widespread discussion

of questions by library schools and librarians. "42   The study
that had the greatest impact on the schools was the survey
of attitudes toward changing the degree structure.   Culminat-
ing in the Foster report cited above, the survey was best
known for revealing the extent of library-school opposition to
any change.   Less noticed was a ripple effect due to the report's bringing into the open the grounds for opposition.
This paved the way for further dialogue and reconsideration.

Influential public discussions initiated by the ALA included the 1945 Council meeting already referred to and the
equally influential follow-up meeting at the 1946 Buffalo Conference, jointly sponsored by the BEL and the Association
of American Library Schools, on "The Place of the Type III
Library School in Education for Librarianship. "43   There is
additional evidence farther on that by the close of that Buffalo Conference the tide of sentiment was turning against the
Type III school.   Of the several papers sponsored by the
ALA, Margaret Rufsvold's "Recruitment and Library Training"44 was the most important.   It deserves consideration
under a separate heading, as follows.

Realignment to Remedy a Policy Failure

Miss Rufsvold's case study of school librarianship in
the state of Indiana, published in 1945, made it clearer than
any previous study that twenty-five years of effort had failed
to produce a workable plan for the development of school library personnel.   She reported on the experience of 734 Indiana schools which were by law supposed to employ licensed
librarians.   Only 49 per cent had been able to comply with
the law.   Of the remaining 51 per cent, some 13 per cent
employed "librarians" with fewer than 16 semester hours of
library science, while 38 per cent had either allowed the post
to go unfilled or had employed a person with no professional
training whatsoever. 45

How was the situation exemplified by Indiana to be
coped with?   The question gained urgency from the fact that
school library service could no longer be dismissed as a
minor segment of the library movement.

The conviction had been growing among experienced
school librarians and others that the problem could be eased
by re-examining the all-or-none policy built into the 1933
accrediting standards.   According to these standards, under-

graduate professional training (in Type III schools) was on a
par with graduate professional training (in Type II schools);
but the training in either case was terminal, so it had to be
taken all in one chunk on whichever level it was begun. By
contrast, the education of all school personnel except library
personnel moved ahead flexibly from lower to higher; undergraduate professional training was not terminal, was more
widely accessible, and dovetailed with advanced work leading
to a fifth-year master's degree.

Following up her field study of 1945 with the BEL-
sponsored paper of May, 1946, Miss Rufsvold proposed closer
alignment of the training practices of the two professions, librarianship and education. In effect, the proposal was for
the library profession to give up the all-or-none principle
and permit approximately one semester of library science instruction at the undergraduate level. This would not be terminal but would dovetail with advanced work leading to a fifth-
year master's degree.

Here in outline is a formula with an appeal so many-
sided that it has to be set down as the most popular put forward to that point. The fifth-year bachelor's degree and the
Type III library school would both disappear. The graduate
library school would be the centerpiece, but the acceptability
of the conventional curriculum for a master's degree was left
to the local institution. Broadening the accessibility of library
science to college students was considered by some as a
threat to standards; but few denied that it would aid in recruitment. A further advantage of the formula was that it
would reopen the opportunity to organize technical training of
subprofessional grade, to be used or not as demonstrable demand warranted. During the early years of the BEL, it was
expected that training of this order would be continued. Pleas
for subprofessional training had been reiterated ever since.
Among such pleas were those of Harold Brigham at the ALA
Council meeting of December, 1945, and Errett McDiarmid
at the GLS Conference on library education in 1948.[46]

Library School Initiative

The reforms that followed publication of the Williamson report and establishment of the BEL were led by librarians whose competence was in administration, not education,
and this influenced what was done and left undone. To borrow the apt phrase of Frederick P. Keppel, their great con-

tributions were to the externalities of education--academic
affiliation, admission requirements, more money for library
school budgets, improved financial administration, etc. By
the mid-1930s, these reforms were well under way, and
minutes of the Association of American Library Schools show
little happening for several years thereafter as stability and
tranquility returned.

Then came the study financed by the Carnegie Corporation and conducted for the University of Illinois by Keyes
D. Metcalf, John Dale Russell and Andrew D. Osborn. [47]
The survey team was selected with a view to examining library education in the context of higher education as a whole.
The resultant suggestions for improving teaching methods
were welcomed by library-school teachers, but the focus was
on overall educational performance. The basic finding of the
study was a lag in this: despite improvements here and
there, the instruction program of library schools was considered "today still far behind the advances in other directions. "[48]

The lag stemmed from a miscalculation of the 1920s
when it was assumed that problems internal to the process
of educating students would take care of themselves if only
library schools were transferred, like other professional
schools, to university surroundings and preprofessional requirements were raised. The transfer succeeded rather in
relocating at universities programs which--as Munthe pointed
out--were not of university standard;[49] and at the same time,
the growing proportion of college graduates increased the
number of young librarians who "remember their library
school year as an academic experience more secondary than
collegiate in character. "[50] The study went on to account for
weak performance, and found it due chiefly to (1) the training and qualifications of library school instructors, (2) the
elementary nature of much of library education, and (3) the
lack of a philosophy of librarianship to add point and depth
to the program.

The study was published in 1943. Other developments
fed into the movement. The same year, the GLS inaugurated
its first-year program. Students were admitted at the end
of the sophomore year so as to make possible two years of
tailored background study, to be followed by an intensive third
year of library science. It was a timely experiment directed
toward better overall planning of the librarian's higher education. At their annual meeting that autumn, New England Col-

lege Librarians devoted a stimulating session to the 1942
working paper.   And it was the year when Ernest J. Reece's
Programs for Library Schools was published. [51] Here was
another, more extensive attempt to justify reinforcing students' knowledge of standard library methods with greater
knowledge both of library resources and of the theoretical
foundations of librarianship.   Its importance is emphasized
by the fact that Professor Reece's Curriculum in Library
Schools of 1936 had adhered to the traditional organization
of instruction in terms of kinds of library work.   His thoughtful 64-page Programs breaks away from this pattern, suggesting instead that the content of librarianship can be gathered up better under the headings: backgrounds of library
science, [52] production and distribution of records, books as
sources, technical organization, library administration and
guidance of clients.

        It was also in 1943-44 that the School of Library Ser-
vice inaugurated curriculum discussions which culminated in
the new master's program in 1948.   These discussions were
prolonged by local circumstances which are not widely known.
Columbia was the only ivy-league university with a library
school.   Abraham Flexner, a frequent visitor on Morningside
Heights, an engaging conversationalist and vigorous protagon-
ist of scholarship unmixed with vocational purpose, believed,
as has been indicated, that library science did not belong in
a university of front rank.   Various senior members of the
University, some in policy positions, agreed and were concerned about the School of Library Service.   As of the autumn of 1943, the School had been established 17 years.   The
trial period was over.   President Butler was nearing retirement.   A new Dean was beginning residence.   A frequently
cited fact was that the door was open for SLS students to
work toward the Ph. D. (through the Joint Committee on Graduate Instruction), but the School was producing no matricu-
lants--although some librarians had matriculated through other departments.   The position was this: the quality of SLS
students commanded respect, but not the curriculum, qualifications of most of the faculty, the degree system or the
School's academic insularity.

        Things were no happier from the School's side.   It
had one of the strongest faculties of any library school, but
morale was low, for two-thirds of the faculty were assistant
professors, some of them with long records of service who
saw little ahead of them but a dead-end street.   A powerful
budget committee, composed (as Young Smith, Dean of the

Faculty of Law liked to say) of deans of "the oldest and best faculties," did not consider them qualified in terms of Columbia standards for rank any higher than that.

While the Dean was on a wartime leave in 1944-45, the faculty under Acting Dean Reece discussed terms for revising the curriculum but came to a halt pending clarification of whether the degree structure was to be rebuilt around a fifth-year master's as the basic professional degree.   Meanwhile the war ended.   It was time to unite on plans for the future.   To this end, the Provost created at the SLS Dean's request an Ad Hoc Committee on the future of the School. Its nine members included two of the School's outspoken critics, three members of the budget committee, two from Teachers College,[53] and two from the SLS faculty, with the Dean as chairman.   The committee was given responsibility for advising on the program, on faculty additions to implement it and on a promotion policy for existing assistant professors.

Members of the Committee agreed that the higher interests of the University and the School were the same and that the big job was to develop a program that would be a credit to both.   Specifications were drawn up for the purpose and presented to the committee in March, 1946.[54]   They envisaged important changes in the curriculum and degree structure.   They left the door open for higher institutions to offer at the undergraduate level a limited range of courses to be approved by state and regional authorities.[55]   Manpower needs were becoming too diverse to be accommodated by "the single curriculum which does all things" for all library workers who require some contact with professional thought and experience.   Second, the main professional program would be one that could be defended as of graduate quality, would be offered for the master's degree, and would be the responsibility of nationally accredited library schools.   The curriculum would emphasize the fundamental aims of the library profession, library resources, and methods of mediating between human needs and intellectual resources for meeting them.   Third, the treatment would bear in mind that the end and aim of every profession is to conduct a branch of public service, which means that the training must be practical, but would stress breadth of comprehension, problem-solving ability, and critical insight more than indoctrination and job skills.   In so doing, instruction would open up problems for further study.   Fourth, centralized control by three Graduate Faculties (Philosophy, Pure Science and Political Science)

over the degree of Doctor of Philosophy raised doubt about
the adequacy of the SLS faculty's authority over advanced
study, but the specifications did not propose a separate degree to be under its own control.   It seemed preferable to
conform to local precedent and try out the use of a special
subcommittee of the Joint Committee on Graduate Instruction
to see whether we could not thereby cope with the problem
satisfactorily. 56

        The Committee was interested and objective.   The
ranking dean of the University, George Pegram, of the Graduate Faculties, welcomed the spirit of the proposals and
noted that for more than a decade universities had been moving away from the use of the master's solely as a research
degree.   Austin Evans, Professor of History, pointed out the
possibilities of interdisciplinary cooperation in the sociology
and social history of librarianship.   Harry Carmen, Dean of
Columbia College, observed that the program would require
mature scholarship and that it would be a University contribution to handle it well.   Hollis Caswell, Associate Dean of
Teachers College, saw in "Foundations of Librarianship" a
parallel to "Foundations of Education," a division of the
Teachers College curriculum which the faculty considered
essential to continuous study and reassessment of educational
theory and practice.

        After full discussion, the Committee approved the spe-
cifications in principle with no change, considered two semesters plus a summer session a suitable requirement for the
master's degree, and supported a broad general education,
in place of an undergraduate major in library science, as
the better prerequisite to admission.   The faculty was agreed
to be of the first importance for success.   It was agreed
that selections for two new positions of interdepartmental interest (foundations of librarianship and subject bibliography)
would be made on the advice of the committee as a whole,
with other nominations to be made by the Dean of the School
with the advice of Dean Pegram acting on the committee's
behalf.

        The volume and character of inquiries indicated that
these Columbia discussions were of interest to the profession
generally, and outside interest was further reinforced by Columbia's seeking, also in 1946, the counsel of some 82 librarians and educators across the country.   Their reactions
to the specifications were not as uniform as those of the Ad
Hoc Committee.   Numerous questions and three principal ob-

jections were raised.   First, whatever might be said about
the conventional curriculum's shortcomings, it was considered
by several to be too well-suited to library needs to require
change.   Second, some believed that a curriculum worked
out in accordance with the proposed specifications would be
too theoretical to meet the needs of beginning librarians.
Third, while it was understood that Columbia itself would not
be directly affected, a generous number of respondents felt
that undergraduate professional instruction should be ruled
out altogether on the ground that it weakens the student's general education and because it acts as an unruly competitor
with graduate professional instruction.   The majority of this
thoughtful but unscientific sample, however, welcomed the
statement as a constructive move toward improvement.   Here
are excerpts from a few of their replies:

> [The suggested specifications for] the reor-
> ganization of the program for the master's degree
> strike me as entirely sound....   The outline ...
> seems to me to provide the necessary professional
> preparation and at the same time to infuse into the
> fifth year the necessary amount of advanced schol-
> arly study to make it worthy of the master's de-
> gree.

> We feel that this is one of the most encour-
> aging documents we have seen in many years.

> I don't think anyone else has proposed so
> sound a solution of a difficult problem.

> You and your faculty are to be thanked most
> heartily for a vigorous attack on the professional
> program.   The fresh re-thinking found in the re-
> port is more constructive than any other pronounce-
> ment on the professional curriculum to date.

The Buffalo Conference of 1946, the first ALA meeting in four years, provided an opportunity to consult the
alumni of the SLS and predecessor schools.   President Lucile Morsch had asked four alumni to take the specifications
apart.   A keynote was struck by one member of this panel
of critics, Ralph Shaw, who said that mistakes were sure to
show up but that many librarians in the field had been asking for action and they were getting it.   It was a stimulating
hour.   When it was announced that the faculty had decided
to go to work on courses to recommend to the University

Council as a program for a fifth-year master's degree, the
news was applauded. Word that a Type I school had made
this announcement travelled quickly through the corridors and
across the land. Inquiries increased. Pierce Butler borrowed Columbia working papers for the use of the GLS committee on instruction, but no one went into the matter more
thoughtfully than Harriet Howe, of Denver, beginning after
breakfast the next morning.

     Another highlight of the Buffalo Conference was the
release at the same alumni meeting of Perry Danton's Education for Librarianship: Criticisms, Dilemmas, and Proposals, 57 the first of two SLS staff studies planned to facilitate a meeting of minds inside and outside the SLS faculty.
In the earnest faculty discussions of 1943-45, four issues had
emerged and were vigorously debated: (1) what should be the
national design or framework into which the basic curriculum
should fit? (2) should the SLS "rock the boat" by offering the
master's as the first professional degree? (3) is education
for librarianship essentially sound or in need of basic improvement? and (4) if the curriculum should be changed, how?

     The brief "Specifications for Developing the School of
Library Service" dealt briefly with all four questions, but
treatment in greater depth was needed, especially of the last
three. As to the propriety of the master's degree, a telling
contribution was made by Professor Emeritus Lucy E. Fay
in a symposium organized by College and Research Libraries
in 1945. Summing up the degree situation, she vigorously
supported a change to a master's degree, to be accompanied
by raising the curriculum to the graduate level. 58 The third
and fourth questions entitled themselves to more searching inquiry, so when Dr. Danton, on joining the SLS faculty in January, 1946, warmed to the suggestion to make an independent
assessment of education for librarianship, his schedule was
arranged to do it. The report, published by the SLS, was
ready in time to let our alumni at Buffalo take the lead in
distributing it as a free service to the profession. A timely
contribution, the Danton report went beyond the Illinois study
both in defining pressing problems and in proposing solutions.
"I would call [the Danton report]," Ralph Ulveling wrote in a
review, "one of the most important documents on this subject
within my professional experience. "59

     The faculty allowed itself two years from that spring
of 1946 to get ready to launch the new master's program. In
its annual report for 1945-46, 60 the BEL refers to the inten-

sive preparations being made by the SLS faculty and to the consultative aid and staff reports that were used to support their efforts. The last of these reports was Ernest J. Reece's The Task and Training of Librarians; a Report of a Field Investigation Carried out in February to May, 1947, to Assist with Curricular Problems Then Pending Before the Dean and Faculty at the School of Library Service, Columbia University (New York: King's Crown Press, 1949). The object was to get from the field a fresh, more reliable picture of high-priority professional competences as an aid to determining what sort of input was needed to improve training. A uniform set of questions was worked out to use for in-depth interviews of well over a hundred librarians in libraries of all types in all sections of the country, and a semester's leave of absence was arranged for the purpose.

The study was Professor Reece's last service before retirement, and one of the most timely. The findings highlighted as no other study had done the interplay between library advances and subtle alteration of demands on library personnel. Imaginative school librarians were working with teachers and students to transform better equipped libraries into live information and learning centers. Special librarians were making skillful information-handling indispensable to the functioning of business organizations and government. Academic librarians were increasingly active in collection development, instruction and research. And leading all the rest were progressive public libraries whose expanding services were challenging and utilizing the most varied professional capabilities. Technical competence in operating procedures remained essential as ever, but to limit library education to this was "simply too narrow and too arid." The evidence brought back supported finding a way to give higher priority than had been granted theretofore to knowledge of information sources, to the nature and problems of administration, to the high-level skill of imaginatively designing services to meet people's needs, to the purpose and place of the library in society, and to research as an aid for problem-solving. A solid fifth year of professional study should continue to be the cornerstone of professional preparation, but should be considered as but one of the stairstep blocks of higher education which should more often continue upward to the doctorate and entail work of an interdisciplinary character.

University Education of Librarians

In the two years between the Buffalo conference and

1948, the SLS faculty and particularly the Associate Deans
(Ernest Reece succeeded by Lowell Martin) worked tirelessly
on details of a set of courses. 61 One is entitled to ask,
why all the bother to do this when new master's programs
were being launched with only minor changes in existing
courses?

     A wag said that the new fifth-year programs had but
one thing in common--the master's degree. Much was said
of differences from one program to another, but it is well to
bear in mind that sponsoring institutions were responsible for
much of this confusion. Columbia did not consider its fifth-
year bachelor's program to be of graduate quality. It was
different at Denver. When the director of its Type III library
school asked how the existing program should be changed to
be acceptable for a master's degree, the reply was that "the
Denver graduate college had always considered the courses in
the college of librarianship as of graduate quality."62 There
is another factor that was at work. In cases where some
change was called for, it was independent faculties who were
responsible for taking action, and it is hardly surprising that
they came up with varied solutions. Nobody would change
this: the price of innovation was to be free "to make mistakes in your own way, shoot them down and try again."
There is a third consideration to keep in mind. The library
school that was asked to make few changes or none at the
outset enjoyed a favored position in that it was left to upgrade its program and staff at its own pace--a rare advantage
when recruiting highly qualified faculty personnel was extreme-
ly difficult. Variations in courses continued, or altered, or
replaced, told us only how a school started, not where it
would be ten years later.

     The point we are leading up to is this. Universities
were independent entities. Their practices varied. There
was no schoolbook definition of what university education was.
But back of the lack of uniformity was a consciousness that
the great service of the modern university had been, and
was, to systematize, transmit, and further advance learning
in one field of human endeavor after another. The new
movement was a groping but widely supported effort to place
library education on better footing in this regard.

     As good a way as any to illustrate this and to relate
the Columbia program to the movement is to sample the
thinking that had gone into it. Following are thumbnail
sketches of four areas. Two were new--study of the goals

or purposes of the profession and its role in society, and
subject bibliography.   Two others, while not altogether new,
had received new treatment.

Foundations of Librarianship.   The faculty used this
term to refer to the social origins and theoretical foundation
of modern librarianship.   The subject deserved study, first,
because the public supports institutions and services that are
known to meet basic and continuing needs.   Many who lived
through the budget-slashing of the depression were sure that
it would have been less severe had librarians' estimates of
the worth of their services been better defined and comprehended.   The worst of the slashing was done on the theory
that library service is a luxury item.   Second, librarians
now had to be equipped to relate the library's service potential to the complex problems and needs of an industrial society.   While the country remained agrarian and libraries
were small, we got along without formal study of the foundations of librarianship, but that time was past.   Banking provides an illustration of the same thing in another field.   When
the American Bankers Association inaugurated its training
program at the turn of the century, the emphasis on technical within-the-walls activities resembled the library-school
curriculum of that day: it consisted of strictly practical
courses on banking and finance, arithmetic, bookkeeping,
typewriting, business correspondence, and the like.   The first
war accelerated industrialization, and the depression made it
plain that the banker who had technical training only was not
equipped to cope with banking problems that really mattered
at the level of social policy.   The solution was to give the
student a better theoretical foundation for the job, with particular attention to banking theory and practice, economics
and banking law. [63]

It can be pointed out that early librarians got along
without formal study of this subject, but it should also be
pointed out that probably no generation had a better-defined
sense of purpose than it had.   Librarians talked of the "library spirit. "   It is a term that stood for their philosophy
and their commitment to translate that philosophy into concrete results.   In a "strictly technical course" on library
economy, there was no formal place for this mystique; but
it poured from Dewey and others like water from a fountain
and accounts for much of the cohesion and driving force of
the modern library movement.

Technical Services.   The inclusion of this new subject

looked like turning the clock back to one alumna, and she
was undoubtedly not alone in needing to know more about it
than the catalog said.   A major recommendation of the Williamson report was to distinguish between professional and
subprofessional duties, to have library schools confine themselves to training for library work of professional grade, and
to leave responsibility for subprofessional work to local library training classes.   The recommendation led to desired
improvements in the study of cataloging and classification,
but led also to the neglect of study and inquiry into technical
services considered--as they must be for imaginative manage-
ment--in their entirety.   One of the best characterizations of
Melvil Dewey I know is that of Henry Watson Kent, who describes his mentor as a great mechanician uncommonly adept
at making the library machine a good one, adding in the next
breath that Dewey stood for the dignity of the profession.
Library schools had wisely outgrown the practice of training
professionals to do subprofessional work, but the designing
and building of the library machine, which is another name
for efficient operational technology, was a modern achievement of the first magnitude; and its further development had
to be treated as a responsibility of library scholarship whether the duties involved were performed by professionals or
subprofessionals.   Twenty-five years earlier, we had tipped
over backwards by lopping off some of this seamless whole.
The intent of the innovation was to correct the mistake and
restore the subject's undeserved loss of dignity.

The Current and Future System of Library Services.
The faculty of that time would have been happy to have someone come up with a stronger name for this subject than "Library Plans and Programs. "   The first object was a course
which afforded beginners an opportunity to find out enough
about libraries of different types to determine which ones
they wished to specialize in, but we also wanted to start
them thinking about the system itself as a phenomenon of
social engineering.   Wartime emergencies had loosened the
imagination and stimulated better planning at higher levels.
Consider the national level in our case and the challenge to
creative effort that awaited us there.   The nominal goal of
the profession for many years had been a system of library
services capable of serving the nation as a whole.   In practice, the structure of the system was that of voluntarily coordinated, locally supported libraries of stated types--public,
special, school, academic and research.   Interlibrary planning had been of an island-by-island type, with regional public library service the most fruitful result.   An unstated sup-

position had been that the sum of good public, special, school
and academic library service, independently governed and supported and informally coordinated, add up to an adequate service program for the nation as a whole. Was this supposition
valid? Was the existing structure of the profession's services
as well designed as it could be to achieve our lofty national
goal, and if not, did the system or the goal need altering?
There were other questions closely related to these. What
stresses in the existing system suggested the need of a stronger network, and were the characteristics of other national library systems the same as or different from ours?

Subject Bibliography. No plan for handling instruction
in subject bibliography had worked out in the past. This all
but terrorized us, and made the new position in the faculty
one of the two hardest of all to fill. Our own SLS and its
predecessor, the School of Library Economy, had had two
instructive failures. An earnest experiment by Melvil Dewey
in the 1880s showed that a series of lectures on the monographic literature of different subjects by outside specialists,
while it could be stimulating, was not the answer. Neither
was a separate course on subject bibliographies, as was
learned in the 1930s. Other plans were tried elsewhere which
had but one thing in common--they were given up.

Our faculty were not yet of one mind on procedure,
and this was healthy; but I believe we were agreed on certain fundamentals. First, we saw subject literature courses
as contributors to the furtherance of general reference, specialized literature searching, and collection development. In
consequence, we approached a body of literature in terms of
the more basic types of information that it supplied inquirers.
This took us into the literature as a whole, the monographic
no less than the strictly reference material; for what was
subject literature but a structured collection of sources designed and published to serve the inquisitive interests of active
minds? If this were true, the task of organizing instruction
would seem to hinge on catching hold of that internal structure and understanding which sources were the more crucial
in each category. We limited attention largely at the outset
to the main categories of reference sources, but some of us
and perhaps all of us looked forward to encompassing the
more crucial substantive works as well.

If the development of subject bibliography as a branch
of study proved feasible--and we were not far enough along
with the experiment to know whether it would--the involvement

of librarians should be a fortunate circumstance. For among
the members of the academic community it was the librarians
who were most interested in achieving social control over information in the broadest sense. The typical scholar's interest, if not limited to the literature of a particular topic,
period, person or place, tended at most to be limited quite
understandably to his own discipline, hence narrower. Scholars and the general public as well as librarians themselves
would be well served by work done from a broader angle of
regard, and we looked forward to the leadership Professor
Hazen hoped to give us in this.

The Ad Hoc Committee counseled on program development, worked out a plan for promoting assistant professors
which enormously boosted our morale,[64] supported an increase in number of positions in the upper professional ranks,
participated in certain faculty selections, but made no contribution more significant than giving the School a fresh sense
of support. It was made to feel at home, and wanted, for
the first time--an intangible of great importance to its faculty, students, alumni and friends. The support strengthened
the School's bid to cope with a very difficult faculty recruiting problem. The prewar shortage of library-school teachers of tested competence had become more critical, obliging
the University to depend more heavily on subjective colleague
estimates. Columbia's ability to cope was complicated by the
practice of making no probationary appointments to positions
at normal tenure levels.[65] And the situation was further
complicated by needing in two new subjects, foundations and
subject bibliography, a degree of maturity that would have to
be developed on the job.

Of the faculty who launched the new master's program,
six veterans had worked on it from the beginning in 1943-44:
Alice I. Bryan, Bertha M. Frick, Hilda M. Grieder, Margaret Hutchins, Hellmut Lehmann-Haupt, and Miriam D.
Tompkins. Ten other appointments were made before 1948.
Three were products of the GLS: Maurice F. Tauber, first
attracted to Columbia in 1944 to participate in the reorganization of the University Libraries, preparatory to entering
the faculty in 1946; J. Periam Danton (1946), untried but so
successful in teaching and scholarship that California soon
called him to head its School of Librarianship; and Lowell A.
Martin (1946), Assistant Professor in the GLS, who was
tapped to succeed Melvil Dewey Professor Ernest J. Reece
as Associate Dean. Three were teachers of demonstrated
competence: Winifred Linderman (1947), with diversified

experience here and overseas and a desire to work toward
the doctorate, was picked to succeed Margaret Hutchins in
reference; Helen R. Sattley (1947) brought to her task a
strong background in both school and children's library work;
and Robert D. Leigh (1947), Director of the Public Library
Inquiry, was drawn into the School part-time because his
social science background qualified him so well to share in
developing study and research on the role of the library in
the communication process.

Four joint appointments were made.   James G. Van
Derpool (1946), Head of the Department of Art in the University of Illinois, School of Architecture, and a beloved teacher, was brought to Columbia as Avery Librarian with the understanding that responsibility for teaching "The history and
literature of the fine arts" would be part of his job.   Thomas
P. Fleming (1948), Columbia's Librarian of the Medical-
Natural Science Libraries, accepted responsibility for developing instruction in science and medical literature. Of the
academic departments at Columbia, English showed the most
perceptive interest in developing subject bibliography as a
branch of serious study, and led us to Allen Hazen (1948),
who was to spearhead the study of subject bibliography, with
special responsibility for the literature of the humanities.
He was to divide his time between the School and the Department of English.   His rapid rise at the University of
Chicago to the posts of Professor of English and Acting Director of Libraries augured well for his capacity to do original work in his area.

Since Chicago was already pioneering a fruitful sociological approach to the goals and the social role of the profession, the Ad Hoc Committee concluded that Columbia could
best complement the work being done there by entrusting the
organization of an initial course on the foundations of librarianship to a qualified historian, and turned to Professor Geof-
frey Bruun, a specialist in intellectual and social history in
Columbia's Department of History, to do the job. He served
part-time in the School in 1947-48 while developing a course
on "Books and libraries in the cultural process," which he
taught that summer, but withdrew upon finding the task to be
such an all-consuming one.   It was getting late; the Committee reversed directions and sought a trained librarian (in
place of a trained historian) who would be undeterred by the
hard climb that conquest of the subject would entail.   Ray
Trautman, commended by his associates for his imagination
and enterprise, accepted the challenge.   As a first step in

his apprenticeship to historical scholarship, he buckled down
to preparing, under the direction of Professor Dwight Miner,
the SLS volume of the Columbia bicentennial history.

In Conclusion

        The main achievements in library education since the
Williamson report were the acceptance of library education
as a university responsibility and a switch to the development
of library education in closer accordance with university
standards.

        The movement to transfer library education to aca-
demic sponsorship produced mixed reactions in American
higher education.   Abraham Flexner, the most outspoken op-
ponent, held that library education was vocational and belonged somewhere else besides the university.   William
Warner Bishop effectively stated the case for accepting library education as a university responsibility.   He emphasized the importance of systematic professional training cast
at the graduate level and the university's obligation in the
matter both in the public interest and its own.

        Friendlier critics than Flexner took the more concilia-
tory position that the usefulness of library schools could be
improved by following the example of better established professions and conforming more closely to university standards.
The views of the deans of two reputable graduate schools
were used to pinpoint the most crucial problems involved in
doing this.   Guy Stanton Ford of the University of Minnesota
held that the test of what belongs in the university is not the
subject per se, but the method and spirit of treating that subject.   In his words, the distinguishing feature of graduate
study of university standard is "the method of inquiry and
research, the accumulation of data, the testing by experiment and observation that we call scientific, and the fearless
drawing of conclusions no matter how sharply they traverse
accepted maxims and practices. "   In the case of librarianship, as with other professions, but most noticeably the newer ones, the spirit of inquiry remained, or seemed to remain,
alien to "training and tradition. "   Charles B. Lipman, of
California, dwelled on the need to infuse greater intellectual
vitality into the first-year program.   He associated librarianship with newer professions whose subject matter consisted
of little more than current practices and skills--professions
in which the educational process amounted to little more than

pouring superficial information about them into passive receptacles.

The rest of this closing chapter has described the progress made in the 1930s and 1940s toward resolving these two problems. The Graduate Library School, established as an experiment for the purpose, convincingly demonstrated the desirability of considering critical inquiry and research essential to the advancement of librarianship. But the School did not assume that, because university professional education at this higher level should foster basic research, it should do nothing else. Instead, the School went on to strengthen professional literature, hold institutes and conduct surveys, and by so doing made contributions on a plane that served better than those of any other agency to meet the higher leadership requirements of a vigorous and rapidly developing profession.

By 1943 when Lipman criticized the first-year program for being of substandard educational quality, a movement toward reconstruction was already forming. There was more unrest and confusion to begin with than cohesion, but an overdue need to revise the degree structure furnished common ground to stand on. Some would consider remodeling the degree structure as being in reality the popular objective of the period, and support for this view is suggested by the fact that initial changes in some library schools consisted for the most part of a scissors-and-paste realignment of existing courses and instatement of a fifth-year master's as the basic professional degree. When a longer view is taken of the movement, however, deeper forces come to light. Twentieth-century librarianship is, as we have seen, not alone among the professions which fell heir to the tradition of apprenticeship schooling. This educational model overstayed its period of greatest usefulness and began in time to break down. The deepening vein of criticism of the 1930s and early 1940s was symptomatic of its inadequacies. The war years saw the tone of negative criticism begin to give way to constructive search by representatives and friends of library education for ways to improve the first-year program by greater conformance to university standards. This creative effort found national expression in the adoption by the American Library Association of the 1951 standards for the accreditation of library schools. The significance of the movement lies not in the amount or character of curricular changes made prior to that date by individual library schools but in the trend which it confirmed toward using an educational model better adapted to twentieth-century needs of those who are preparing for careers as professional librarians.

REFERENCES

1. "Standards for Accreditation Presented by the ALA Board of Education for Librarianship and Adopted by the ALA Council, Chicago, July 13, 1951," ALAB, 46, 1952, 48-49.

2. Russell, John Dale. "Professional Education for Librarianship," Library Quarterly 12, 1942, 775-93.

3. The thinking back of the 1951 standards is presented more fully in a companion document, Statement of Interpretation to Accompany "Standards for Accreditation," Adopted by the ALA Council, July 13, 1951. Chicago: American Library Association. Committee on Accreditation, April, 1962. Mimeographed. It spells out some 16 objectives for guidance in planning the five years of the librarian's higher education.

4. Flexner, Abraham. Universities: American, English, German. New York: Oxford University Press, 1930, pp. 152-53, 172, 195.

5. Bishop, W. W. "The Status of Library Schools in Universities," Association of American Universities. Journal of Proceedings, 1933, 124-37.

6. Ford, Guy S. "Professional Education at the Graduate Level," Association of American Universities. Journal of Proceedings, 1930, p. 104.

7. Ibid., p. 107.

8. Lipman, Charles B. "Vocational and Professional Training at the Graduate Level and Its Effect on the Academic Graduate Work," Association of American Universities. Journal of Proceedings, 1943, 55-65.

9. Works, George A. "The Graduate Library School of the University of Chicago," Libraries, 34, 1929, 310-14.

10. "Dr. Works Resigns from Graduate Library School,"
     Libraries, 34, 1929, 317-19.

11. Waples, Douglas. "The Graduate Library School, Uni-
     versity of Chicago," Library Quarterly, 1, 1931,
     26-36.

12. Thompson, D. Seymour. "Do We Want a Library Sci-
     ence?" LJ 56, 1931, 743-46.

13. Waples, Douglas. "Do We Want a Library Science?
     A Reply," LJ 56, 1931, 743-46; Thompson, C.
     Seymour, "Comment on the Reply," LJ 56, 1931,
     746-47.

14. Dr. Frank D. Fackenthal was Provost of Columbia Uni-
     versity for many years and concluded his career as
     Acting President following President Butler's retire-
     ment in 1945. He spoke good-humoredly of periodic
     calls made by the first Secretary of the BEL to
     "keep the University in line" with its duty to the
     young School of Library Service, which he helped
     bring into being.

15. Shera, Jesse H. The Foundations of Education for Li-
     brarianship. New York: Becker and Hayes (Wiley),
     1972, 246.

16. Butler, Pierce. Introduction to Library Science. Chi-
     cago: University of Chicago Press, 1933. (Studies
     in library science, no. 1).

17. Carnovsky, Leon. "Why Graduate Study in Librarian-
     ship?" Library Quarterly 7, 1937, 246-61.

18. American Political Science Review 29, 1935, 906-07.

19. Wilson, L. R. and M. F. Tauber. The University Li-
     brary; Its Organization, Administration, and Func-
     tions. Chicago: University of Chicago Press, 1945.

20. American Library Association. Committee on Post-
     War Planning of the American Library Association.
     Post-war Standards for Public Libraries, prepared
     by the Committee on Post-War Planning, Carleton
     B. Joeckel, Chairman. Chicago: American Library
     Association, 1943.

21. Wilson, Louis R. The Geography of Reading; a Study
     of the Distribution and Statistics of Libraries in
     the United States. Chicago: American Library
     Association and University of Chicago Press, 1938.

22. Wilson, Louis R., ed. Library Trends; Papers Pre-
     sented Before the Library Institute at the Univer-
     sity of Chicago, August 3-15, 1936. Chicago:
     University of Chicago, 1937.

23. ALAB 31, 1937, 340.

24. Journal of Higher Education 10, 1939, 55.

25. Chicago. University. Library Institute. Current Issues
     in Library Administration, ed. with an introduc-
     tion by Carleton B. Joeckel. Chicago: University
     of Chicago Press, 1939.

26. LJ 64, 1939, 510.

27. Shera, J. H., op. cit., p. 248.

28. "Is Personnel Adequate for the Job: a Discussion by
     the Council at its Meeting in Chicago on December
     28," ALAB 40, 1946, 89-95.

29. Dean, Hazel. "Dilemma of the Library School," Cali-
     fornia Library Association. Bulletin 7, 1946, 115-
     17.

30. Wheeler, Joseph L. Progress and Problems in Educa-
     tion for Librarianship. New York: Carnegie Cor-
     poration of New York, 1946.

31. Howe, Harriet E. "The Type III Library School," LJ
     71, 1946, 949-52.

32. Foster, Jeannette H. Library School Opinion on De-
     grees and Curriculum. A. L. A. Board of Educa-
     tion for Librarianship, 1945. Mimeographed.

33. Howe, Harriet E. "The Type III Library School," LJ,
     1946, 952.

34. Howe, Harriet E. "The New Program at the University
     of Denver," ALAB, 41, 1947, 450-53.

35. LJ 48, 1923, 1066.

36. Roos, Jean. "Laying the Foundation," ALAB, 34,
      448-54.

37. White, Carl M. "The Place of the University Library
      in the Modern World," ALAB, 34, 1940, 440-45.
      Also appeared in Educational Record 21, 1940, 454-
      69.

38. Welles, Sumner. The Time for Decision. New York:
      Harper, 1944, p. 90.

39. White, Carl M. "The Program of the Library School,"
      Journal of Higher Education 16, 1945, 358-63.

40. ALAB 36, 1942, 689.

41. ALA Board of Education for librarianship. "The Li-
      brarian in Wartime," ALAB 37, 1943, 359-62.

42. ALA Board of Education for librarianship. "The Li-
      brarian in Wartime," ALAB 38, 1944, 360-62.

43. ALAB 40, 1946, P95-P96.

44. ALAB 40, 1946, 151-53.

45. Rufsvold, Margaret I. School Library Personnel in In-
      diana. Bloomington: Indiana. University. Coopera-
      tive Research and Field Service Bureau, 1945.
      (Bulletin of School of Education). Other contem-
      porary documentation of fact and opinion on school
      librarianship includes two widely read reports:
      (1) Hoyle, Nancy. Report on Progress and Prob-
      lems in Training for School Librarianship. Chi-
      cago: ALA, 1946. Mimeographed; and (2) Southern
      Association of Colleges and Secondary Schools.
      Library Committee. Summary of the Third South-
      ern Library Planning Conference on Training for
      School Librarianship. 1946.

46. McDiarmid, Errett W. "Training for Clerical and Sub-
      professional Workers," in Berelson, Bernard, ed.
      Education for Librarianship; Papers Presented at
      the Library Conference, University of Chicago,
      August 16-21, 1948. Chicago: American Library

Association, 1949, 232-48.

47. Metcalf, Keyes D. and others. The Program of Instruc-
     tion in Library Schools. Urbana: University of
     Illinois Press, 1943.

48. Ibid., p. 7.

49. Munthe, Wilhelm. American Librarianship from a Euro-
     pean Angle; an Attempt at an Evaluation of Policies
     and Activities. Chicago: American Library Asso-
     ciation, 1939, 130-39.

50. The phrase is Robert A. Miller's. LJ 69, 1944, 549.

51. Reece, Ernest J. Programs for Library Schools. New
     York: Columbia University Press, 1943.

52. As used in the Programs, this phrase means "the story
     of libraries," but Reece envisages a treatment more
     penetrating than the descriptive history then com-
     monly offered. The first course entitled, "Back-
     grounds for Librarianship," so far as is known,
     was organized at Illinois in 1941-42. It was short-
     lived because no one could allocate the time it took
     to prepare for it. It was planned as "an interpre-
     tation of the development of libraries and of the li-
     brary profession, of the role of libraries in modern
     life, of the qualifications, the assorted duties and
     varied opportunities ... of library service." Illi-
     nois Library School Association. Fifty Years of
     Education for Librarianship. Urbana: University
     of Illinois Press, 1943. p. 66.

53. Some of the School's critics bandied about the possibil-
     ity of transferring it to Teachers College, which
     is affiliated with Columbia but has its own board of
     trustees.

54. These specifications were included in the annual report
     of the Dean, 1945-46, presented in draft to 82 li-
     brarians and educators for criticism, and published
     early in 1947. The statement had shortcomings,
     but two things about it deserve notice. It served
     to unite a divided University behind its library
     school. Second, it served as a call to action based,
     not on further criticism of library schools of which

there had been enough, but on a package of affirmative proposals as to what should be done.

55. There were at the time more than 120 undergraduate programs, and the number was increasing. Conditions that accounted for the trend seemed unlikely to go away.

56. Regulations of long standing empowered a Joint Committee on Graduate Instruction under the Dean of the Graduate Faculties (Philosophy, Political Science, and Pure Science) to approve programs of study toward the Ph. D. proposed by students in professional schools. The Committee was further empowered to determine when such a candidate qualified as a matriculant and to authorize the awarding of the degree on satisfactory completion of a dissertation. In practice, the amount of work required in other departments for matriculation (which formally marked completion of all course work, examination in two foreign languages, and passing a qualifying examination) largely cancelled any advantage of registering in the SLS. For purposes of strengthening SLS participation in planning Ph. D. work for its students, a new procedure was introduced in 1948. On the recommendation of the Dean, the Associate Dean was designated as Adviser to the Dean of the Graduate Faculties in setting up all programs of doctoral study in library science. Various students undertook work toward the Ph. D. under this arrangement. It helped, but not enough, and was abandoned in favor of a separate degree of Doctor of Library Science, awarded on the authority of the Faculty of Library Service.

57. Danton, J. Periam. Education for Librarianship; Criticisms, Dilemmas, Proposals. New York: School of Library Service, Columbia University, 1946.

58. Fay, Lucy E. "An Over-all View, " College and Research Libraries 6, 1945, 276-78.

59. College and Research Libraries 7, 1946, 371.

60. ALAB 40, 1946, 367. See also ALAB 41, 1947, 378.

61. The most lucid interpretation of the Columbia program

as it approached finished form was contributed by
Lowell Martin in an article, "Proposed Program
of Library Study at Columbia, 1948," New York
Library Club Bulletin, February, 1948.

62.   Op. cit., ALAB 41, 1947, 452.

63.   Schneider, Wilbert M.   The American Bankers Associa-
      tion; Its Past and Present.   Washington, D.C.:
      Public Affairs Press, 1956, 53-67.

64.   The boost was short-lived.   Postwar inflation hurt Co-
      lumbia.   One of the very hurtful effects was the
      delay in clearing these scheduled advancements.

65.   The rationale of the policy is instructive.   "We prefer
      living with a few mistakes to weakening tenure at
      tenure levels" [Dean Pegram].   "There is little
      risk.   A gentleman is going to move on if he can't
      handle the work." [Dr. Fackenthal]

INDEX

Compiled by Dorothy Gray